DEVELOPING TEACHERS

Fifth Year Programs for Outstanding Students

Edited by

Joseph O. Milner
Roy Edelfelt
Peter T. Wilbur

University Press of America,® Inc.
Lanham · New York · Oxford

Copyright © 2001 by
University Press of America,® Inc.
4720 Boston Way
Lanham, Maryland 20706

12 Hid's Copse Rd.
Cumnor Hill, Oxford OX2 9JJ

All rights reserved
Printed in the United States of America
British Library Cataloging in Publication Information Available

Library of Congress Cataloging-in-Publication Data

Developing teachers : fifth-year programs for outstanding students / edited by Joseph O. Milner, Roy Edelfelt, Peter T. Wilbur.
p. cm
Includes bibliographical references and index.
1. Teachers—Training of—United States. 2. Education—Study and teaching (Graduate)—United States. I. Milner, Joseph O'Beirne.
II. Edelfelt, Roy A. III. Wilbur, Peter T.
LB2165 .D48   2000   370'.71'173—dc21   00-048855 CIP

ISBN 0-7618-1891-X (pbk. : alk. ppr.)

∞™ The paper used in this publication meets the minimum requirements of American National Standard for Information Sciences—Permanence of Paper for Printed Library Materials, ANSI Z39.48—1984

To teachers who teach teachers and are reviled by fools and charlatans from within and without.

Contents

Preface

Introduction

Chapter 1	**Perspectives**	1
	New Teachers for New Schools Barbara Kelley	3
	The Teaching Habit of Mind: **A Harvard Student's Perspective** Allyson Mizoguchi	13
	Master Teacher Programs: **A Student's Perspective** Alice Sy	17
Chapter 2:	**Students**	23
	The Master Of Arts Program: **Admissions Procedures** William S. Palmer Xue Lan Rong	27

	Students: Recruitment, Selection and Funding Ruth S. Bettandorff, Ph.D.	33
	Admission to the University of New Hampshire Teacher Education Program: Criteria for Success Eleanor Abrams Michael D. Andrews	39
	Response Margo A. Figgins Carl A. Young	45
	Students: Recruitment, Selection, Funding **A Plenary Conversation**	47
	Discussion Response Margo Figgins Carl A. Young	55
Chapter 3	**Academic Programs**	59
	Rice University Teacher Preparation Program Lissa Heckelman	61
	Dispelling the Myths of Teacher Preparation through Interdisciplinary And Integrative Studies Christopher Roellke	69
	Balancing Tensions: The Liberal Arts and Professional Education in Wake Forest's Master Teacher Fellows Program R. Scott Baker	81

	Academic Programs Discussion	87
	Discussion Response
Leslie Quast	99
Chapter 4	Internships	103
	Improving the Student
Teaching Experience
Lawrence Wakeford	107
	Preparing Teachers through Professional
Development School Partnerships
Angela Breidenstein	115
	The Internship in a Professional
Development School: The Power
of Place
Richard H. Card	125
	Response
Alan J. Reiman	133
	Internships Discussion	139
	Discussion Response: Designing
Coherent and Effective Teacher
Education Internships
Alan J. Reiman	147
Chapter 5	Research	159
	The Personal Inquiry: An Example of
Teacher Research in a Fifth-year Teacher
Education Program
Eileen Landay	161
	Research Times Two: A Model of Formal
Research and Personal Reflection
Leah McCoy and Robert Evans	171

An Evolution in Action Research from Improving Practice to Personal Authority Joseph McCaleb and Jeremy Price	177
Research Discussion	193
Response Paper Charles B. Myers	199

Chapter 6 Induction — 205

Professional Development Schools and their Influence on Developing Teachers in an Integrated Program John R. Mascazine	207
Preparing Teachers with Staying Power Rosemary Thorne	215
Induction Discussion	221
Induction Response **Michael Andrew**	225

Chapter 7 Program Profiles — 227

References — 275

Index — 283

Preface

Developing Teachers came to life in my mind as I considered my wife's work in medical education as I thought about how I should respond to a RFP that focused on universities' use of clinical faculty. Suddenly everything made perfect sense: our student teachers should not be apprenticed to one master but observe a variety of experts as do medical students so they might construct their own excellent practice. My model was taken from medical education but, in spite of the lack of parallels between the two professions, the model was well liked and the proposed program was funded.

With $50,000 annual support for a new approach to teacher education we began our work immediately: we built the locomotive as it rolled out of the station. We constructed our program with much gusto and high hopes. After a somewhat faltering first year, outstanding candidates began to apply to the program. When Wake Forest President Hearn gave his support to a cooperative venture I arranged with the local superintendent to offer stipends on top of our full scholarship, the program lurched forward perceptibly. Because we had a strong methods faculty with discipline knowledge and public school experiencing, our program was extremely attractive to academically strong students. All we needed was this very special incentive to set us apart and help us compete with highly respected universities across the country. The full scholarship with an additional $4,000 fellowship to help with living expenses made our very solid program attractive to students from Washington Sate to New Hampshire, from Florida to Texas. We found that applicants were tempted enough by our financial support that they were sending us their GRE scores alongside Harvard, Brown, Stanford and other fine universities.

As we began to have greater confidence in what we were doing and the capacities of students who we were admitting to the program, we began to experiment with new ideas like video tape interviews, action research in our Master Teachers' classrooms, distinguished visiting scholars, and electronic portfolios as an induction tool. We began to feel so strong about our program that in a pitch of hubris, I decided we needed to gather directors and faculty from similar programs for a short, working conference where the best ideas from the best programs could be put on the table for full exploration. A great coincidence helped matters considerably. A prospective science teacher who joined our program from Brown let me know that her undergraduate advisor, Larry Wakeford, had ties in North Carolina. He had indeed. I had met Larry a few years earlier when he was touring our state as teacher-of-the-year. With such a likely link, I began plans for an invitational meeting at Wake Forest's Graylyn Conference Center. John Anderson's deep interest in best practice prompted him as Vice President for Planning and Finance to support my proposal. After further planning, I called Larry Wakeford to ask if he would like to work with me to develop a best practice conference that Brown and Wake Forest would sponsor. He was very positive from the beginning, so the idea was fully born and a list of schools to be invited was drawn up. I found additional support from Sam Gladding who was able to allocate funds to us dedicated to leadership activities. The right people and the right support mechanisms were in place for a good idea to be realized.

Regular meetings of professional groups are not difficult to bring to fruition. Thousands of details must be mastered for such conferences, but if one is built, the regular attendees will come. A new venture is something else again. Ours was an idea that had real merit, obvious usefulness; but attracting busy professionals to yet another meetings was not easy. The idea of focusing on five clearly significant parts of a graduate program for prospective teachers made great sense. Anyone interested in creating a strong program would find each of them compelling. We wanted to ask for enough substance and forethought that the presenters would offer us something strong and new. At the same time, we wanted the sessions to be fresh and lively, so we created a response period that was longer than the time allotted for the three presentations. The resultant conversations that grew out of those papers were rich, free flowing, and spontaneous and thus difficult to weld into a clear linear progression of thought. We also wanted to hear critiques of our ideas from two directions: the world of highly respected teachers and the small province of new teachers who had been nurtured by programs like ours. Barbara Kelley, who chairs the National board for Professional Teaching Standards was the perfect representative from the world of classroom teachers. Graduates of the Harvard and Wake Forest programs were eloquent spokespersons for the programs themselves. Added to these ingredients was the Program Profile for the score of universities who were invited participants in the conference. Things fell into place in a charmed way and at the same time made perfect sense in creating a text that captures the effervescence of the moment while providing an enduring record of the firm ideas that emerged as learning built on learning during those brief hours of our gathering. Thus the ideas were conceived; thus the text emerged. This text would not have been possible without the dedication of its contributors.

Joseph O. Milner

Introduction

Developing Teachers grew out of a conference attended by educators from some of the elite universities of the nation. Its task was to examine five critical dimensions of Fifth Year/MAT programs so as to find what works well and discover what an ideal program might look like. The five focal areas present a comprehensive review of such programs: Students, Academics, Research, Internships, and Induction. These important dimensions of a graduate education program form the five major sections of this text. In addition, a Perspectives section is included where two teachers who prepared to teach at these institutions reflect upon those programs' effectiveness. This section also includes an essay by Barbara Kelley, President of the National Board for Professional Teaching Standards, that critiques the contribution of such programs to the teaching profession.

Each of the five chapters includes a set of essays by teacher educators who examine the topics at hand. The essays are followed by a transcript of the conversation that grew out of participants' response to those essays as well as response papers by discussion leaders. This important part of the book has a mosaic rather than a strict linear cast. Each of the five sections is introduced briefly with a statement that points to the national context for the essays and speaks generally about their content.

Another extremely valuable feature of *Developing Teachers* is the Program Profiles which offers detailed information submitted by each of the institutions that defines more precisely the five topics examined in the book. Prospective students, deans, faculty members at similar programs, secondary school administrators, human resource officers, and educators generally will find the book helpful because it serves their own interests but also because they can see that it lights the way toward a strong future for American education.

Chapter One

Perspectives

To introduce our exploration of teacher education programs, this chapter presents the perspectives of three individuals who are not members of education department faculty, but whose lives have been and continue to be directly affected by the shape of these programs.

The first piece is by Barbara Kelley, the chair of the National Board for Professional Teaching Standards. Kelley gives a personal account of the challenges she faced as a pioneering student in an early fifth-year education program. She then argues that today's fifth-year and MAT programs should be structured around the standards of the National Board. Since these standards are developed and implemented with strong input from practicing teachers, they carry the weight of field-tested authenticity. The National Board has also developed its criteria with induction and retention of excellent teachers in mind, no small issue in a time of looming teacher shortages.

The final two essays are by practicing teachers, both of whom are recent graduates of graduate education programs. Their testimony offers a revealing glimpse of the problems and successes of these programs in preparing teachers for careers in schools.

New Teachers for New Schools

Barbara Kelley
Chair, National Board for Professional Teaching Standards

When I was about twelve, I decided I wanted to become a physical education teacher. I maintained that conviction through high school, and became acutely aware of the low esteem in which teachers were held. My high school was a highly competitive private school for girls, and 135 of the 137 members of our graduating class went to college—many to Ivy League and other prestigious institutions. It was the late 60s, when career opportunities for women were just beginning to open up. My choice of career was both mystifying to my peers and clearly a disappointment to most of the influential adults in my life. The fact that my chosen discipline was physical education appeared to be an even greater source of anguish among the well-meaning adults who challenged my decision. When I was president of our National Honor Society, the high school principal asked me not to mention my anticipated major at our induction ceremony for new members, because it was important our top students keep their aspirations high. As I look back, the most disheartening aspect of that memory is the number of teachers who advised me to choose a more challenging career. Of course, as a stubborn adolescent, their advice only served to cement my conviction that my true destiny lay in physical education! I never wavered in my goal—well, maybe once, when our senior math class took an hour-long train ride into Brooklyn, NY to see a computer, and test out our semester projects. When that technician fed my hundred cards with blackened circles into the huge machine, and my little program actually worked, I did experience some moments of significant soul searching!

At the college level, my first actual experience in a classroom came my senior year, when I student taught in Fairfax County, Virginia. I spent five weeks at a brand new high school, one with thirteen physical educators on staff. I then spent five more weeks at an elementary school, teaching first through fifth graders. The job market was very tight in the early seventies, and I considered myself lucky to get a job in a poor, rural Virginia district that was instituting elementary physical education for the first time. Thirteen first-year teachers were hired for the entire county. My student teaching experience in resource-rich northern Virginia had done little to prepare me for my new job. I had a small section of blacktop behind the school with two basketball hoops, a tick infested field of foot-long weeds, and four basketballs. The children filled Clorox jugs with gravel to serve as field markers, and we made racquets out of panty hose and wire hangers for use with homemade yarn balls. The classes and expectations at each grade level were tiered by so-called ability, but the correlation with skin color and socio-economic status was blatant. There was no curriculum guide, no department head, no mentor teacher, and no support for me or for any other novice teacher. There were no accepted standards against which to measure my practice, and at my school, prompt attention to trivial bureaucratic tasks was valued more highly than skilled pedagogy. In May of my first year, the district laid off all thirteen physical educators: it was a tight budget year, and ours was the last program in—so the first program out. When my principal spoke with me about my plans, he told me he'd been authorized to offer me a job teaching reading. Even though I was desperate for a job, I knew I was neither qualified nor did I desire to teach reading and I turned him down. That was the year I learned hard lessons about student equity—within a school, within a district, and within a state. And I was very aware I would never have been offered that reading job in northern Virginia.

It was sheer luck that a notice in the national physical education journal caught my eye—about an internship program at the University of Maine at Orono. For an annual stipend of $2300 (which at the time was a little more than a third of a first-year teacher's starting salary), licensed teachers could work full time in a public school system, earning their master's in a year. The university had worked out an arrangement with the local school systems in the area. The districts paid both the stipend and the interns' tuition to the college, in exchange for full-time licensed teachers to staff their physical education programs. My application to the program was accepted, and I headed off to Maine.

It was a brutal year. Three credit hours were earned each semester through the submission of lesson and unit plans to my college advisor, who also observed my teaching several times during the year. It was not like student teaching: there was no mentor teacher. Interns were scheduled for three courses in the summer. I took home $99 every two weeks. I practically lived in the campus library on the weekend. My ordeal was less rigorous than the others': I was the only one who had teaching experience beyond student teaching, and had taken a graduate course on learning disabilities at the University of Virginia the prior year which I was able to transfer.

It is somewhat ironic that I am writing in a text that discusses attracting highly qualified candidates to the teaching profession, and teacher preparation programs—specifically fifth-year programs. I was the beneficiary of a fledgling fifth-year program more than two decades ago, although it was one that enrolled only those already holding a teaching license. In some ways, so much has changed in education since I went through my initial teacher preparation program. In other ways, there are things that remain the same, not the least of which is that I am afraid we have not come all that far in promoting teaching as a profession for those with exemplary academic credentials.

Not surprisingly, my first concern is the need to attract talented individuals to the teaching profession. Teaching has never been, and will never be, an easy job. It requires physical stamina, emotional stability, intellectual rigor, and an incredible commitment to students and their learning. The teaching profession cannot be a default career—one on which to fall back if you are unsuccessful at something else. The responsibility for student learning in this country must be placed in the hands of a highly qualified, competent, and knowledgeable teaching force. Those of us already in the profession need sustained and systemic professional development to enhance and enrich our skills. Considering the demographics of our country's teaching force, projections indicate a potential turnover of 50 percent of the current workforce in the coming decade. Who will be the candidates for those positions? How can we ensure the level of talent needed to accept the challenge of teaching? First, laissez-faire recruiting at the high school level is insufficient. Our son, an honor student, graduated from high school two years ago. Although he had made no mention of entering the military, he was actively pursued by the armed forces. He was provided with abundant information, contacted repeatedly by phone, and made well aware of the financial benefits and scholarships available. I would urge an equally aggressive approach to recruiting talented high school students to teacher preparation programs. Thinking back to my experiences in Virginia, there need to be strong support systems in place within teacher education programs for students whose K–12 experiences inadequately prepared them for the rigors of higher education. Please make no mistake about this: I am advocating high standards for entry into teacher education programs, high standards to remain in a teacher education program, and high standards for entry into the profession. But I am well aware that all students do not receive an equitable education across the country. Until we remedy that situation, we must find ways to invest appropriate time and resources in students who have unrealized potential to enable their success at the college level. Otherwise, we are ignoring a potential pool of teachers who could serve our profession and our students well.

Another pool of talented individuals lies in what was previously considered non-traditional education students: for example, people who might enter teaching as a second career, graduates of liberal arts programs who choose to pursue a graduate degree in education, and paraprofessionals who have worked in the schools and who now want to become teachers. The recruitment of these individuals poses a different dilemma. It is unlikely the prospective salary scale will serve as a significant inducement, particularly to those seeking a second career. The appeal of a teaching position may be lessened further by working conditions in which access to a telephone is frequently rare, and practitioners often have little or no say over policies and purchases that affect their students' learning. Although I will speak later about positive steps states and local districts might take to support new teachers, issues such as salaries and teacher empowerment must be addressed when recruitment and retention of qualified teachers is discussed. If we can attract them, many of these people will enroll in fifth-year and MAT programs, which are uniquely positioned to provide them with model preparation and induction support. My personal bias is that four years of undergraduate work does not provide enough time for teacher candidates to acquire the knowledge and skills needed to function independently in a classroom. There are no shortcuts to good teacher preparation. Programs most likely to produce the strongest teachers are ones in which the relationship between the faculty and the new teacher does not end abruptly when coursework is complete: there needs to be a strong support component during the first several years of induction.

That thought brings me to my next topic: local and state policies that can support teachers' continued professional development. In the ideal situation I see teacher preparation and professional development as a seamless process, so I would like to discuss first elements that I consider essential to pre-service training of a new teacher, then discuss ongoing support for teachers that can be provided by the teacher education community, local districts, and states. What are the standards we want teachers to meet? It will come as no surprise that my thoughts parallel the core propositions of the National Board for Professional Teaching Standards. Early in its history, the Board established these propositions as the basis for all our standards, regardless of the content area or developmental level of the students. Commitment to students and their learning means we must be willing to invest the time in getting to know our students—as individuals. We must understand the principles of child development, through adolescence and young adulthood. Up-to-date, in-depth content knowledge is critical. So we must ask if the coursework we offer our prospective teachers in the education department measures up to the rigor of the coursework offered in the colleges of arts and sciences. In the past, members of our profession have been criticized, and at times justifiably so, for an incomplete grasp of content knowledge. Comprehensive understanding of subject matter must be accompanied by a solid grounding in pedagogical skills. Incoming professionals must be provided with multiple teaching strategies to address the diverse learning styles of their students. They must know how to assess their students' learning, and how to individualize instruction based on that assessment. They need a full range of approaches for managing their classrooms. Teachers who enter a classroom with the ability to reflect on their practice, who have a systematic method to learn from experience and improve their instruction on the basis of their analyses, have been provided the most important tool for success. Teachers should enter the profession with the understanding that good teaching does not occur in isolation: collaboration with colleagues, parents, and others is an integral part of the job. When examining programs that prepare teachers, the degree to which these core propositions are addressed in a systematic, coherent fashion would be a key quality indicator.

Multiple experiences in diverse classroom settings under the guidance of both a mentor teacher and college or university faculty should be hallmarks of a good teacher preparation program. The selection of mentors is a crucial one. Until the culture of teaching changes, this may be the only opportunity the novice teacher has to work collaboratively with an accomplished teacher. True professional development schools in which best practices are consistently modeled provide nurturing environments for new teachers. The classrooms of National Board certified teachers are ideal placements for those just beginning to acquire pedagogical skills. These teachers have been assessed by their peers, and have met high and rigorous standards established for accomplished teaching. Mentoring is not simply an intuitive process; it is equally important for teacher educators to provide professional development for any veteran teachers who will be serving in that capacity.

In my role as Chair of the National Board for Professional Teaching Standards, I have had the opportunity to interact with teacher educators, pre-service teachers, new teachers, and veterans. There are two themes common to many of their comments about teacher preparation. The first goes back to the concept of respect: in what esteem are the professors and the education students held on campus? And if that is not as high as it is for the students and professors in other professional preparation programs, we must determine the reasons why, and address them. The second is an equally important concern: how recently have the teacher educators actually taught in a pre–K through 12th grade classroom for a sustained period of time? It is difficult to imagine lawyers being trained by professors who rarely, if ever, practiced law—or doctors being educated primarily by physicians whose contact with patients had been limited to observations of interns.

I wrote earlier of the need for an extended relationship between the university faculty and the new teacher beyond the scheduled end of his or her coursework. The induction period is probably the most critical time in a teacher's career, and I applaud the approaches that include mentoring by both regularly engaged teachers and continued support from colleges and university faculty. A crucial tool possessed by veteran teachers is the ability to rely on prior experience and to apply that knowledge to other situations. Incoming professionals lack that critical component, and need a mechanism through which they can access the experience and judgment of other professionals. As this process becomes more common, I hope it will be a catalyst for a change in the culture of teaching. Too many veteran practitioners are isolated from peers, and collaboration falls victim to time constraints or fear that seeking another's judgment may be perceived as a weakness rather than a strength. The incoming professional is not the only beneficiary of a formal structure for collaboration; experienced teachers invariably attest to significant professional development experiences when working with a teacher just beginning his or her career.

To return to the responsibility of policy makers, there are policies that can be established in local school districts that would provide support for both incoming professionals and veteran teachers. I mentioned teacher salaries and empowerment as recruitment issues earlier. In addition, new teachers are frequently given the most challenging assignments, multiple preparations, and then left to fend for themselves. Whether new teachers are placed in wealthy or poor districts, the critical resource of time is invariably in short supply. Although it is particularly difficult to adjust schedules at the elementary level, enlightened administrators can provide a schedule that enables additional planning time and/or peer assistance within the school day for beginning teachers. Unfortunately, until the induction period is recognized and accepted as a continuation of teacher preparation, this policy tends to engender animosity among long-time educators working in the same school with a full schedule. The problem is sometimes compounded by the perception that a new teacher has been hired specifically to bring new techniques and knowledge to a veteran faculty. I recently attended a gathering of first- and second-year teachers in Maine. These teachers were nominated by their administrators as outstanding practitioners. (Several of them, by the way, came from the University of Southern Maine's highly acclaimed five-year teacher education program.) When they shared their experiences, many of them remarked about the resentment they sensed from their colleagues. In several cases, administrators had indicated to the veteran teachers that their new colleague would "shake them up," or enlighten them on the most up-to-date methods for increasing student achievement. It's no wonder they were not welcomed with open arms upon their arrival, but the unfortunate result was that they felt they had no natural allies to whom they could turn for support.

It is particularly helpful when college or university programs establish partnerships with school districts that go beyond the mere placement of their students. A team approach which involves teacher educators, administrators and classroom teachers can have an effect well beyond the individual interns. Teacher education can work with administrators and practitioners on recognition of best practice and on problems most commonly faced by incoming professionals. Together they must begin to put in place a systematic and supportive induction process in school systems. Advocates for reduced class loads, increased planning time, mentoring, and collaboration can be enlisted. The false walls between teacher educators and classroom teachers begin to disintegrate when a true team approach is employed. Models in which accomplished pre-K–12 teachers are employed as adjunct faculty, and teacher educators are provided sustained opportunities to teach in elementary or secondary classrooms can dismantle those walls altogether. Among our two communities, there is a tremendous knowledge base about that art and science of teaching. The future of the teaching profession is too important to allow that wisdom to accumulate in separate silos.

The responsibility for student learning in this country rests primarily in the hands of the states, and clearly, state policies that address teacher quality issues will affect student learning. Well-publicized scholarships that attract talented students to teaching can help address the recruitment issue. Loan forgiveness programs are also effective tools, particularly in targeting high-need areas such as math, science, and special education. Some states provide funding for local support teams for new teachers. The trend toward performance-based licensure will have a profound effect on teacher quality and teacher preparation programs. It takes away the traditional reliance on credit counts, transcripts and seat time as indicators of readiness to be entrusted with the education of students. It enables diverse teacher preparation programs to be placed on a level playing field. State policies that also provide incentives for National Board Certification reinforce the states' commitment to a teaching force that continually seeks to reach high and rigorous standards.

Earlier I mentioned the somewhat bleak situation when I first entered the teaching profession. A quarter of a century later, I'm afraid that scenario still occurs in places across the country. But I'm becoming convinced that ten years from now, that will no longer be the case. Initiatives have been underway, thanks in no small part to the advocacy of other authors in this volume, to ensure that all students benefit from working with well-prepared, highly skilled teachers.

Because of my position with the National Board for Professional Teaching Standards, it is probably not surprising that I view the defining of standards for what constitutes accomplished teaching as the most important development in the profession over the course of my career. What is surprising is that I initially opposed the concept of National Board Certification. I was convinced that teachers would not be involved in the process, and that standards and assessments simply could not be developed that would apply equitably to all teachers. I was dead wrong on both counts. The National Board Standards provide a framework and a challenge against which to measure one's practice. For those who choose to participate in the assessments, the rigorous process provides meaningful professional development, regardless of the teaching environment. The incredible involvement of practicing teachers in every aspect of the National Board has assured authenticity. Board-certified teachers are already having an impact serving as adjunct faculty, mentor teachers, and demonstration teachers. Not only must we attract strong candidates to teaching, but it's crucial for our students that we keep our best teachers in the classroom, and National Board Certification is providing an incentive for them to stay. We are also finding that the standards are affecting teacher preparation programs across the country, and that many of the performance-based licensure systems being instituted in states are based upon National Board Standards. Graduate programs and partnerships with colleges and universities are being developed to familiarize teachers with the standards and/or to support them through the assessment process. There are Master's programs being developed that tie directly to our five core propositions. In one decade, this single reform has had a profound systemic impact on the profession, an impact that continues to grow.

I would like to close by sharing my own performance standard for measuring progress in the collaborative effort by teachers, teacher educators, and policy makers to improve and professionalize teaching in this country. Ten years from now I envision the principal of a secondary school proudly requesting the president of the National Honor Society to proclaim his or her intent to be a teacher—because the principal wants the top students in that school to keep their aspirations high.

The Teaching Habit of Mind: A Harvard Student's Perspective

Allyson Mizoguchi

My decision to become a teacher was irrational at best. I was not thinking about educational theories, philosophies, or other lofty, intellectual matters. I did not know what the word *pedagogy* meant, nor did I know of any alternate uses of the terms *jigsaw* and *scaffolding*. I was an education ignoramus; I had been an English major, and I simply wanted to be a high school English teacher.

My expectations for teacher education school were simple and unsophisticated: I wanted to learn how to be a teacher. I expected to fill a bag of tricks with clever lesson plans, classroom management skills, group facilitation skills, and public speaking skills. Back then, in my mind, that bag of tricks—the mechanical "how-tos" and "whats"—stood between me and a teaching credential. I knew that there was more to becoming a teacher than learning how to hold chalk and use the Xerox machine; however, I vastly underestimated the mental and emotional challenges I would face as I donned the role of teacher for the first time.

Before I began my year at the Harvard Graduate School of Education, I wanted to learn how to *do*. Little did I know that I would be learning how to think about teaching. I didn't realize that unless I could *think*, I would never be able to *do* my best.

Harvard did not promise to churn out accomplished educators in ten months' time, although there was a part of me that wanted Harvard to make and fulfill that promise. Harvard did not propose to chisel away at each individual in exactly the same way, creating a mass of Harvard-indoctrinated teachers who would fearlessly charge ahead into the world of education. Rather, Harvard's statements of purpose contained statements such as, "Candidates should *not* view what the programs profess as doctrine," and "it is hoped that candidates will use the philosophical contentions of the programs as a *template* for their own beliefs about teaching and learning."

This open approach to teaching education was enlightening but frightening. *I* was to determine—perhaps reshape—my way of thinking about learning, understanding, and hence teaching, by talking with others, reading literature, and reflecting. Teaching, I was to realize, is not about technical skills, but about habits of mind.

One cathartic moment that pointed me toward this new mindfulness occurred in the fall. I remember Vito Perrone, the director of the programs, asking my class to write a paper about something we truly understood—not just knew, but *understood*. I mulled over the difference between knowing and understanding for the first time in my life. Sadly, I realized that I didn't know a whole lot. I knew pieces of information, but true understanding must entail knowing how to use that information, even being able to teach it. My classmates brought in papers about making black bean soup, changing a flat tire, DNA replication. What did I write about? Shooting a basketball. Thirteen years of school and four years of college, and all I understood was how to shoot a basketball. And even that was a bit shaky. My new notion of understanding would later lay the foundation of my goals for my own students. As an English teacher, I want them to *understand* literature, not just know how to read it.

Besides learning and understanding, I began to question why. Once again, one of Vito's early paper assignments asked a vital question: "Why English?" In other words, why is English taught? What are my purposes as an English teacher? What should students of English eventually understand? Yes, reading and writing—but why? I had never before asked why. I had simply assumed and operated according to the given. Slowly, I began training my mind to think in terms of purposes while planning lessons in addition to strategies. Being purposeful lent new complexities and rewards to being an educator.

My decision to go to a teacher education program certainly had professional implications, but in teaching I soon discovered that the personal is inseparable from the professional. After only seven months of being a credentialed educator, I identified myself with the title of teacher with as much pride and inevitability as I would identify myself as woman, human, daughter, or sister. *Teacher* defines the way I live my life, the way I think, and the way my heart functions; it does not simply explain what I do for a living.

Being a teacher is not just a job, so teacher education should not be mere job training. It should engage, nurture, and educate the whole person, not just the professional exterior, but the personal, social, political interior. If teacher education could seep into the bloodstream, it would be welcome and useful there too. Teaching runs that deep.

Even with my knowledge of purposes, of learning and understanding, I found myself standing in front of my class during my student teaching stint, feeling completely naked. I wrote the following in my journal in October:

> I hate the feeling of not being on top of things, of not running a crisp class. I know what crispness tastes like. On Friday I had a tiny taste of that—productivity, we're all clicking together and moving in a prescribed, definite direction. Yesterday I felt like I was holding on by a thread. I felt like the entire period was a battle between me and them. I felt angry at them, and eventually angry at myself and disappointed in my teaching. I need to be aware of my expectations. I need to be firm and observant in my classroom; I need to enforce those rules I set without expectation.

I know now that education school did not need to teach me how to hold chalk, or how to keep grades organized, or how to make a seating chart. These and countless other skills are lessons learned in the trenches. Just as I became a conscientious driver by driving alone in the car without a passenger, I am learning the tricks of the teaching trade by working on my own, with nothing else to fall back upon.

However, I craved, ached for these "practical" pieces of knowledge during my year of education school. Like my students do, I figured that learning "stuff"—the technical know-how behind teaching—would make me an efficient, seamless teacher. During my first teaching experience, I didn't know what to do, but I knew how to think.

Unfortunately, as a first-year teacher, I am too busy putting out fires (and starting them, of course) to hone my "habits of mind." The furious pace and daily scramble at times still cries out for the lifesaver of more tricks, more tried-and-true methods, some magic bullet to get me through the moment. Yet I have come to realize that no sane person can have a meaningful life, or profession, living from harried moment to harried moment. There need to be threads; there needs to be a consistency of purpose. Because of my lack of experience, that consistency can only come from inside. The lessons from last year have found their context.

As the months have passed, I find myself still afloat—miraculously. The lifesavers have turned out to be inside of me all along: my brain, my heart. Harvard did not give me a new brain or a new heart; Harvard helped me to understand and reshape them. I am beginning to be able to pay attention to what I think and how I feel for the first time in a long while. The School of Education at Harvard prepared me to be a reflective practitioner of teaching rather than a technician. The word *practice* in *practitioner* reminds me of a continual effort, the need to practice what I do, and the inherent existence of imperfection.

It is impossible to fully train a teacher, as it should be. Teaching is too dynamic, too personal, and too deep to be teachable. The exhilaration of teaching comes from its unpredictability and its freedom of creation. Being a technician would not allow me the freedom to flex my mind and actually teach for understanding; being a practitioner does.

Master Teacher Programs: A Student's Perspective

Alice Sy

The success of a teacher is often judged by her students' preparedness upon leaving her class to proceed to the next level of education. In evaluating a teacher, it is also important to gather reactions from students regarding their opinions of the class. Was it interesting? Was it challenging? Did the students enjoy attending class? Do the students feel that it was worth their time? Do they feel ready for what lies before them? Having been the subject of these evaluations for two years, I now have the opportunity to step into the shoes of the evaluator. I have been asked to share the student's perspective on the Master Teacher Fellows program at Wake Forest University and other similar programs. In reflecting on my time spent at Wake Forest, I have asked these same questions. I hope my answers will offer some insights into the success of these programs.

Student Expectations

A student's decision to attend a graduate program such as the Master Teacher Fellows is based on certain expectations for academic quality, for the teaching internship, and for the selection of the other program participants. Fulfilling all of these expectations requires careful planning and design. I believe that many graduate teacher education programs are successfully meeting most of these expectations as outlined below.

First and foremost, students who are interested in and are recruited by these programs usually have strong academic backgrounds. These backgrounds are in the core subject areas, and usually do not include extensive coursework in education. While potential graduate students do have an interest in pursuing a career in education, they also value the academic rigor of their undergraduate coursework. In fact, many of them may have intentionally steered away from a focus on education because of its reputation for having an easier course load. While in reality teaching is one of the most intellectually challenging careers, courses designed for teachers are often disparaged. Therefore, presenting a strong academic program is essential to attracting quality students.

For example, when I chose to attend Duke University for my undergraduate work, my decision was based on the quality of the overall undergraduate education Duke could offer. While I could have attended a local teacher's college near home and received the necessary training, I understood that the experiences I would have at Duke would have a tremendous impact on the quality of my eventual teaching. I knew that this choice meant additional coursework after college to receive certification, but the importance of a solid foundation in my discipline was valuable to me, both personally and professionally. Therefore, as I began to research graduate programs the emphasis placed on academic rigor in the graduate school setting was a key element in my initial evaluation. For many students this rigor is found in the research component of the graduate program. Creating and maintaining a meaningful research project in the master teacher programs is crucial to attracting students who have the academic preparation to succeed as teachers.

However, academic preparation is but one facet of many that makes a teacher exceptional. Undoubtedly, the best teachers are those who have a passion for what they do each day in the classroom. As a Master Teacher Fellow, I expected that my peers and my professors in the program would demonstrate this passion. I did not want to be surrounded by graduate students who had entered teaching as a second or third choice career. I wanted to learn with people who had an essential desire to become teachers. In addition, I certainly expected my professors and my mentor teacher to share this enthusiasm. Creating a community in which excitement about education is fostered is crucial.

Areas of Concern: Then and Now

If I had been asked to identify weak elements of my program at Wake Forest immediately following my graduation, my concerns would have been focused on one issue: discipline. Despite the number of times that we were assured by professors that there really was no way to "teach" discipline to future teachers, I left the program thinking that perhaps they just had not thought it through well. I knew there had to be a way. In retrospect, less than two years after my graduation, I feel differently for two reasons. First of all, now I know they were right! I realize now the infinite combinations of circumstances that can occur, circumstances that I could not have imagined as a graduate student. Second, and perhaps more important, the program did prepare me for classroom discipline through my teaching preparation. While I recognize the multitude of situations that can arise, I have learned that the majority of these situations do not play out when my teaching is on target. When a series of teaching moments are strung together to make a great class, most problems disappear. Classroom control problems do not prevent good teaching; good teaching breeds an environment where children are too interested to misbehave.

Now, as a teacher seasoned with at least a little experience, I see different areas for improvement that I would not have been able to identify even a year ago. Foremost among these areas is the need to strengthen cross-curricular interaction. While science education students may take courses with English education students, these courses focus on general education issues. However, it is important for teachers in all disciplines to know what the best practice and best methods are in areas other than their own. As a science education student, I know what science teaching can look like at its best. Yet I am left wondering what a truly great Spanish teacher does for her students, or how the best history teacher can make the Revolutionary War come alive. I believe that my teaching would be enhanced by knowing what my students do in school the other six hours of the day. While I would love to have time to observe my coworkers on the job, the reality of daily life makes this nearly impossible. Exposure to the methods employed by teachers in other areas should be explored more during the graduate school experience.

Idealistic Preparation—Realistic Results

Upon leaving Wake Forest and entering the real world of teaching public school in Atlanta, I was initially concerned that my preparation from the Master Teacher Fellows program was not realistic enough. I feared that I would not be ready for the challenges that would present themselves as 150 faces in the seats in front of me each day. As I questioned my graduate experience, I was able to define its purpose more clearly. I concluded that my program had provided me with two things: a high standard for the art and practice of teaching, and a plan for continuous professional development.

One of the main purposes of a teacher education program should be to expose students to true excellence in the teaching profession. However, students of education should not only be able to identify exceptional teaching, but they should also be challenged to demonstrate this quality to the best of their ability. This may mean placing students in teaching internships where the situations are less realistic than in many schools, but these less than realistic situations allow student teachers to focus on their craft. The opportunity to practice in a teacher-friendly environment allows student teachers to recognize great teaching in themselves, not just in others.

For example, I was placed in a teaching internship where I taught two physics classes and two Algebra III classes. Except for some unmotivated or talkative students, the students in my classes were above-average in intelligence and attitude. Other teachers in the school would comment that I was not really being exposed to the true nature of education since I did not have to face serious discipline problems or deal with special-needs children. While I agree in their assessment of the ideal circumstances that I was working under, I disagree with the idea that it was not the true nature of education. The work that I did during this period was the best work I have done to date. Sure, I made mistakes and had some boring classes, but overall, I think my teaching was excellent for a first attempt. While I have not returned to the consistent level of quality that I set for myself during the internship, those weeks stand before me as a reachable goal. Many days, my teaching has taken second chair to the real struggles posed by discipline problems, emotionally deprived children, uncaring parents, endless committees, and faculty meetings. I learn lessons in these areas each day, and as I learn how to incorporate these new experiences into my teaching style, I approach the bar that I originally set for myself. I expect to reach the bar soon, and to move it up a few notches. However, had I never been sure that I could be a great teacher, I wonder where the bar would have been set. Unfortunately, too many teachers set the bar low, for they have never known how high it can go.

The second responsibility of a teacher education program is to model and encourage long-term professional development. We all know the negative effects static teachers have on their students. When a teacher fails to be a learner, the students follow suit. There are many ways in which Wake Forest's program fostered this ideal of professional development in its students.

First, the selection of mentor/master teachers to participate in the program requires that these participants are interested in more than simply having a student teacher. They are genuinely interested in collaborating on research projects, engaging in seminars with the graduate school, and learning about current trends in education. I am still amazed at the enthusiasm displayed by my mentor teacher in developing new methods for teaching. His teaching is excellent, yet he continually strives further, understanding that a good teacher can never be completely satisfied. His desire for growth and learning spills over into the lives of his students. Certainly, this model of professional development has made a lasting impression on my career goals.

Second, the development of a professional teaching portfolio during the last summer of the Master Teacher Fellows program emphasized both the work that goes into career development, and the satisfaction achieved from these times of self-reflection. Although we had taught for less than twelve weeks, we were asked to model the process for National Board Certification. Forcing students to articulate their goals for the immediate and the distant future is critical. After all, if you do not know where you are going, it is impossible to get there. As we strive to offer guidance and direction to our students as they face tough choices in adolescence, we must have direction in our own lives, or our advice will ring hollow to the ears of these perceptive young minds.

Conclusion

In closing, I want to share some thoughts from a recent faculty workshop held at my school. The leader of the workshop discussed the need for each teacher to know who she wanted to be—as a teacher, a spouse, a child, a parent, or a community member. If you know who you want to be, then each time you make a choice you can come closer to that vision of yourself. Wake Forest's Master Teacher Fellows program allowed me to develop a clear vision of who I want to be as a teacher.

Now, each time I speak with a child, plan a lesson, confer with a parent, or design a lab, I do so with this vision in mind. Most of the time, I choose to move toward that vision. When teachers do not have an ideal in mind, they can become frustrated with where they are, and the effect of this frustration on students can be devastating. Those of us who are committed to education in the deepest sense must insure that we are helping to create and define the visions of future teachers. As our nation's schools face a shortage of qualified teachers, programs such as the Master Teacher Fellows and others of its kind must shape the future of teacher education programs by insisting on raising standards across the board.

Chapter Two

Students

Attracting and selecting outstanding students is where it all starts. If teacher education programs don't select able and committed students, it is where it all ends. The confounding fact is that most studies have found that the very students that such outstanding programs recruit are the ones least likely to remain in the profession. The effectiveness of our programs and the effort we expend in the induction process for such bright students can mitigate this dreadful and stubborn fact but this ironic situation creates a serious dilemma for all of us. The decision that many of us have made to help solidify these young teachers' ties to their state and national professional associations and to help them take on leadership attitudes may strengthen their commitment and make the selection of such academically talented students seem less naive.

Academic achievement during the undergraduate years is often the yardstick used to select students for such programs. Some institutions admit very selectively and focus on the traditional criteria of GPA, GRE and letters of recommendation. These standards have been attacked for both their cultural bias and their lack of depth, but they still remain useful as a means of certifying a level of intelligence needed to teach effectively and predicting success in graduate studies. Other programs rely much more heavily on interviews and personality profiles as a way to determine candidates' personal engagement, empathy and commitment to teaching. Still others allow people who are successful in initial school internships or demonstrate strong professional interest in other ways to join their programs. Scholarships, stipends, and other incentives are far too scarce in this area of real need. States such as North Carolina have established lateral entry sites as a way to attract able undergraduates into teaching after they graduate, but recent research shows that the intent to attract a more academically talented group of students by this means has not been effective because new teachers who enter the profession through such backdoor operations do not perform as well on the General Knowledge section of the NTE Praxis exam as do those who enter through regular teacher education programs at colleges and universities.

National loan programs and state awards for teaching service are badly needed to attract good people into the rapidly depleted teaching ranks. The findings of *Teaching and America's Future* make it clear that serious school reform must begin with excellent teachers, so the attraction, selection, and support of outstanding prospective teachers needs to be the first order of business for all of us.

In the first essay, Palmer and Rong describe the University of North Carolina's reliance on its substantial name recognition and its superb academic reputation to attract strong candidates to its Graduate Teacher Education Program. Their task is to select the best in-state (70 percent) and out-of-state (30 percent) students who apply to the program. Typical measures such as GRE, GPA and letters of recommendation are used to select the best-qualified students. No financial aid is available but the institution's fine reputation allows the program to attract outstanding prospective teachers.

Bettandorff's paper outlines Agnes Scott College's entry into graduate teacher education as the demand for new teachers rose steadily through the 1990s. The strength of the institution's English faculty caused the program to focus on the preparation of English teachers and, though it is a small program, it has attracted 80 percent of its students from other institutions and 20 percent of them have been minority teachers. Agnes Scott does not have a regular scholarship award to attract students but it has discretionary funding for students who have financial need and can delay tuition to help prospective teachers ease the strain of an additional year of tuition expense.

Abrams and Andrew speak of the special way their program at New Hampshire admits students who hope to teach. They reject most of the academic formulas used by the majority of professional schools to determine who will be admitted. Teachers, they believe, are different from lawyers, entrepreneurs, and doctors, so candidates for their program must prove that they have the special skills needed for the classroom to be admitted. Because they have seen these skills in action and require a year's internship, they boast of a much lower attrition rate than most other programs. Their people unfailingly become career teachers.

Wake Forest uses multifaceted videotape interviews to admit a small number of academically talented students who are awarded full scholarships and $4,000 to $8,000 stipends. Vanderbilt allows much larger numbers of students to enter the graduate teacher preparation program where their commitment is tested by the rigor of the program. So, a wide variety of recruitment and selection processes are available to able students who hope to enter teaching at such academically elite institutions.

The Master of Arts Program: Admissions Procedures

William S. Palmer
Xue Lan Rong
University of North Carolina

University of North Carolina-Chapel Hill offers graduate preparation for prospective teachers of English, Latin, mathematics, science, and social studies in grades 9–12, and prepares teachers of foreign languages (French, German, Japanese, or Spanish), and music for grades K–12. The program is designed to prepare candidates for initial licensure in North Carolina. More specifically, the program provides opportunities for students to accomplish three general objectives: (1) to expand content specialization in methodology; (2) to gain an understanding of curriculum and instruction primarily at the secondary level (in foreign languages and music, there is a K–12 subject area focus); (3) to acquire knowledge and understanding of the social and psychological foundations of education.

The MAT program is a twelve-month, full-time, school-based, and student-centered program. It relies on partnerships between public schools and the university and utilizes the realities of the classroom as the motivation for students to connect theory and practice. Clinical placements include multiple settings and levels of instruction. Methods courses are subject-oriented; however, the contexts of schooling courses, learner and learning courses, and topical seminars are interdisciplinary and are ongoing over the entire twelve-month period.

Several interrelated Strands of Knowledge run through the program. The Teaching and Methods Strand focuses on the structure of discipline, tools of inquiry, and methodologies concerned with instructional strategies, planning, and assessment in varied learning experiences and communities. The Learner and Learning Strand assists teachers in the designing and implementing of learning experiences for students based on subject matter knowledge, the nature of the learning process, and the nature of learners. The Context Strand focuses on teacher-student-community relationships in schools and classrooms. Students prepare case studies of each type of relationship, analyze them from cultural, historical, and pedagogical perspectives, and develop strategies to address these issues in practice.

Admissions

Recruitment Procedures

At the national level, we recruit in two basic ways. For potential applicants, we send an attractive brochure outlining our MAT program, its description and justification, its course sequence, as well as content-area faculty members and their individual telephone numbers and e-mail addresses. Frequently the content-area faculty members conduct telephone interviews, write e-mail messages, or conduct other types of interviews to answer specific questions of the many out-of-state applicants.

At the local level, we receive many referrals from the arts and science faculty members at our own institution because they come to know students well who are earning a B.A. They refer their students who are interested in a teaching career to us for MAT program admission. A large number of our applicants also come from the North Carolina Teaching Fellows program, a four-year program for outstanding high school students who wish to teach in North Carolina.

We encourage local undergraduate students who are interested in becoming teachers to make early contact with us, thereby establishing an informal mentorship between the content-area faculty and potential candidates. This way, these students will receive accurate and timely information on the criteria for MAT program admission, including courses needed in their content area, preparation for teaching-related experience, information about required tests, and other matters related to admission procedures or the program itself.

We take several steps to recruit minority students. Our MAT brochures, along with our expressed intention to increase the diversity of our programs, are disseminated by our faculty members who advise minority student associations, both at the school and university levels. We also distribute posters containing MAT program information to ethnic study programs such as African Studies, Asian Studies and Latino Studies in the School of Arts and Sciences, hopefully encouraging interested minority students to contact the Associate Dean of Student Affairs in the School of Education as well as professors who teach the specialty content areas in our MAT program.

Selection

We know that the students with the highest GPA or standardized test scores do not automatically become the best candidates for an MAT program. We believe that what makes a good teacher actually involves many intricate factors such as an applicant's academic preparation and intellectual potential, personal attributes (maturity, flexibility, dependability), social skills (interpersonal and interpersonal, communication ability, organizational skills, and leadership style), positive and logical thinking ability, and the ability to exercise good judgment and to make wise decisions. Good teachers also need to be reflective, ethical, and emotionally responsive. Therefore, the successful selection of candidates for our MAT program is a complex procedure that includes some crucial steps.

The MAT Planning and Steering Committee receives the application files and distributes them to subcommittees that consist of the faculty members who specialize in each of the three Knowledge Strands. Specialty area subcommittees thoroughly examine the file of each applicant and make recommendations and select the most promising and qualified applicants to our program. The MAT Planning and Steering Committee then selects the most promising and qualified applicants using the recommendations from the subcommittees. The Associate Dean of Graduate Studies reviews the recommended applicants in relation to Graduate School requirements as well as School of Education requirements and selects applicants for admission.

Requirements for admission include a completed bachelor's degree from an accredited institution (with an undergraduate major in the content specialty area to which the applicant is applying); Graduate Record Exam (GRE) verbal and quantitative scores; a University of North Carolina at Chapel Hill Application completed and on file (including three recommendation letters and a statement of purpose); a list of verified experiences working with young people; and successful completion of a computer literacy test.

Rarely are students recommended for admission if they do not possess an undergraduate GPA of 3.0 or better in their content specialty area. Similarly, students are rarely considered for admission if they do not receive a 500 score or better on both the verbal and quantitative components of the GRE.

There are three justifications for the relatively rigorous requirements we have developed for a candidate's quantitative credentials in our selection. First, we believe that appropriate preparation in the chosen content area is of major importance; with such strong academic requirements, we believe there will be little chance that students will lack content knowledge during student teaching and first-year teaching. Second, our past experience has shown that applicants who have inadequate background in their content areas and who are less competitive academically may have substantial difficulties working inside a cohort of students who are very competitive. Third, we must consider the Praxis and other testing requirements for licensure in North Carolina. Many less academically competitive students have higher failure rates on these required tests.

We have reminded ourselves, however, not to overemphasize the quantitative criteria at the risk of ignoring other qualities essential to good teaching. In all cases, the applicant's three required letters of recommendation play an important part in the selection process. Moreover, each applicant's statement of purpose is read carefully to assist in selecting the most promising applicants. If there are conflicting selection data and marginal information in a few of the selection categories, then references and applicants are contacted by phone or e-mail to obtain more background information before the final selections are determined.

Accepted Applicant Pool and Funding

From the total pool of accepted applicants, 70 percent come from in state and 30 percent from out of state. Typically, we recommend approximately ninety students each year for acceptance into our MAT program, but only an estimated thirty applicants attend. This attrition is caused by a variety of variables, but the following two predominate. First, the majority of applicants in the pool apply to a number of top institutions throughout the country. Typically, these applicants are outstanding, with remarkably high credentials, and seek acceptance first at institutions other than UNC-CH. Secondly, many applicants hope to receive a stipend as part of their degree work, but we offer no such funding at present to applicants admitted to our program.

Program Rationale and Conclusion

We believe that a baccalaureate degree in the Arts and Sciences is the minimum requirement and a strong prerequisite to teacher education programs, especially at the secondary level, for two reasons. First, a strong liberal education can be a foundation that provides the basis for students to explore and experience much interdisciplinary learning, while at the same time developing an in-depth knowledge of an academic discipline for later use as teachers of specific content areas. Second, in order to meet the requirements of the General College and each specified academic discipline, our previous undergraduates majoring in secondary education had little time to pursue a coherent and in-depth program of professional studies in education. Therefore, our present fifth-year MAT program is conceptualized in order to integrate program strengths with students' experiences and their teacher training needs.

Students: Recruitment, Selection and Funding

Ruth S. Bettandorff, Ph.D.
Agnes Scott College

Background

As a highly selective-admission liberal arts college for women, Agnes Scott College has a long and proud tradition of preparing outstanding educators with a strong background in the liberal arts. Throughout most of its 109-year history, the college has had a non-degree undergraduate teacher education unit through which future teachers have developed extensive field experiences and theoretical knowledge in education to supplement the content knowledge developed in their major academic areas. The focus of teacher education has always been toward excellence in education in the public schools and the training of teachers for public school teaching careers.

In 1991, in response to the college's strategic planning process calling for new and innovative programs, the faculty of the departments of English and education developed the college's first graduate program, The Master of Arts in Teaching Secondary English. In June 1992, the college began offering its first graduate and first coeducation program (federal law mandates that all newly created graduate programs cannot deny entrance to students on the basis of gender, race or creed). This program came about as a response to data from the Georgia Professional Standards Commission (1990) which showed that during the 1990s as much as one-third of the current pre-college teaching force would retire and that the national teacher demand was expected to increase by more than 24 percent. More than half of the hiring was to take place at the secondary level. In Georgia, the graduates of teacher education programs do not currently satisfy even half of the demand for certified personnel. For many years the English and education faculty at Agnes Scott had been watching and discussing the trend of declining writing and grammar ability of students graduating from high schools throughout the nation, particularly in public schools, and the impact of this trend both on preparation of students for college and for future generations of students.

What is the program?

The Master of Arts in Teaching Secondary English program at Agnes Scott College is designed specifically for students who have completed a bachelor's degree in English (or a closely related field such as communications or journalism) but who did not complete a teacher certification program at the undergraduate level and who want to teach secondary English in the public schools. The program is fifty-one semester hours, with twenty-five hours in education (including methods and student teaching) and twenty-six hours in English literature and pedagogy. Students must complete a minimum of forty-five graduate hours at Agnes Scott. Classes are small with average class sizes of ten to twelve. The program cycle for full-time students is June through August of the following year. Part-time students and students who do not meet the prerequisites of an undergraduate degree (or equivalent hours) in English enroll for two or more years. Students who do not have the necessary prerequisites or who want to be part-time are the only students admitted in the fall or spring semesters; all others begin the program in June.

The MAT program specifically focuses on preparing teachers who are trained to address issues of gender equity in our public school classrooms. As a women's college, Agnes Scott is uniquely sensitive to this concern. The program is designed to raise consciousness on gender issues and to provide teachers with methods and strategies which are effective in ensuring gender-fair education in the classroom. Special emphasis is given to multicultural experiences and cooperative learning experiences.

Who are the Students?

The program enrollment is fairly evenly divided between students of traditional age who enter the program shortly after graduating from their undergraduate program and return-to-college students who want to pursue teaching after another career or after raising children. The profile of the thirty-five students registered (both new and returning) in June 1997 was:

- 90 percent full-time; 10 percent part-time
- 90 percent female; 10 percent male
- 80 percent white; 15 percent African American; 5 percent other
- 60 percent ages twenty to thirty; 25 percent ages thirty-one to fifty; 15 percent over fifty
- 80 percent non-Agnes Scott graduates; 20 percent Agnes Scott graduates
- 100 percent U.S. citizens

How are Students Recruited?

Recruiting is the responsibility of the Director of Graduate Studies. Students are recruited through a combination of internal and external publicity and personal contacts. A marketing plan has been developed which includes:

- Direct mailings to inquiry data bases, colleges, and universities, area school systems, graduating Agnes Scott students, Agnes Scott alumnae, and career planning offices
- Paid advertisements in newspapers and on radio
- Internal campus publicity
- Flyers at various community and college functions
- Attendance at graduate recruiting fairs
- Agnes Scott Graduate Studies Web Site
- Web site listings at commercial graduate program sites
- Listings in national publications such as Peterson's Guide and The Graduate School guide

- Membership in the National Association of Graduate Admissions Professionals

Personal contact is one of the most effective recruiting tools of the program. When prospective students calls to inquire about program specifics, they are referred to the director. A personal relationship is established, careful notes of questions and dates of calls are recorded, and students are encouraged to make further direct contact whenever needed. If a student calls a subsequent time, the record of previous calls and any follow-up action is available. This individualized attention is critical to a student's choosing our program instead of larger, less-expensive public programs available in this area.

Every inquiry about the program is logged on a Marketing Survey/Mailing List form allowing us to track where students learn about the program, dates they were mailed information, and dates they were entered on the inquiry data base.

What is the Admissions Process and Requirements?

When students calls to inquire about the program, they are mailed an admission packet (and entered on the inquiry database for future mailings) which includes the name, telephone, and e-mail address of the director. This information often leads to the direct contact which we consider crucial to leading to an admission.

Admission requirements include:

- A bachelor's degree in English
- Minimum undergraduate grade point average of 2.75
- Passing score in PRAXIS I (or SAT, ACT or GRE)
- Admissions interview with the MAT Admissions Committee when requested
- Two-page Statement of Purpose for Graduate Study
- Portfolio of two writing samples
- Three letters of recommendation attesting to fitness for a teaching career

Completed applications are reviewed by the MAT Admissions Committee which is comprised of the chairs of the English and education departments and the Director of Graduate Studies. Well qualified candidates are sent letters of admission and other qualified candidates are scheduled for personal interviews with the committee. Originally we interviewed every candidate but this became too time consuming and we now only interview those for whom questions are raised.

Admission categories include Full-Standing, Conditional Status for one semester only, or Graduate Special-Non Degree for twelve hours maximum (usually for transfer or certification purposes).

How are Students Selected?

Students are selected following review of the entire admissions packet listed above by the MAT Admissions Committee. The key elements are academic credentials; evidence of interest in becoming a teacher of high school-age students; and strength in writing, grammar, and literature. The average undergraduate GPA for admitted students in the last four years is 3.19. In addition to the academic credentials, the committee looks for past experience with teenagers, a sense of excitement and enthusiasm for teaching, creativity in thought, strong communication skills, self-confidence, and projection/appearance. When an interview is required, each interviewer completes an Interview Response Sheet and results are tabulated for use in the admission process.

How are Students Funded?

The Agnes Scott College Board of Trustees initially approved the MAT program with the basic understanding that the program was to be self-supporting and, if possible, revenue-producing. Data collected from other comparable graduate programs showed that graduate students needed some type of financial assistance and that a typical amount was 50 percent of undergraduate tuition. Projections of enrollment and revenue led us to propose to the Board of Trustees that graduate students be charged one-half of undergraduate tuition and that no additional Agnes Scott financial aid be available to them. The board accepted this proposal and that has been the operation policy. Admitted students are, if they qualify, eligible for federal loans. Several have received educational assistance from employers or other sources.

To apply for federal financial aid, MAT students contact the Office of Financial Aid and are given assistance in filing the required forms. The Office of Graduate Studies mails financial aid forms to applicants who indicate on the admission form that they want them. Graduate Studies does not provide any financial advising.

Agnes Scott has a payment plan which allows students to spread tuition payments over a ten-month period. Graduate students are eligible to do this; however, to date none have applied. A fund for student emergencies is maintained in the Dean of Students Office and graduate students may apply for emergency, short-term funding (amounts of less than $500) if needed.

One interesting aspect of funding involves those students who are Agnes Scott graduates. The College has a fifth-year recruiting plan for undergraduates which promises them free tuition the year (fall/spring or spring/fall) immediately following graduation to take any courses they wish, from one course to a full load on a space-available basis. Included are teacher certification courses and the MAT program. Students entering the MAT must pay summer tuition but can attend fall and spring semesters without charge.

Admission to the University of New Hampshire Teacher Education Program: Criteria for Success

Eleanor Abrams
Michael D. Andrews
University of New Hampshire

The Context

Our Master of Arts in Teaching program dates back to the early 1960s. It has now become integrated with an undergraduate-graduate program, a so-called five year program which began in 1973-74. Two populations are served:

- Undergraduates who take several education courses at the undergraduate level at UNH and then continue for a year or more of graduate work including a full year internship.
- Graduate students who have taken few, if any, education courses at the undergraduate level. This latter group is comprised of recent graduates (no post-college job experience) and graduates who have

been out of college for a few years and in most cases have had career experience, but not in education.

Importance of Admissions

Much of what makes a good teacher is determined by whom we choose to admit to our programs. Teaching is not doctoring or lawyering. It has almost nothing in common with conducting surgery or piling up legal precedents. It has to do with managing, motivating and mentoring twenty to thirty active young children at a time—sometimes up to 150 of them a day—many of whom don't want to be taught. In no other profession is the following combination of qualities requisite: effective interpersonal skills for dealing with both children and adults; organizational abilities; outstanding communication skills; good academic skills; clear thinking; intellectual curiosity; flexibility; perceptiveness; the ability to exercise good judgment and make decisions in a complex, rapidly changing environment; ethical behavior; and a commitment to care for each and every child. Most of these prerequisites for good teaching are well established when candidates for teaching are admitted—especially when they are admitted at the graduate level.

Not everyone can be a teacher; therefore, we need to refocus on those essential qualities of good teaching as we admit people to our programs or our hope to develop a specialized, scientific body of procedural knowledge will be of little use.

Personal Qualities as Predictors of Teaching Success

In 1995 we conducted a study of our best and our weakest interns (Andrew, Lent, Moorhead, Moss, Singer, & Woolf, 1996). We asked forty university supervisors to identify their strongest and weakest interns over a four year period. For each intern identified, the supervisor filled out an open-ended survey indicating major strengths and major weaknesses of 100 interns. Overwhelmingly, the most important qualities of outstanding teachers were personal qualities such as the ability to deal positively with children and adults, professional commitment, willingness to work hard, enthusiasm, reflectiveness about their work, and a good sense of humor. The next most important qualities found in strong teachers were content knowledge followed by knowledge of the teaching and learning process.

The best predictors of success or failure in the teaching internship were estimates of those essential personal qualities as judged by teachers who worked with interns in early field experience courses. GRE scores were useless predictors as were age of teaching candidates, or (unhappily) judgments of education professors. Undergraduate GPA had only moderate predictive value.

We have come to value early, direct experience in classrooms as an essential part of the admissions process. Graduate students who are just entering the teacher preparation program start with an initial summer experience called Live, Learn, and Teach. Positive recommendations from this experience are prerequisite to continuation in the program. The seven-week program serves as a recruitment tool, a screening experience, and a foundation of educational philosophy and real school experience. Taught by an experienced team under the direction of UNH faculty members, Live, Learn, and Teach is a challenging seven-week program designed for prospective teachers to learn how to design and implement activity-centered and community-based curricula. The program begins with a Wilderness Week in New Hampshire's White Mountains where participants engage in hiking, writing, rock climbing, and sharing daily tasks. The emphasis is on developing collaborative problem-solving methods that can be adapted to teaching. Participants return to Durham, NH to plan and lead Summer Learning, a five-week, activity centered, interdisciplinary summer program for children (grades 1–12) from Durham and the New Hampshire seacoast area. Team meetings, individual conferences, and workshops are integral to the program. Communities of support and communities of inquiry are a recurring thread throughout our teacher preparation program.

When students complete the Live, Learn, and Teach summer program their work as teachers is assessed by both the cooperating teacher and the university faculty who teach the seminar. Students are also involved in their own self-assessment. This is the foundation of our admissions process.

Graduate Admission

Candidates for admission to the initial certification program must go through a rigorous admissions process. Successful completion of Live, Learn, and Teach, including a positive recommendation to continue, is an important step to admission. Over the past ten years from 20 to 30 percent of candidates have been denied admission at the Teacher

Education Graduate Program. This is a competitive process and an individual must meet specified admissions standards.

We have ten criteria that guide the admissions process. In the assessment of each applicant we seek evidence that our students have the following knowledge, abilities, and dispositions:

1. Motives to teach that include a strong social commitment to contribute to society through education.
2. A disposition to care for each and every one of their students.
3. An ability to interact positively with children and adults.
4. A capacity to win the respect of their peers and be effective in group interactions, showing openness to the needs and views of others.
5. Well-developed communication skills, including speaking, writing, and listening skills as well as an ability to engage others in both the giving and receiving of information and feelings.
6. Perceptiveness—the ability to identify and process the relevant details in their environment, especially in the context of a classroom.
7. The ability to make reasonable judgments in a context of complex situations that change from moment to moment.
8. The capacity for clear thinking and an ability to translate their thoughts into simple and clear explanations.
9. Superior academic skills: extensive knowledge of at least one major discipline, intellectual curiosity, and the ability to be open to the unknown.
10. A disposition to take charge of their own learning, which includes the active pursuit of feedback and the willingness to take thoughtful risks. We believe that by admitting students who demonstrate such abilities, knowledge, and affective skills, we will produce high quality teachers.

The Graduate School application process requires a standard UNH Graduate School data form; a personal résumé; a written narrative stating the reasons applicants want to become teachers; their relevant qualities for teaching; their life experiences that have shaped their beliefs about teaching and learning; three letters of recommendation with accompanying assessment rating scales; an undergraduate transcript; graduate transcripts where applicable; and GRE scores. Once all required materials have been submitted to the UNH Graduate School, admissions staff calculate the applicant's cumulative grade point average (GPA) from all institutions attended, complete an admissions action sheet, and send a copy of the completed file to the Coordinator of Graduate Studies in Education. The Coordinator adds the Live, Learn, and Teach recommendations and the student's self-assessment paper. The completed application files are forwarded to the Teacher Education Program Admission Committee.

Selection Process

After the Teacher Education Admissions Committee receives the admission files, subcommittees thoroughly examine each application. Each subcommittee consists of the faculty members who specialize in the relevant area of teacher education and content area specialists. This committee uses a scoring rubric based on the agreed upon admissions criteria which each member scores (a range of 4 to 1) and comments in writing on an applicant's grades, GREs, personal statement, personal recommendations, the Live, Learn and Teach recommendations and the self-assessment paper.

In determining admission of students to the graduate teacher education program, several criteria are used:

1. The undergraduate record. The undergraduate grade point average of the middle 50 percent of students admitted to the graduate programs in teacher education falls in the range of 2.93 and 3.48 with a yearly average of 3.1 to 3.2 for all admitted students. Both the content and education courses are examined.
2. Scores on the GRE. Scores of the middle 50 percent of students admitted to the graduate programs in teacher education fall in the following range: Verbal 440–560; Quantitative 460–620; Analytical 500–650.
3. Positive recommendations from Live, Learn and Teach, and from those able to offer information about a candidate's performance in other teaching situations or related areas.
4. Positive recommendations regarding academic ability, motivation, and interpersonal skills.

The subcommittee meets, discusses each case and makes a recommendation to admit or deny admission. The application, the scored recommendations and individual written comments, and the final subcommittee recommendation are then reviewed by the Teacher Education Admissions Committee. The Departmental Admissions Committee and the Graduate School approves the decisions for denial or admission to the Teacher Education Program.

Conclusion

To be effective, the Teacher Education Program must begin with a sound admissions procedure; it is our most important task. A careful dialogue can help us identify those essential personal attributes, dispositions, and skills which are at the heart of good teaching. Our admissions process focuses on the qualities we think are important for future teachers to have in the classroom. Some of these capabilities can be measured with quantitative methods such as content and pedagogical knowledge through GPA and GREs. However, knowing the discipline is not enough. Our students, as future educators, need to be able to choose the appropriate content knowledge and to teach it effectively to each and every student, each and every day. This is truly a daunting task for any professional. Through the use of early field experiences, directed personal statements, and student self-assessments, we can gain insight into those prerequisites necessary for the type of teachers we want in our classrooms.

The best environment to make assessments about potential for teaching is in the classroom. A strong teacher preparation program should begin with this kind of experience, and structures should be in place to use this experience as a basis for student self-selecting for teaching as well as for informed admissions decisions.

Response

Margo A. Figgins
Carl A. Young
University of Virginia

The requirements for student admission across institutions include satisfactory undergraduate record, GRE scores, and recommendations. While the nature of the admissions process for MAT-type programs at the University of New Hampshire, Agnes Scott College, and the University of North Carolina at Chapel Hill share certain basic admissions requirements in common, a number of differences distinguish them. New Hampshire's focus on personal qualities such as positive interpersonal skills, commitment, good humor, and reflectivity are impressive because they are assessed in a field-based teaching experience called Live, Learn and Teach. This is an innovative way to give balance to the admissions process which traditionally favors quantitative data such as GRE scores and undergraduate GPAs. Using its own research into the personal qualities of its "best" and "weakest" interns, the New Hampshire program is able to assert the importance of early, direct experience in the classroom as an essential part of the admissions process. The input of both co-operating teachers and the students themselves foreshadows one of the discussion themes that follows: the role played by clinical faculty in the admissions and acceptance process.

In the case of Agnes Scott College, its program's setting, that of a selective liberal arts college for women, sets it apart from the other coeducational institutions represented and shapes some of its program concerns such as the commitment to gender equity, which necessarily commutes to admissions criteria and processes, and to the admission of male and age-diverse, as well as female, populations. With its history of not requiring the GRE until 1997, a change imposed by the Georgia Professional Standards Commission, its application process is more extensive than many; it includes a statement of purpose, a portfolio of written work and an interview process, all of which provide the opportunity for qualitative data to offset quantitative data for those students who do not test well. The Agnes Scott program also responded to the data indicating an extreme rise in demand for certified personnel in the state of Georgia. Not unrelated is the awareness of a need among graduate students for financial assistance averaging about 50 percent of tuition costs. That awareness led to the policy that graduate students be charged one-half of undergraduate tuition. In addition, Agnes Scott has a unique recruiting plan that offers its undergraduates a year of tuition-free study in the MAT program. While Agnes Scott does not have a specific minority recruiting plan, this focus on funding undoubtedly gave rise in the discussion of admissions procedures to more general questions of funding for MAT students and, more pointedly, to special incentives to attract minority candidates.

The MAT program at the University of North Carolina at Chapel Hill program has a very rigorous application process but an unusually high attrition rate (17–20 percent), which was attributed to a lack of funding, as well as changes in the program which resulted in the program taking longer to complete, thereby exacerbating student financial need. So, while the overall reputation of UNC ("the southern part of Heaven") as a public Ivy has made the recruitment of talented MAT candidates a simple chore, the realities of completing the program have made its effectiveness in contributing teachers to the field problematic. Perhaps the most distinguishing feature of the UNC program that relate to New Hampshire and Agnes Scott is the involvement of the arts and sciences faculty. A steering committee receives three strands of input, one of which is an arts and sciences-based committee. This information adds to the interest in who has input into the admissions process, and emerged as a crucial aspect of the discussion.

Students: Recruitment, Selection, Funding

A Plenary Conversation

Participants: Lawrence Wakeford, Brown University; **Ruth S. Bettandorff,** Agnes Scott College; **William Palmer** and **Xue Lan Rong**, University of North Carolina; **Michael Andrew**, University of New Hampshire; **Joseph Milner** and **Leah McCoy**, Wake Forest University; **Rosemary Thorne**, Duke University; **Beverly Carter**, Stanford University; **Margo Figgins**, University of Virginia; **Alan Reiman**, North Carolina State University; **Charles Myers**, Vanderbilt University.

Wakeford: I'm interested in the role clinical faculty members play in admissions. What's their role in the admissions and selections process for candidates?

Bettandorff: They do not have a role in the admissions selection process at Agnes Scott right now.

Palmer: We have a number of clinical members faculty but they are not proportionate to the content areas in the MAT program. I'm thinking of someone like Susan Bellage who works with Xue Lan

[Rong]. We often don't have them officially as part of the selection committee, but if they come to us and say, "three of our students are very strong and are going to apply to our program, look carefully at these and I will send you a recommendation personally," I always record that.

Andrew: At New Hampshire, the committee that governs teacher education voted last year to include teachers who work at our professional development sites in the admissions process. We've yet to implement that because of several problems, not the least of which was legal issues raised by the graduate school regarding access to confidential references when they did not have the same status as tenure track faculty. That has now put our plan on the back burner.

Milner: The way we avoid that problem is to use videotapes. Right now those tapes are at East High School where our clinical faculty in English and students who are in the program are selecting four people who are going to be invited to join our program next year.

Wakeford: So, people buy and submit a tape?

Milner: They have to submit a tape because we have people applying from distant places; it wouldn't be fair to have to come here. So we use a videotape interview; students respond to a set of questions that are sent to a faculty member at their university or to an appropriate adult.

McCoy: That is the second level, but first there is a formal application process that includes GRE scores, recommendations, and GPAs. After that initial screening, we invite finalists to participate in the videotape interview.

Palmer: All of the people we have admitted have been observed in a classroom situation by classroom teachers. I tried to make that clear in our presentation. That is our biggest predictor of success. We use that very heavily. The teachers have a role in that but they don't sit on the committee that makes the final decision. They have input, but they do not participate in the final decision.

Thorne: We have a lot of teachers who send people to us who have taught our student teacher but who are not on the committee. We do have one of our mentor teachers who sits on the admissions committee and reviews every application and also helps us conduct interviews. The way we get around the confidentiality issue is that our mentors are adjunct faculty of the graduate school, so they are entitled to see all of the applications.

Carter: At Stanford we have selection committees that are subject-matter specific. They include the methods instructors, a student, university supervisors, and others who read these applications and we have never had the legal issue raised. The only restriction is that our students may not read applications of current Stanford students. Each of them uses rubrics to rate the application and the rubrics go to the faculty sponsor and me to admit and we recommend them to the Associate Dean for Admissions. Actually, having people in different kinds of roles really helps us to see those applications better. People pick up different things in those statements of purpose that we might not be able to see otherwise.

Palmer: It impressed me that clinical teachers—mentor teachers—and students were on admissions committees. What I find is that our applicants are so good, it is so hard to accept one over another. They are outstanding in many ways. Occasionally we will find one or two that we can easily not accept. So we need a lot of people screening such fine applicants. The difficult issue for us is a political one where I will get a an e-mail from the Dean saying, "So and so, who is in governor Hunt's office, has just sent me this about one of the applicants for your MAT program." Does that mean that I am supposed to accept that person just because the governor's office has called?

Rong: There are a lot of people who make a very political statement of, "I want that person in the MAT program." Sometimes it's really easy to do. Say it's music, for example; if there is a space available in music for that person, then nothing is said. But, if it is a very competitive area like English where we can only take 20, and there are three applicants who are good but not better than the others who are being pushed by people, it makes me most uncomfortable to make a decision based on that kind of political clout. I think having a great variety of voices on a committee and making the whole committee accountable for the selection of the most qualified applicants would help in that kind of a decision-making situation. I'm curious if any of you find that situation at work in your program occasionally. It is not a dominating factor, but it's there.

Figgins: I'm wondering about minority recruitment. What kind of processes or systematic attempts are made in that direction?

Palmer (UNC): At UNC we give special fellowships through Student Services. There are not many: only four. We invite minority MAT applicants to apply for them. Often two or more will end up in our program.

Bettandorff: Our attempt to recruit both male students and other minorities into our program takes a little different twist. The male students that come to our program have almost always had some kind of real strong mother or wife or some female in their life that has made them able to come into the women's college environment. Because we are located in Atlanta, and because our mission is to improve the teaching in public schools, we want to have as large a number as possible of minority candidates. So, we do try to spend a lot of time recruiting those students.

Wakeford: How do you do that?

Bettandorff: By talking to principals, teachers, and other students who know students who might come into the program. We also follow up on our minority undergraduates; we encourage them to apply to the program. They are subject to pretty much the same college admission criteria, so they are excellent candidates.

Reiman: One of the things we have done at our institution is to have a peer mentor program in place for minorities. When minority students come to the campus—it's a large institution dominated by white students—there will be people there who help them make the transition to this huge new culture. That has been a very successful program because there are some unique issues that come up and having a peer mentor they can go to and confide in has been really significant.

Wakeford: is that for the whole school?

Reiman: That is for the entire university. Not just for the college. Within every one of the academic colleges there are minority advisors who work with the peer mentors and minority students. That also has been extremely helpful because it's not just a student link, but it includes an administrator that has a great sensitivity to the particular issues and the needs of minorities.

Myers: on the issue of minority recruitment at Vanderbilt, I have to talk about it in terms of all of the graduate degrees in teacher education; we have an MAEd program as well as an MAT. Financial aid does not make a distinction between the two. We were successful a number of years ago in convincing our dean that there were a certain number of slots needed that were half tuition: slots for master's degree people, people who have an academic degree and either come to college soon after that or are career change people. Once we did that, we asked the dean if a certain number of minority students could come free as opposed to just half tuition. So we have created six slots where applicants don't have to pay the tuition. Of course they still have living expenses. We have never filled the six slots so it means that minority students can come free. We invite these students because we know that everyone taking the GRE indicates their majority/minority status, and the institutions that receive their scores, so we receive that data from the ETS Minority Locator and then write all of the students in that national pool to say that if you want to be a teacher, you can be admitted to our institution and will not have to pay any tuition. For us, tuition is between $850–900 per credit hour so it's substantial. It's just a commitment that we've made. And it's kind of interesting that we don't really advertise that any more. Any institutions could do it. It was very interesting, because we started to get a lot of calls. I got all the calls: "I want to come to your minority teacher education program." I let them know it's not a minority teacher education program, but if they fit into this classification there is a special pot of money that deals with tuition funding. Actually the dean didn't want to do that after a while because he got too much flack from other programs. So what we basically say now is apply and if you qualify and if you are a minority, we will consider offering you aid. Now if we had thirty-five minority applicants that fit the bill, we would be in trouble, but we're only talking about two and three a year. The academic credentials are what hurts, because you don't have a whole lot of minority students who want to be teachers who test that well and have above a 3.0 GPA from a prestigious academic institution. We still have very few minority applicants and it's probably because we have all those artificial academic criteria.

Wakeford: One thing that has helped us it the Multicultural Alliance. I don't know how many of you are familiar with that group but they have been very helpful over the past four years helping us to attract minority students to our program. I don't know if this is true of every institution that they are affiliated with. The students from our class actually teach in a local independent school as their student teaching experience. They are paid for teaching part time. By agreeing to modify our program, it has allowed us to attract some very high-quality minority students. Once we get a student in there, they talk constantly about our program. That's the one thing that has helped us attract minority students.

Discussion Response

Margo Figgins
Carl A. Young
University of Virginia

Two central themes emerged in the conversation following the presentations on the admissions component of teacher education programs: the role of clinical faculty in the selection of new students, and minority recruitment, admissions, and retention.

The Role of Clinical Faculty in the Selection of Students for Admission

Involvement of clinical faculty in the admissions process ranged from none to informal to formal. Several participants observed that legality, while an issue, need not be an obstacle. Wake Forest has devised a creative solution: the videotape interview. At Duke, because teacher mentors are considered adjunct faculty, clinical faculty involvement is a non-issue. The practice of these two institutions offers inventive ways in which to include clinical faculty.

Stanford's perception is that having people in different roles reviewing applications makes it possible to see aspects and nuances to the application that might otherwise go unnoticed. The implication is that clinical faculty members have a distinct contribution to make to the admissions process and that teacher education programs should more systematically involve them in ways similar to those structured by Wake Forest and Duke.

No one questioned the possible down side of clinical faculty involvement in the admissions process, but programs may need to consider the problems that may arise. For instance, is there anything that might be gained by the exclusion of clinical faculty? Assuming that they are involved, how many clinical faculty members should be involved and in what proportion on the admissions committee? What are the criteria for selection of these clinical faculty members from the larger pool of those available? What are the possible effects of some clinical faculty members being chosen while others are not? What advantages does informal inclusion in the process have? What are the disadvantages? What advantages and disadvantages does formal inclusion have? What should be the nature of their involvement? To what criteria are they uniquely prepared to speak? Should all subject matter areas and grade levels be represented in the process?

While there is no indication that politics played a serious role in the admissions process, the fact that it was mentioned suggests the need for vigilance in this area. Future discussion of such pressures, external or internal, that might adversely affect the admissions process should include how they might be effectively countered, through diverse committee membership and other means in the decision-making process.

It would seem that further discussion about admissions criteria is also needed. If teacher educators agree with Abrams and Andrew that personal factors such as commitment, enthusiasm, effective interpersonal communication, and reflectiveness should weigh in as importantly as the candidate's age, previous experience, undergraduate GPA, and GRE scores, then the traditional admissions process needs to be changed to include these personal measures. Such change suggests the need for carefully designed rubrics and the training necessary for accurate rubric scoring. It further suggests the need for follow-up research to determine if stronger teacher performance in fact results from a selection process that includes these personal qualities.

Finally, the assertion that the selection process should begin in the classroom has enormous implications for programs that seek applicants located beyond the immediate vicinity of the teacher training institution. It is unlikely that many such students would be willing to uproot their lives and make financial commitments to a summer classroom-based program which would determine their acceptance into the graduate teacher training program. While the idea of beginning the admissions process in the classroom has efficacy for assessing a candidate's personal qualities, we must consider alternative admission structures that are sensitive to candidates already involved in the risks attending career selection.

Application portfolios represent an intriguing solution for assessing qualitative attributes from a distance. Just as master teachers are developing portfolios for national board certification, prospective teachers might create portfolios that portray their interactions with youth: significant related events such as artistic performances, service projects, and camp experiences; and their personal as well as professional goals that make clear the appropriateness of teaching as a career choice. Such a portfolio, in effect, would provide applicants with the occasion for their own self-assessment to become a part of the admissions process.

Of course, of real concern is the recruitment of individuals with the time and means to create such a portfolio presentation. With teachers in increasingly high demand and few formal incentives such as funding to support their choice of teaching, are we in a position to broadly require such measures? On the other hand, an application portfolio might provide a viable alternative for those who do not test well. Finally, are there analogues in other professional schools from which we might learn in reviewing our admissions and selection instruments?

To say that the quality of tomorrow's classroom learning depends upon those we choose today for that crucial work is, perhaps, stating the obvious. But those at the Best Practice Conference expressed an awareness of the complexities in such choices as well as the limits of current selection criteria and prevailing admissions processes. The challenge remains apparent: we must examine the limits of existing procedures and find ways to enhance the selection and admissions process in ways that will identify and open the doors to the very best people.

Minority Recruitment, Admissions & Retention

A number of recruiting methods to supplement more usual methods (web sites, program brochures, and other internal and external publicity tools) were mentioned, from direct personal contacts with principals to ads in local minority newspapers and bulletins in church announcements. Given the under-representation of minorities in teacher education programs, we have to continue to pursue inventive ways of reaching minority populations.

A related concern is the successful retention of minority candidates. We must build support structures such as the peer mentor program at NC State that make it more possible for minority students to make the transition into the university or college culture successfully. We also need to know more about the issues unique to minorities so that our programs can work more consciously to address them. As a part of that planning process, it may be that we need to look more closely at the composition of our teacher education faculties for their minority representation. How many teacher education programs would be able to staff a team of minority advisors, as exists at NC State, to work with minority students and their peer mentors? We need to consider how we ourselves can become a more diverse community of teachers and mentors.

It was interesting to note that, while various strategies have been developed to offer special funds for minority candidates, the obstacle of academic performance in graduate courses remains and, in some cases, has resulted in these special funds going unutilized. Two interpretations seem viable: 1) there are not enough high-ability minorities interested in a teaching career; and 2) the academic criteria imposed are "artificial," biased against minority success. While either/or explanations rarely account for such realities, both explanations need to be examined: How can high-ability minorities be attracted to the teaching profession? How can the admissions process be more sensitive to cultural differences, especially those which affect academic performance as defined and measured by the dominant culture? Is it fair to say that when exceptions are made on GRE and GPA criteria, those minority students typically don't make it? Or, do we need to seek ways to not only attract but to sustain minority candidates?

Teacher education programs might more systematically take advantage of minority recruiting programs such as the Institute of Recruitment for Teachers at Andover. At the same time, our programs must more assiduously grapple with the ongoing problem of attracting minorities and males into the profession, without the sense that selection criteria are being compromised, a compromise most find objectionable. What might it mean to modify, as opposed to lower standards? How do we make such a distinction? And as we consider that difference, we might also consider how to move from the language of "guideline exceptions" and "escape hatches" to more positive representations of non-dominant culture candidates whose cultural knowledge we desperately need to inform and help with the mentoring of rapidly increasing K–12 minority student populations.

The issues raised by minority recruitment, admissions, and retention are intimately commingled with issues of admission standards. The call for data-based decision-making seems judicious; we need strong research that informs our decision-making process. But how can we expand the territory of our data? Does this mean more flexible admissions criteria for minorities? Are admissions criteria hindering males, majority or minority, as well? Is Vanderbilt's policy of accepting all minorities who apply a potential way of broadening the data terrain? If the mechanisms of support, supervision, and screening are an integral part of such a policy, might we begin to see a change in the data reported? Ultimately, we have to ask ourselves what risks we are willing to take in order to change the culture of our schools, both K–12 schools and teacher education schools. Whom are our teacher education programs keeping out? And how is that affecting the quality of learning in K–12 classrooms?

The conversation lumps all minority students together under the general term *minorities*. The danger, of course, is in the homogenizing effect of such categorization. Future discussions might focus more specifically on the different minority populations and how all aspects of our teacher education programs can be more culturally sensitive to their distinct differences. The language we use constructs the realities wherein we do our work. To change our realities means to change our language—such change may need to be the first level of institutionalized change out of which others, suggested by this conversation, may more effectively follow.

One of the measures of a good discussion is the questions it provokes. Our questions are not meant to be portrayed as those of everyone in attendance. Nor are they meant to be exhaustive. We are sure that readers will have added many more of their own. It is such questions that form our future agenda as teacher educators. Clearly, that agenda and the issues surrounding it are substantial, issues that this initiating discussion at the Best Practice Conference candidly engaged. Through this discussion, conference participants made notable headway which, in turn, will surely inspire future innovations that will make our best practices better.

Chapter Three

Academic Programs

It is not a simple matter to design the academic portion of a teacher education program. A number of factors can influence the design and implementation of particular course work. These factors include (but are not limited to) the choices a program makes regarding the size of its enrollment, the length of its program, and the academic level of the program (i.e., undergraduate or fifth-year); the grade levels and subject areas of preparation; its philosophy, purposes, and intentions regarding teaching and learning; how it defines teacher education—as teacher training, teacher preparation, or a continuum of professional development; the balance it strikes among "why" (purposes), "what" (content), and "how" (process and pedagogy); the relative importance it assigns to principles of progressive or traditional education; whether its focus is on urban, rural, or suburban education; how it defines the role of context in teacher education, curriculum design, and instruction; its definition of the teacher's role in educational reform; how it treats the relation between policy and practice; the balance it strikes between course work and field work; its relationships with schools concerning interns' placement, partnerships, professional development activity, and/or induction programs; its relationship with the arts and sciences; how its courses of study integrate theory and practice (and the degree to which the program practices what it preaches); the kind and use of assessment it uses to inform and improve the performance of the program and its candidates; the role it assigns to reflective practice in teacher education, classroom practice, professional development, and educational reform; how it addresses the constraints and possibilities of degree and state certification requirements as well as of expectations of national accreditation and professional organizations; and how it responds to the expectations of various funding agencies.

The three programs that are presented in the following pages—Rice University, the University of Richmond, and Wake Forest University—tackle these choices with integrity and a strong sense of mission. They all define teaching as a practicing profession, acknowledge the value of student-centered teaching and learning, and reinforce the importance of reflective practice. They are all dedicated to providing their candidates with the most intense and rich curricula possible. Yet, their academic programs are quite distinct as well. The following reflections about the design and implementation of academic programs serve to remind us of the complexity of the venture we call teacher education.

Vicki A. Jacobs
Harvard University

Rice University Teacher Preparation Program

Lissa Heckelman
Rice University

Teachers of today's youth must be experts in their content areas yet receptive to continually learning more. They must be deeply committed to challenging each student academically and accepting responsibility for the achievements of whole classes, while knowing that they are not in control of all the factors required for success. Further, they must be optimistic and fully involved every minute, yet willing to respond to student challenges, even apathy, professionally rather than personally. Beginning teachers coming from academically rigorous institutions of higher education have additional challenges of recognizing that teaching is not a profession that allows the 100 percent success rate they usually expect, and that all students are not as well prepared or motivated to achieve academically as they and their peers are. Fraught with challenges as the profession is, educating our youth is the best hope of harmonizing society and of maintaining and improving our record of human achievement. It can also be a source of deep personal satisfaction. The best and the brightest teachers inspire students of every ethnicity and economic status to achieve their best, both for themselves and for the world in which they live. Members of the Rice University education department strive to prepare students in the teacher preparation program to inspire academic achievement by their students in the schools. We have created and continue to refine a multifaceted and cohesive program that allows students to master the fundamental concepts of teaching and to act reflectively to improve education.

Master of Arts in Teaching Program (Fifth Year)

Our fifth-year, Master of Arts in Teaching (MAT) students generally complete the program in one-and-a-half years, beginning with their theoretical studies and content preparation courses, and concluding with employment within a secondary school in the Houston area. MAT students must earn a total of thirty-three semester hours of graduate credit for the degree. The required eighteen hours within the education department, twelve hours of academic course work, and six hours of student teaching are supplemented with an individualized program of study that allows students to tailor their preparation according to their academic needs and interests.

An entering MAT student meets with an education department advisor during orientation week to establish a plan of study for the degree. The student's transcript is compared to the requirements for certification that have been established through negotiation between Rice University and the Texas Education Agency. Requirements include the education course work, evidence of competence with computers, completion of state-mandated tests, and the course work within each discipline in which we certify teachers. Each academic department in which certification is offered has created a list of required and optional courses, totaling between twenty-four and forty-eight academic hours that a student must complete to earn certification within that discipline. One member of each of the academic departments serves on the Teacher Education Council and becomes a second advisor to each MAT student. Thus, each MAT student has at least one academic department advisor who monitors and approves course work within the discipline, and an education department advisor who monitors completion of the required courses and supplemental course work to enhance the student's preparation to teach.

The majority of our MAT students enter the program with a strong preparation in their chosen field of study. Most have completed the equivalent of the Rice University requirements within their academic discipline and have at most one or two required subject area courses to take. These students have several options for their remaining course work. Generally, they may select any Rice University upper-level courses that they feel, in consultation with their advisors, would enhance their preparation and allow them to pursue their own intellectual growth.

Optional Course Work

Several optional courses are recommended for all MAT students. "Sociology of Education" and "Minorities in School Process" are very helpful for understanding schools in Houston because students examine socioeconomic and multicultural issues that are prominent in the school culture. More direct experience with urban classrooms is offered through upper-level research courses in education. The ethnographic research skills students gain in "Studies in Teaching and Learning" enhance their observation skills as teacher-researchers and provide extensive opportunities to observe a variety of effective teachers in local schools. Students are also encouraged to take foreign language and ethnic literature courses to enhance their ability to understand and reach students in urban classrooms.

Required Education Academic Courses

MAT students are required to take twelve academic hours within the education department. In the fall of the first year, they take two courses, "Historical and Philosophical Foundations" and "Fundamentals of Secondary Education." In the Spring they take "Psychology of Human Learning" and a methods course in the appropriate discipline: art, English, foreign language, math, physical education and health, science, or social studies.

Each of the fall classes includes a large observation component. While students study the "Historical and Philosophical Foundations of Education," which emphasizes the historical roots of education, the changes the system has undergone, and the possibilities for change in the future, they spend fifteen hours observing classes in the variety of secondary schools found in the city. All students are encouraged to observe in middle and high schools, and public and private schools. Houston Independent School District has a strong magnet program allowing students to observe teaching in a variety of classes within the public school system, from magnet schools which draw diverse student bodies for special groups of students such as the gifted, the artistic, and students interested in law enforcement, to neighborhood schools which serve a largely homogeneous population. As our students observe in these classrooms, they begin to recognize the roots of the systems within which they operate, and become able to articulate their own philosophies of education. Revisions of those initial philosophies of education are made throughout the program.

In the fall course, "Fundamentals of Secondary Education," students engage in fifteen hours of observation that lead to group ethnographic research that focuses on one urban school. At the end of the semester, groups of students present an in-depth analysis of each targeted school, incorporating contemporary themes of effective school organization and practice with their first-hand experience at the school. Through this course, students identify themselves as teacher-researchers who are able to identify issues worthy of study within schools, to carry out the research, and to communicate their findings to an audience.

Students concentrate on learning theory and practical application in the "Psychology of Human Learning" course. They spend several hours in the schools doing directed observations of concepts such as student motivation, classroom management, student development, and learning styles. This course, offered in the spring, offers a bridge between theory and practice as students develop learning theories to complement their philosophies of education.

The methods courses are constricted by the state of Texas, which limits the number of hours students may take in such courses. The course is more an experience in professional development than a course with the traditional hours and grades usually associated with these courses. In this course students accomplish three main objectives: they use curriculum theory as they develop curriculum for the six-week class that they will teach in the Rice University Summer School for Middle and High School Students; they master the vocabulary and methods associated with their own disciplines; and they practice the skills that any teacher needs to have in his or her repertoire, including creating a variety of methods of assessment, devising strategies for classroom management and discipline, dealing with a diversity of students in one classroom, and using the skills of best practice in teaching such as reinforcement and effective questioning techniques. Each of these components is a course in itself, as our students soon recognize. The course, therefore, is a cooperative group effort with students being supported by all the members of the education faculty within their academic disciplines and by master teachers. Master teachers are certified, experienced teachers from the Houston area who are carefully selected for their excellence in all facets of the profession. Our students observe in their master teachers' classrooms where the teaching exemplifies the philosophy we are trying to foster in our courses and in the nature of the teacher education program itself. Master teachers are found in urban and suburban public and private schools; collectively they bring experience in teaching all kinds of children in all kinds of settings. Each MAT student works closely with two master teachers, one supervising each course the student is preparing to teach.

The major assignments that students complete in the methods courses center around plans for the courses students are developing for use during student teaching in the summer. Near the end of the first month of the class, the students complete course unit plans that include an overview of the content, goals and objectives, and methods they will use to teach each course. Near the end of the next month they complete the first two weeks of lesson plans for each course detailing the objectives, procedures, materials required, assessment procedures, and source of each lesson. The following month they submit the final four weeks of lesson plans. Students receive detailed feedback on each assignment from their master teachers, from the professor of their discipline-specific methods section, and from the director of summer school. Plans are also shared with peers in their classes. Though students have plenty of sources for ideas, resources, and methods, they make the ultimate decision about what goals they will try to meet in their classes and the methods they will use to achieve those goals.

Summer School Student Teaching

During the six-week Rice University Summer School for Middle and High School Students, the student teachers put their ideas into practice by teaching the classes they have so carefully planned and revised during the methods course. Established in 1964, the summer school is a tuition-based day school. It is open to rising seventh- through twelfth-grade students on a first-come, first-served basis, and offers courses in all the disciplines in which Rice recommends student teachers for certification. Teaching in the summer school is a required part of the preparation of all teachers certified through Rice. This first part of the student teaching experience is supported through the efforts of a number of people including the education department faculty and master teachers who have already established a strong relationship with the student teachers, and, financially, by the parents of secondary students from the community.

In summer school the student teachers have the opportunity to engage in many facets of the teaching profession in a supported environment. They teach their classes daily and receive written and oral feedback from their master teachers and their peers; they observe other teachers, experienced and novice, at their work; they assist a master teacher in a class that individualizes learning; they attend weekly department and biweekly faculty meetings; and they even perform campus supervisory duties during the session. From the first day of summer school the emphasis changes from the carefully created plans of the student teachers to an engagement with the secondary students in their courses. Student teachers coming from a summer school experience have the confidence that they can establish goals for their students, that they can enhance curriculum to achieve those goals, that they can establish themselves in the classroom, and that they have resources of people, materials, and techniques to turn to for ideas and guidance when they encounter difficulties. These are large advantages to be taking into their first classrooms, whether the students they teach are in public or private, privileged or economically disadvantaged schools.

Internship

Following a successful student teaching experience, MAT students are eligible for an internship. To complete an internship, students must apply for, be offered, and accept a teaching position in an accredited secondary school in the Houston area. Though they are responsible for finding their own jobs, the education department faculty assists them by alerting principals about the ability of the candidates preparing to teach, by referring principals to students and students to schools, by writing references, and generally by maintaining contact with the schools and programs in the area that are receptive to and supportive of beginning teachers. Students sign a one-year contract with the school or district they select for their first year of teaching and begin work as a first-year member of the faculty. By agreement with the local schools and districts, the interns are hired and paid as first-year teachers. The student teachers earn their final three credits of student teaching through attending a weekly seminar during the fall semester and by allowing a member of the education department to observe their classes and give them written feedback approximately once each three weeks. In the internship seminar the teachers continue their consideration of effective practice as it now plays out in their own classrooms in the city. More important, they regularly establish ties with their colleagues, ties which will hopefully last much longer than the internship semester itself.

Teachers from the Rice Teacher Preparation program enter the profession with a number of advantages. They have a thorough grounding in their disciplines, and an understanding that no discipline is ever fully mastered. They must be, and model being, lifelong learners. They have observed and analyzed a wide variety of classrooms, in public and private, large and small, middle and high schools, studying the education system itself with the goal of creating and using best practice for teaching in our schools. And in summer school they have created their own classrooms where they develop a curriculum, establish classroom routines, manage student activity, assess progress, and document achievement, not only with numbers and grades, but also in narratives which involve a variety of alternative assessments. Student teachers in summer school teach for understanding, even as they demonstrate the effectiveness of the concepts themselves. The teachers who leave the program are prepared to meet their first classes with confidence and resources, and they have the ideas and expertise to become leaders in the profession.

Dispelling the Myths of Teacher Preparation through Interdisciplinary and Integrative Studies

Christopher Roellke
University of Richmond

At a recent social gathering at my daughter's preschool, I was asked by an arts and sciences colleague, "where is the education department and what exactly do you do?" I promptly responded, "our department is housed on the third floor of North Court, above Classics and Philosophy, and our job is to prepare future teachers." Underlying my colleague's question was a genuine interest in understanding the *modus operandi* of our department and our role within the arts and sciences at the University of Richmond. The colleague's question was a timely one, given the substantial changes that have occurred in our department in recent years. Since 1994, two of our five full-time faculty members have been hired and several teacher preparation programs, including our fifth-year masters of teaching program, have been restructured and expanded considerably. Reflecting the renewed national interest in educational issues, demand for our courses is at an all-time high and an increasing number of students are pursuing careers in teaching.

An examination of our role within the arts and sciences is also timely because of a broader university initiative to make interdisciplinary and integrative study a fundamental part of the institution's identity. This initiative provides a special opportunity for us to educate our colleagues about our department and to illustrate how we can link ourselves meaningfully and coherently across the campus. These linkages are particularly important for our fifth-year masters of teaching program, since we must rely on our colleagues in the arts and sciences for required and elective courses, methodological and professional assistance within the disciplines, and mentoring of pre-service teachers.

Brief Historical Background

The movement to strengthen the University of Richmond's commitment to teacher preparation and to better integrate our department with the arts and sciences is occurring when education programs at other prestigious liberal arts institutions are struggling to survive. Historically, a primary purpose of small, liberal arts institutions has been to prepare teachers for the schools, and ministers for the churches. At many of these institutions, education departments were a source of institutional prestige and solvency (Burgess, 1990). While many of these colleges and universities still prepare teachers, few would claim that the preparation of teachers is central to their mission. Part of this shift in institutional mission can be explained by the rapid expansion of higher education in the last century. This expansion of (and subsequent competition among) institutions offering teacher education has made it easier and even attractive for private, liberal arts colleges to focus on developing their "liberal" and non-vocational character.

As a result, the number of undergraduate students pursuing teacher preparation within the small, liberal arts context has declined substantially. As recently as thirty to forty years ago, many liberal arts colleges enrolled 50 percent of their students in teacher education programs. Today, some of these same institutions enroll fewer than 5 percent of their students in education programs and some no longer prepare teachers at all (Goodlad, 1990). Increasingly, students pursuing careers in teaching are drawn to larger, state institutions.[1]

Criticized for being pre-professional and lacking academic rigor and connectedness, teacher education programs, particularly within small, liberal arts universities, have become an endangered species on the brink of extinction. Despite student demand for course work in education, many elite colleges and universities have either closed or reduced the size of their teacher preparation programs. A recent and notable casualty is the Educational Studies Program at my own alma mater,

Wesleyan University. Wesleyan, nationally recognized as a leader in undergraduate teacher preparation, offered its last education course in 1996.

A faculty panel at Dartmouth, where teacher preparation has long been a stable and productive part of the liberal arts curriculum, recently recommended terminating its education department. Both Wesleyan and Dartmouth were founding members of the Consortium for Excellence in Teacher Education (CETE), a group of selective private colleges and universities committed to producing teachers with a broad liberal arts background. No longer members of CETE, Wesleyan and Dartmouth have succumbed to critics who claim that certifying teachers for service in public education is peripheral to the primary mission of liberal arts institutions. The collapse of these exemplary teacher education programs has come at a time when critical shortages of qualified classroom teachers are projected.

Myths Surrounding the Preparation of Teachers

What accounts for this precarious position of teacher education within the liberal arts? I argue that part of the answer lies in a mythology that has emerged surrounding the preparation of teachers. This mythology has gained momentum in recent years and can be lethal to education departments within the liberal arts university. In order to preserve its rightful place in the arts and sciences curriculum, the field of education must confront these common misconceptions about the preparation of teachers:

- Preparing teachers is peripheral to the mission of liberal arts institutions
- Teacher preparation courses lack intellectual rigor
- Teacher preparation is strictly pre-professional and cannot be integrated with the arts and sciences
- The least capable students pursue teacher education

It is the responsibility of teacher educators, university administrators, colleagues within the arts and sciences, and professionals in education to eradicate these myths through open communication and dialogue. Most importantly, teacher educators must counter this mythology in their own professional practice through the development of courses that are interdisciplinary, intellectually rigorous, and linked coherently to the arts and sciences curriculum.

Myth 1: Preparing Teachers is Peripheral to the Mission of Liberal Arts Institutions

In defending the decision to close its Educational Studies Program, Wesleyan's Vice President, Joanne Creighton, argued that certifying teachers for service in public education was "peripheral to the University's primary mission as a liberal arts institution" (personal correspondence, July 1994). This myth, that preparing teachers is somehow incongruent with the goals of the liberal arts, has emerged despite a strong tradition of teacher preparation within these contexts. The reality is that the curriculum aims of teacher education programs have consistently advanced the purposes of a liberal education. A long held goal of the liberal arts, for example, is to yield a well-educated citizenry that can lead society judiciously to good ends. This is precisely the goal of any high-quality teacher preparation program: to produce well-educated problem solvers who can think creatively to improve the human condition. Our discipline, not unlike others in the arts and sciences, promotes full realization of what is means to be human and intelligent, and seeks to equip students with the tools necessary to address societal concerns and problems.

Peter Kelman, a former education faculty member at Dartmouth and currently Vice President of Scholastic, Inc., wrote this following Wesleyan's decision to phase out teacher education:

> I can think of no study more central to the liberal arts than the study of education. . . . At Dartmouth, where I taught hundreds of undergraduates over a six-year period about the role of education in America . . . I observed that the majority of these students experienced important intellectual and emotional changes in the course of these studies. In studying education, they were engaged in a critical meta-cognitive activity, one which clearly met the definition of a liberal arts education. (open letter to the Wesleyan community, July, 1992)

Teacher preparation, by its very character, is focused on humanistic, ethical, and inquiry-oriented approaches (Davis and Buttafuso, 1994). With this in mind, the cohabitation of teacher education curricula and the liberal arts is a natural one and should be encouraged.

Myth 2: Teacher Preparation Courses Lack Intellectual Rigor

Courses in education are mistakenly perceived as intellectually vacant. Critics often assume that the field of education lacks a sufficient knowledge base and methodology to promote student engagement in meaningful analysis and critique. The consideration of educational problems, however, has always been at the center of our intellectual and philosophical history. Plato, Aristotle, and Locke were all intimately concerned with how we construct knowledge and each worked to understand the relationship between this knowledge and the functioning of society. More contemporary theorists such as Dewey, Freire, Vygostsky, and Gardner have continued to direct intellectual energy to uncovering how learning processes can be improved to benefit humankind.

The philosopher Rudolph Weingartner has outlined the intellectual virtues expected of college graduates, which include an appetite for learning, imaginativeness, and creativity; respect for the viewpoints of others; tolerance for ambiguity; and the ability to reason and think critically (Weingartner, 1993). These are exactly the dispositions we seek to foster in our pre-service teachers. Course work and field experiences in education are inherently linked to the pursuit of these goals.

In our educational policy course, for example, we have adopted a dialectical approach, a strategy which requires the student to examine critical educational issues from divergent perspectives and viewpoints. The basic structure in dialectical reasoning is to pit one argument (thesis) against another (antithesis) to develop a synthesis which is superior to either (Nelson, Carlson, and Palonsky, 1996). Students are forced to challenge their assumptions about issues such as school choice, multicultural curricula, and academic freedom. Often frustrated by the ambiguity that permeates this approach, students tend to leave the course with more questions than answers, an outcome consistent with Weingartner's framework. Prospective classroom teachers must engage in this kind of intellectual activity if they are to have any hope of developing cognitive capacities in their students that have social usefulness.

Similar approaches are taken in our teaching methods courses. Rather than advocate one particular type of pedagogy over another, we encourage students to explore a variety of theoretical models and apply them to their own disciplines and anticipated classroom environments. This pluralistic approach requires the prospective teacher to draw from the full range of options before making curricular and instructional decisions. In their micro-teaching experiences, students design their own lessons and then implement them in front of their peers. In these experiences, heavy emphasis is placed on self, peer, and instructor evaluation. The goal, of course, is to produce "reflective practitioners," who utilize theory, research, and learner/observer feedback as a basis for consciously and consistently examining their craft. More importantly, the strategy requires liberal arts undergraduates to develop skills in problem solving, active listening, data analysis, and assessment, all skills which will be in high demand in future organizations.

Myth 3: Teacher Preparation is Strictly Pre-Professional and Cannot Be Integrated with the Arts and Sciences

Contributing to the precarious status of the field of education within the liberal arts is the myth that teacher preparation is strictly pre-professional and hence cannot be integrated with the arts and sciences. Liberal education is purported to be learning without reference to preparation for any specific occupation. It follows then, that any curriculum centered specifically around classroom teaching, or any other profession for that matter, violates a fundamental premise of liberal learning. Does our department require students to acquire specific skills that can be applied to classroom teaching? The answer is undeniably yes. Providing this kind of attention to professional skills, however, is quite consistent with our colleagues in biology or computer science who work with their students to develop specific laboratory and technical skills so that they have a reasonable chance of being employable. We would be doing a disservice to students if we failed to provide them with these skills.

While we work hard on skill development and ensure that students are thoroughly oriented to the teaching profession, the cornerstone of our teacher preparation program is the integration of study in the arts and sciences. Focusing this liberal and integrated study on the organizational behavior of schools and classroom interaction does not, in and of itself, make a curriculum vocational. The acquisition of specific teaching skills is meaningless without a liberal arts foundation. No matter how well a pre-service teacher is prepared in terms of pedagogic skill and classroom management, he or she will not succeed in the classroom without strong content knowledge and the ability to think critically, the hallmarks of a liberal education.

Similarly, the liberally educated teacher is doomed to fail without prerequisite teaching skills and the ability to apply theories of learning and motivation in the classroom. In the film *Mr. Holland's Opus*, the lead character, despite strong grounding in the subject matter, delivers uninspiring lessons and fails to engage his music students in any kind of meaningful learning. Finally admitting to his students that he had little or no impact on them for the first six months of the school year, Mr. Holland is forced to rethink his pedagogy to make his lessons relevant and accessible to his students. His eventual success as a classroom teacher requires a combination of deep subject matter understanding and sound professional practice.

Moreover, if we accept the notion that teacher preparation is strictly pre-professional, it would be expected that nearly all of the students enrolled in education courses plan to become teachers. The reality is that many students enroll in our program with no firm career plans. Some are considering careers in counseling, social work, or other human services and want course work that can provide them with prerequisite knowledge and skills. Others are contemplating graduate school to study medicine, law or psychology. Consider the case of Reginald Skinner, one of our education students who was elected by his peers to speak at the university's commencement ceremony last year. Certified as a middle school and high school social studies teacher through the University of Richmond, Reggie used his undergraduate course work in education and economics to study disadvantaged youth. Currently conducting research for the NAACP on equity issues in education, Reggie has enrolled at Harvard University in a joint program in law and public policy. In addition to rejecting the "strictly pre-professional" arguments, Reggie Skinner's story illustrates the kind of curricular balance that is possible in teacher preparation.

Myth 4: The Least Capable Students Pursue Teacher Education

Reggie is also just one example of the kind of student who can dispel the myth that the least capable students pursue teacher education. The field of education has long battled the cliché, "those who can't, teach." Teacher preparation is misperceived as a simplistic curriculum reserved for those students not able to succeed in other arts and sciences disciplines. Teacher licensure is inaccurately viewed by many as "something to fall back on" should students fail in course work leading to promising careers in law, medicine, or engineering. Many of our first public school teachers were, in fact, poorly educated and untrained, and the profession has battled this reputation ever since. Teachers in colonial New England were often social misfits and teacher incompetence was commonplace (Farris, 1996). This reputation has unfortunately been perpetuated by the continued existence of a handful of poorly prepared teachers in our school systems.

Selective liberal arts institutions, with their competitive admissions profiles, can play an important role in combating this problem by guaranteeing a pool of high-quality teacher education candidates. A direct beneficiary of the university's growing academic reputation, our department enjoys a steady supply of outstanding students. Last semester, thirty-three of our students were inducted into Kappa Delta Pi, an international education honors society. A comparable number of our students were recognized at Honors Convocation for outstanding achievement in their chosen academic discipline. Students in our program exemplify the kind of intelligent, motivated scholars that can preserve and promote the role of teacher education within the liberal arts. Eva Travers, Associate Dean at Swarthmore, and Susan Sacks of Barnard College have articulated the view that liberal arts institutions are a key national resource for producing excellent future educators:

> Our students are likely to be the kind of bright, well-prepared and highly motivated individuals who will exert disproportionate influence in schools. ... The entry of talented liberal arts graduates into teaching—exactly the sort of individuals that the national reform reports are seeking—must be actively promoted, not indirectly discouraged. (Travers and Sacks, 1989)

With more new teachers expected to be hired in the next decade than at any other time in our nation's history, this is not the time for liberal arts universities to abandon teacher preparation. Furthermore, it is disconcerting, if not unethical, for universities to decry the state of public education and then recommend that liberal arts institutions have no interest in trying to improve it. Prestigious liberal arts institutions, the University of Richmond among them, can and must play a vital role in the ongoing restructuring and betterment of our school systems.

Dispelling the Myths Through Interdisciplinary and Integrative Studies

Although evidence has been provided here to reject the mythology surrounding the preparation of teachers, it is important to note that myths emerge for a reason. In some situations, myths emerge and gain momentum because they are based partly in truth. In other instances, they emerge because no other logical explanations have been provided or empirically tested. The mythology discussed here has emerged for both of these reasons. With its concerns for professional study, teacher preparation has endured an awkward existence within the liberal arts context. The vocational dimension of teacher training, coupled with divisiveness between education departments and other social science disciplines, has stimulated many important questions surrounding the intellectual focus of education faculty and their courses. The continued existence of poorly prepared teachers in our nation's classrooms provides additional fuel for critics of teacher preparation programs.

The field of education has also done little to disprove its critics by providing theoretical and empirical evidence to dispel these myths. In order to survive and thrive within colleges and universities, teacher preparation programs need to demonstrate how they can be linked coherently and meaningfully to the study of the liberal arts. In a paper delivered to the World Assembly of the International Council on Education For Teaching (ICET), Elaine Traynelis-Yurek and I outlined a series of recommendations for teacher preparation programs to gain stability and strength. Held in Amman, Jordan, the World Assembly was focused on how teacher education can be improved to complement the broader movement to reform schools around the globe. Our recommendations, based on a framework adapted from Soder and Sirotnik (1990), included:[2]

- Make meaningful linkages with the arts and sciences through interdisciplinary study and integration of programs into the broader academic and social life of the campus
- Provide pedagogical and other professional development training for the broader university faculty
- Legitimize and clarify the role of graduate study in education, including fifth-year masters of teaching programs
- Illustrate the effectiveness of teacher preparation programs by tracking the success of graduates

Several situations have emerged which have led to better integration between the Teacher Preparation Program and the School of Arts and Sciences at the University of Richmond. First, teacher education students at the University of Richmond, whether they are preparing to teach in elementary or secondary schools, must major in the liberal arts. In addition, the general curriculum of the School of Arts and Sciences requires every student to complete courses in six different fields of study. The School of Arts and Sciences recently granted field of study status to our introductory course, Perspectives in Education. This course, which draws from a wide range of social science disciplines such as economics, history, sociology, law, and psychology, satisfies the area of social analysis. In addition to providing much needed visibility for our department, the course yields many opportunities for interdisciplinary study. The course was just ranked among the top three courses at the university in a recent survey.[3]

The education department has also strengthened the membership and role of the Teacher Advisory Committee. This committee is made up of a contact person in every academic department who has an endorsement area in the secondary program as well as professionals from schools in the community. Faculty in the education department are ex-members of this committee, which addresses curriculum issues by periodically updating courses and programs to meet state licensure standards. Recently, our discussions have centered around the role arts and sciences colleagues can play in assisting our fifth-year students with methods within the disciplines.

We are also working on establishing a liberal arts mentor program which would greatly enhance the practicum experiences of our fifth-year master's students. Our preliminary ideas include having our students "shadow" faculty members in their selected discipline. This shadowing might also involve assisting faculty members as they prepare and implement introductory college level courses. We have experimented with this kind of teaching apprenticeship program in our own department and it has been highly successful. The liberal arts mentor would be asked to engage in ongoing dialogue with our students about methods and other discipline-specific issues. During the capstone student teaching experience, a liberal arts mentor would be asked to supervise his or her student teacher with the same level of commitment that would be provided for a thesis student. Several faculty members have already committed to this model and we look forward to further developing these ideas through internal and external grant opportunities.

The education department also recognizes the importance of becoming a resource to the faculty of the university. Our faculty has collaborated with instructors in psychology, leadership studies, and political science to provide seminars for the broader university community. Our guest lecture series, which brings prominent scholars and practitioners to the campus, is open to all members of the faculty and interested members of the Richmond community. The challenge is to the members of the education department to continue to make progress in this area so that expertise in teaching and scholarship is shared.

In addition, the university has established a center for housing professional development resources for faculty. The Program for the Enhancement of Teaching Effectiveness (PETE) will be expanded in the next five years to support new teaching initiatives that foster students' active engagement in learning. A priority for the Department of Education is to become actively involved in the professional development activities of PETE, both as participants and providers of faculty workshops. PETE provides mini-grants to faculty members to initiate instructional innovations within their classes and to attend conferences that will improve their teaching. Several faculty members within our department have taken advantage of these resources and are in the process of designing professional development activities that will be of value to the university as a whole. The conceptual linkage between PETE and the Department of Education is a natural one and we are looking forward to expanding and strengthening this relationship.

It is also vitally important that teacher preparation programs take steps to strengthen and legitimize graduate-level study in education. Several controversial reform reports of the last decade, including those produced by the Holmes education deans (1986) and the Carnegie Forum (1986), have urged that teacher preparation occur in two separate phases: 1) baccalaureate level work devoted to liberal education with strong subject matter preparation, and 2) master's level work focused on professional courses and teacher training. It is our view that divorcing education courses from the undergraduate experience may have important deleterious effects, including limiting the pool of high quality teaching candidates. Many undergraduate students arrive on campus without a clear career path in mind. Without a solid array of undergraduate course work in education available to them, these undecided students may overlook opportunities within the field.

This is *not* to suggest that teacher training should occur solely at the undergraduate level. Providing graduate level options is advantageous to many individuals and institutions of higher education. Our own master of teaching program is designed to provide opportunities for students to integrate the liberal arts and graduate-level teacher preparation. An important feature of our fifth-year program is its integration with the arts and sciences. In consultation with their advisors, fifth-year students are encouraged to select two of their graduate courses outside the field of education. Students may pursue course work within their content area, or elect to complete a research project/thesis that crosses disciplinary boundaries.

Tracking the success of graduates has proven to be an excellent vehicle for promoting legitimization of our graduate programs. Recent follow-up surveys of teacher education graduates from the last decade (1986–1996) indicate that our programs are very effective. Our graduates give us consistently high ratings and report that our course work is responsible for developing the skills necessary to deal with the complexity of the classroom. In addition, many of our former students hold leadership positions in schools, state education departments, and higher education. Documenting and publicizing this success has provided us with credibility across the campus and in the broader Richmond community.

We view these positive assessments as a function of the integration of a strong liberal arts education with the acquisition of specific skills in pedagogy and curriculum design. It is this integration which has allowed the University of Richmond to withstand the challenges made to teacher preparation programs in small, liberal arts contexts. Our hope is that further development of intellectually rigorous, field relevant, and interdisciplinary teaching and research will continue to stabilize and strengthen the presence of teacher preparation at the University of Richmond and other selective liberal arts institutions. We welcome the opportunity to engage in teaching and research collaborations to foster interdisciplinary study across the campus and view it as our responsibility to stimulate and promote these partnerships.

Notes

[1] Although the majority (approximately 65 percent) of institutions who have teacher preparation programs are private, liberal arts colleges and universities, most of our nation's new teachers (approximately 75 percent) are educated in large, public universities (Darling-Hammond & Cobb, 1996).

[2] For detailed discussion of these and other recommendations, and departmental efforts to implement them, see Traynelis-Yurek, Roellke, and Stohr-Hunt (1996).

[3] See "The Best and Worst of UR," *The Collegian*, February 26, 1998.

Balancing Tensions: The Liberal Arts and Professional Education in Wake Forest's Master Teacher Fellows Program

R. Scott Baker
Wake Forest University

At the heart of most debates about teacher education is a tension between the liberal arts and professional training. For more than a generation, many policy makers and politicians have seen more rigorous requirements in the disciplines as a panacea for the problems that plague public education. While not opposed to training in the liberal arts, many educators have emphasized the importance of a specific body of professional teaching knowledge in teacher education. I want to use this tension to frame a brief description of the Master Teacher Fellows program at Wake Forest University examining the ways in which we balance the tension between liberal arts and professional training.

Modeled after the MAT programs of the 1960s and 1970s, the Master Teacher Fellows (MTF) program at Wake Forest trains between twenty and twenty-five students annually in a one year master's program that offers certification in English, foreign languages, math, science, and social studies. Supported by the state of North Carolina and the university, this program provides tuition and living expense stipends to well-trained college graduates with majors in these five disciplines. The success of the program here and at other universities in North Carolina that are part of the Model Clinical Teaching program suggests that financial incentives can play an important role in attracting, if not always retaining, very promising young people to the teaching profession.

One of the reasons we are able to balance the tension between the liberal arts and professional training is that the Master Teacher Fellows come to us with broad and deep backgrounds in the subjects they plan to teach, having completed the requirements for majors in academic subjects at selective colleges and universities in the South. Each year, area advisors in our department, who have academic strengths in the five disciplines, select four or five fellows from a large pool of applicants. While the fellows take common courses in, for example, the history and philosophy of education, much of what they do at Wake Forest involves close collaboration with their area advisors and other fellows in their disciplines.

Most of the courses the MTFs take at Wake Forest are in education, but we do require that fellows complete three concentration courses in their major. The courses that students take vary. In English, many take advantage of a department that has rich offerings in British and American literature; in social studies, students typically take courses in geography and non-western history that are needed for licensure. In many cases, students who have spent the last two years of their undergraduate career digging deeply into a particular dimension of a discipline are allowed to enroll as special students in an undergraduate survey course that will help orient them to the kinds of issues they will teach about at the secondary level. For example, social studies fellows who have developed expertise in a specific historical field benefit from a survey course in American, European, or world history.

These courses not only broaden and deepen students' understanding of the disciplines, in some cases they allow fellows to complete courses in broad teaching fields such as social studies that are required for licensure. The experience of our students in science and social studies suggests that fifth-year programs need to make some provision for the completion of courses in these cluster disciplines so that students can meet certification requirements. Even more important, advanced graduate courses in the disciplines help students come to terms with the structure of their discipline. English students, for example, who take a literary criticism course, or Biology majors who take a course in the philosophy of science begin to develop an overview of their discipline that may not have been achieved during their undergraduate years.

Another way Wake Forest balances the tension between the liberal arts and professional preparation is by building bridges between liberal arts disciplines and education. We begin doing this in June when the Master Teacher Fellows enter our program. Students take four courses during two intensive (some say exhaustive) summer semesters. Courses in the history and philosophy of education, qualitative research methods, adolescent psychology, and curriculum and instruction combine theoretical and practical perspectives, providing students with several different ways of seeing and understanding secondary schooling. In June, students take a history and philosophy course and a qualitative research methods course. While students might discuss the origins, growth, and development of the American high school or consider E.D. Hirsch's recent attack on progressivism in the morning, they study the methods that educational researchers use to answer specific empirical questions in the afternoon. During the second summer semester in July, students take courses in adolescent psychology and curriculum and instruction. In the morning, the Master Teacher Fellows explore the problematic passage from childhood to adulthood taught by a practicing adolescent psychologist; in the afternoon, they discuss the research on best teaching practice in their specific disciplines, situating what and how they will teach their subject in the context of adolescent growth and development. Creating bridges between the liberal arts disciplines, the subjects they have mastered as undergraduates, and the schools and classrooms they are about to enter as prospective teachers, course offerings during the summer session prepare students for intensive field experiences during the fall that include observations and ethnographic research on a specific dimension of teaching.

We continue to balance this tension during the fall term when students take two graduate concentration courses in their discipline, participate in Teaching Rounds, and develop research reports that are presented at the annual Research Forum in December. One of the unique aspects of our program is what we call the Teaching Rounds. Modeled after rotations in medical education, this paradigm assumes that good teaching takes many forms. Students observe four master teachers in different schools, seeing the different approaches taken to pedagogy and curriculum. During the rounds, the MTFs see how some of the curricular and instructional issues they examined in the summer are played out in practice. Meeting once a week with their advisor and other fellows from their discipline, students discuss what they have seen, and begin to talk about the master teacher with whom they would like to work. Drawing upon their knowledge of their discipline, coursework in the summer, and the teaching rounds, students craft empirical research questions that they investigate and attempt to answer through qualitative research in the classroom and the library. Last year, students explored such topics as "Teaching Methodologies for ESL students in Secondary Science," "Error Correction in the Foreign Language Classroom," and "The Effects of Race and Gender on Students' Perceptions of Social Studies." In December, students present their findings to fellow students in their discipline, cooperating teachers, advisors, interested members of the department and the university, and undergraduate secondary education students. These presentations generate rich discussions on many pedagogical issues in the teaching of the disciplines, setting the stage for the most significant and intense part of our program: the teaching block.

We connect courses in the disciplines, methodology, and pedagogy in an intensive six-week teaching block. Although students complete courses in special education and technology, the core of the block involves helping students learn how to make what they know about their subject accessible and meaningful to secondary school students. Methods classes meet for two to three hours a day, five days a week. Approaches vary, but most pedagogical faculty use a current research/best practice model. In the English Block, for example, the Master Teacher Fellows study basic models of English instruction; approaches to drama, poetry, and fiction; the use of film in the classroom; and writing strategies. Toward the end of the block, students plan lessons and units planning, and complete micro-teaching assignments at Wake Forest and in the schools. During the last ten weeks of the semester, the fellows student teach in the schools under the supervision of master teachers, some of whom are graduates of our program, and our faculty.

After the Master Teacher Fellows have completed student teaching, they return to campus to complete a professional development seminar and a course in the teaching of Advanced Placement subjects. Modeled after the requirements for national certification, the professional development course requires students to develop an electronic portfolio that includes a statement of their educational philosophy, videotapes of their teaching, and sample lessons and assignments. The MTFs also complete an exit interview where they respond to questions from a panel of teachers, school administrators, and university faculty. While students apply for North Carolina teaching licenses, our hope is that this professional development course will help these promising young teachers obtain National Board Certification as soon as they are eligible. During this final term, students also participate in an Advanced Placement Institute and a brief observation and internship at the North Carolina Governor's School, where the AP Institute's course knowledge and the pedagogy related to such special students can be applied. Building on the broad and deep base of subject matter knowledge that the Master Teacher Fellows bring to Wake, our program provides students with the professional knowledge they need to teach their subjects.

While we balance the tension between liberal arts and professional training well, the Master Teacher Fellow Program at Wake Forest University, like other fifth-year programs, is not without its problems. The strength and the weakness of the teaching block, like our program as a whole, is that it forces faculty to cover significant bodies of information and knowledge in a relatively short period of time. Material can be covered but not fully digested. Faculty can feel drained, and students overwhelmed and anxious. Limiting the number of education courses students take and the time devoted to them allows students to deepen their knowledge of the subjects they teach, but it also increases demands on the faculty in the program. The burden of balancing tensions between liberal arts and professional training is borne by both the faculty in education and the cohort of twenty-four Master Teacher Fellows.

As the field of teacher education moves toward-fifth year programs, we need to consider how this burden can be more equitably shared. The steady stream of horror stories about teachers who have not completed any coursework in the subjects they teach will likely increase demands for more subject matter coursework. As secondary school populations become more diverse and as standards for secondary school graduation are raised, it is also likely that demands for new competencies will also grow. Wake Forest's Master Teacher Fellow program provides a useful model of how to balance tensions between liberal arts and professional training.

Academic Programs Discussion

Participants: Vicki Jacobs, Harvard University; **Leah McCoy, R. Scott Baker**, and **Joseph Milner**, Wake Forest University; **Margo Figgins**, University of Virginia; **Alan Reiman**, North Carolina State University; **Charles Myers**, Vanderbilt University; **William Palmer** and **Roy Edelfelt**, University of North Carolina; **Christopher Roellke**, University of Richmond; **Lissa Heckelman**, Rice University; **Greg Smith**, Lewis and Clark College; **Eileen Landay** and **Lawrence Wakeford**, Brown University; **Allyson Mizoguchi**, English teacher; **Beverly Carter**, Stanford University; **Rosemary Thorne**, Duke University; **Richard Card**, University of Southern Maine.

Jacobs: It occurs to me that we are all dealt the same bag of groceries, although some will vary a little according to state requirements and national expectations. The meals we make, however, are going to vary as well as our seasonings. As I said to an interested candidate the other day, some programs cater to the crab crowd and the others to the vegetable crowd. I'm looking forward to hearing you all share what is on your plate.

McCoy: At Wake Forest we are helped by the state in that there is a Department of Public Instruction requirement that students have a 2.5 [GPA] to be admitted to teacher education. At Wake Forest 2.5 is a good grade point average. Lots of people graduate from Wake Forest without a 2.5. Our students are in most ways better than the average students on campus.

Figgins: Scott [Baker], just a clarification. People in your fellows programs are funded?

Baker: Yes, there are two levels of funding. For all MTF students tuition is fully paid and they receive a $4,000 stipend; that is sort of subsistence level. Maybe Alice [Sy] can talk about how she tried to supplement this amount in order to make it through the year. Minority students receive an $8,000 stipend that is funded both by the state of North Carolina and Wake Forest. That's very important in terms of the quality of students we are able to attract. The down side is that when we attract highly qualified students they can say, "I've got a BA from Virginia." I use Virginia as an example because a few of our more promising students come from UVA. One very able English student came here for a year, but the English department at Virginia lured her back into its Ph.D. program. We invested a good sum of money in someone who will probably teach in higher education and may be a better university teacher for it, but it is one of the difficulties we face in attracting such able students.

Figgins: The other thing I want to ask Scott [Baker] is, do you see yourselves actually beginning to shape these teachers for National Board certification? You mentioned that you encouraged them to move in that direction. I was wondering how much of the National Board certification standards and shaping of the teacher is behind what your doing in your courses.

Baker: I think one of my colleagues can comment on that.

Milner: I don't think it in any way shapes what I do in an English Methods course, but Leah McCoy and I teach a course together in which students develop a portfolio modeled entirely on National Board standards. They do that after they have finished all requirements of the program; it is the way they exit our program. Leah [McCoy], you may want to say more about that because you have basically defined that course.

McCoy: We consider that a part of our research strand. We take the standards and break them up. Our students are required to reflect on what they did here, what they learned about their teaching, and what they propose to do in the future based on that framework.

Reiman: Leah [McCoy], do you also address the INTASC standards? They are going to be used for inductees in almost any program they enter as first year teachers. Where is the link there?

McCoy: We have been discussing that fairly recently. To me, the INTASC standards look more relevant and easier to apply, but I think the two approaches may end up at the same place. Right now we are going to stay with National Board standards, but in the future our students may have a choice of which outline to follow for their reflection. I'm not quite sure where we will go with that. I would be interested to know if anybody else is doing something like that.

Myers: I was about to ask the same question and I would like to make a comment. As NCATE moves toward performance-based standards (I am very heavily involved in that right now), its standards are almost exactly parallel to those of INTASC. Both of those are tied very directly to the National Board. We all are going to face the same situation. I'm going to spend next week at Central Michigan University helping to revise its future education program for the year 2000 when it comes up for its next NCATE review. And it's based on the performance standards. Already there are fourteen states that have said they will no longer have content subject matter standards that are different from the national standards of the various groups, in my case the National Council for the Social Studies. Therefore, I'm starting to run around the country dealing with the question, "What is it that you want?" I chaired the task force for the National Council for the Social Studies to establish those standards last year. And they are being built into state licensing requirements! No social studies teachers will be allowed to get a license in those fourteen states unless a team of the National Council for Social Studies votes on their institution's program and says that it does, in fact, meet their performance standards. Just to give you an idea on how fast that's moving, three years ago there were no states. In three years, it went from three to fourteen states.

Palmer: Scott [Baker] really did a lot of fine work with building up an ethnographic framework for integrating liberal arts and teacher education, and I kept thinking, "Why is that such a big trend today?" At Carolina, we have to answer to NCATE and the national subject matter standards. We have to form a team of people from the foundations area and the content areas to get the whole concept going or we get no integration at all. So if we can document this or that particular standard that we want to meet, it is an NCATE as well as a national content area standard.

Myers: To what extent does that process foster an understanding of integrating subject matter or helping understand the purpose of the high school? Every one of our graduates should have a concept of what the high school is all about or what should happen to students that go through high school.

Baker: That is something I try to focus on in the summer in the history of philosophy course. I focus on the history of high school, on problems of race, class, and gender; I think that by planting that seed in students' minds when they first enter the program, they are receptive to it because this is really their first course and they are thrilled to get into it and dying to learn.

Edelfelt: Returning to the idea of integration of subject matter, we have done this in the past in block programs of English and social studies, for example. It is true as well in science. Some schools are doing that again now. I'm just wondering whether you address that and how that fits into what seems, on the other hand, to be a very strong second-subject emphasis.

Baker: I think we operate on a more discipline-centered model. Joe [Milner] can speak to that. Each ship sails its own course.

Milner: Each ship sails its own course and we like it that way. Really strong people lead each of those programs and there isn't any self-conscious integration. I think integration *is* extremely important: the Governor's school where I taught for many years was built totally on integration. But I worry sometimes about integration, that it can shortchange students' serious investigation in their discipline, what really needs to be understood about social studies or language arts. Sometimes you start getting integration that is flimsy and doesn't have much substance to it. I worry about that. I think we should investigate that much more carefully.

Roellke: We have almost been forced to integrate because of our size. We are a small faculty with just five people. I appreciated Scott [Baker]'s comment that a lot of the burden has been placed on the foundation faculty to make these linkages happen. There are only so many things we can do. The sheer number of our faculty, the smallness of our faculty, the smallness of our department, forces us to go out and do things, and one of the things we're working on right now is expanding the role of our teacher education advisory committee which is made up of arts and science faculty members in all the endorsement areas. That committee meets once a semester to make sure that the endorsements are in line with the discipline. We're looking to expand their role dramatically, so that from those faculty who have already expressed an interest in education by serving on the committee, we can find a committed and knowledgeable person who can supervise a student teacher to help them with methodologies with which we're not familiar. For example, my background is in social studies and I've got students in my classroom who want to teach mathematics or foreign language or other things, and I can't assist them as well as I think my colleagues can. Again, they get to see the student teaching experience and they get to see how tremendous it is, and how difficult it is, and how rigorous it is, and that word gets out. Some research opportunities, I think, also emerge for them, and they get excited: "Hey, this is a really interesting thing, I would like to work with this teacher, I'd like to engage in some collaborative field-based research." Then that kind of research and that kind of work gets higher esteem in the arts and sciences, and we all win. The thing steamrolls, and although the reasons might seem selfish in that we're trying to get some of our workload shared by our arts and sciences colleagues, I think we all win in this positive situation.

Heckelman: I wanted to say that at Rice the integration comes into the subject through the example that the students present us as they are planning their courses. They have many interests and they try to bring them all together into a course. Because so many people are looking at the plans that they are creating (their peers, the master teachers who are working with two or three students), these ideas come to the fore through the example of what the students have presented us. That seems to be the most effective way to integrate, when student teachers are actually developing what they will be doing in a classroom. It is for us the most effective way we have found to bring about this kind of multi-subject incorporation into their own work.

Palmer: I'm concerned that if we don't make attempts at integration and do keep the content areas separated as much as they have been, what happens from the faculty point of view is that we perpetuate the old program in a new structure. If we don't have a cohort concept and if we don't do any integration with the foundations, we will remain stagnant. Just in evaluating people for promotion and tenure I have had to go to one lecture in leadership and one in social foundations. I learned so much more from a lecture on inclusion, from another one on magnet schools, and another one on research issues in communities than from a narrow pedagogical strand that I realized the teaming part is more than a word. It means that in order to team well I have to get a foundation person and a cultural studies person to work on a team plan to observe each other and say, "What do we do well? Do we overlap? How can we do it differently?" and "How do we build a richer program for ourselves as well as our students?" And if we don't do that we're going to end up returning to our old program because that teamwork takes so much work. And, yet, the cohort concept may not work well for the students either because they'll be getting it in dribbles. So the more that I hear from the two presenters today, three really, but two in particular, I think it's given me all the more reason for trying to form realistic, authentic teams that really work hard at listening to each others' classes on planning and on demonstrating the model to chink together and to develop a very new kind of model. It extends us way beyond where we are today. So, I feel now as though we'll defeat the old ways. But we, all the people, have to change. And, I'm talking about myself as well.

Smith: Integration is a different question. Oregon is now moving towards a four licensure program with early childhood, primary, middle, and high school. And what we've tried to do is create a program that will allow people who complete our program to earn both the middle school and high school licenses. And to address the whole teaming question, we have created two new summer courses. A week-long intensive writing class and another week long intensive class in quantitative reasoning will be required of people in all disciplines. So actually it would be their first experience, hoping that experience will prepare them for the kinds of issues they are likely to run into in middle school teams. So, we'll see how that goes. We're excited about the possibilities. My question relates to ways in which people, across any number of programs, are trying to work with incoming teachers, novice teachers, to really get to the heart of their disciplines to figure out what really are the core concepts and theories and methodologies. We find that people who have gone through very traditional graduate programs are generally dumbfounded when asked that question. And we've taken to heart a lot of what's going on in schools. We have thought a great deal about the issue of what the essential questions are. What are the essential issues here? And we find that it's a struggle in the short amount of time that we have with our interns to get them to grapple well and successfully with those questions. Are any of you having any luck with that? It seems to be a curriculum planning issue because so much of curriculum planning is deciding what to leave out and what to include. Unless you are able to make wise decisions about what is essential, you can't do that. I'm not always sure that the state standards in particular (the national standards are better) really are able to answer that question. Can you give us any guidance here?

Landay: Well, this is very informal, but English in particular has been problematic in terms of how to define the discipline. The day after our students arrive I ask them that question. I ask them to write about it and then I create a concept map showing their version of English. I collect them and after we go through the summer program, I give them back and ask them to revisit what they thought English was and say again what they think English is. We do the same thing during the next academic semester. So we keep returning to that question and I think, from my perspective anyway, my goal, aside from having them develop a strong tool box that will allow them to put their beliefs into practice, is to be able to answer that question with confidence. So, the formal process by which they do that is to write a statement of purpose that they put into their portfolio which talks about how they define the core concepts in that discipline. It's really simple. But we keep coming back to it, over and over again.

Roellke: I want to ask everyone just what the faculty member in the sciences might have as an incentive to volunteer to supervise a student teacher? One of the incentives we have developed is that the student teacher would in return, perhaps, serve as a teaching assistant to them in an introductory level course that they might teach on campus. The fear, though, is that they'll go into college teaching rather than public school teaching after they see how easy it is, even though it's really not that easy. This process paves a two-way street between the content discipline expert and the student who's going to have to be somewhat more of a generalist in the school system. So the students have to pay back a little bit while they are learning more methods, even though they are college-level methods. They usually receive one academic credit or something for independent study or something like that. I think it's a nice idea. I'd like to see it done more.

Jacobs: Allyson [Mizoguchi], how do you respond to Greg [Smith]'s idea about the structure of the discipline.

Mizoguchi: Yeah, Greg [Smith], I don't know if this is in answer to your question, but as a recent graduate of an English program, I can tell you that we do something similar at Harvard. We wrote a "Why English?" paper or "Why History?" and up to that point I didn't know "Why English." I knew it was reading and writing and that was about it. I came to realize why students need to know that. The paper was instrumental in helping me think about that. I also, as part of the program, took an undergraduate course simultaneously with some education courses. I was surprised how much content defined my confidence when I began my student teaching. That was something to fall back on. I knew a little bit of what I was talking about because if I didn't know everything about how to teach, at least I knew a little bit about that. That's how I was able to present myself as not just scared stiff that first year.

Jacobs: Scott [Baker], do you want to respond to Greg [Smith]?

Baker: I guess what I was trying to say at the close of my paper is that we need to put pressure on colleagues in arts and sciences. I find that curriculum in a lot of the disciplines, to be really blunt, is totally incoherent. It's fragmented. It's a buffet. Whenever they want to add something, they just put it on a new serving table at the end of the counter. I think that we've really got to go to our colleagues and say, "here's what the state is asking teachers to know and what they need to have taken to earn a license," so I think your questions are great ones. Here are the questions that we're going to ask our people at the end of the program and maybe we should send those responses back to our colleagues in these disciplines and say you know you're turning out people who can't define what English is, what history is.

Wakeford: I recently was lamenting to a colleague in the biology department that the students finishing my program were still struggling with the issue of what's the difference between science and English and these other disciplines. But my colleague from biology said you wouldn't want to ask that question of most of the biology professors. It's a good answer to your concern. So, he was sort of saying to me you're asking a lot of your teachers if the people at your campus who spend all of their lives doing biology might not be able to give you a very good answer. But, if you don't answer that question, I don't know how you can really teach a discipline if you can't show kids the differences there are. We do things differently in science than she does in English. She doesn't do any lab safety at all, for example.

Carter: Well, we too have different subject matter areas at Stanford, but I'd like to echo what Allyson [Mizoguchi] said about the issue of knowing why we teach whatever it is we teach. Some of our subject matter people really emphasize that. Another thing that's very interesting, and I'd love to see it across all of our disciplines, is that in the social studies area they actually design lesson plans around central questions so they're not only thinking about their lesson planning and their themes and objectives around those central questions, but they are also in the process of revisiting the question, "What are the basic questions behind history and social studies?" I think that's very powerful. It's a very interesting way of teaching that gets beyond just teaching fragments of subjects; it gives a broader view. So I recommend that to you. I wish I had Larry Cuban here to tell you exactly how to do that.

Jacobs: We've got an approach that has its own problems. There is a core course that all students take—teaching and the curriculum—that is all about developing curriculum around teaching for understanding as well as the subject questions. I mean they're all related. And it is against those purposes that they then determine what it is they want students to understand and how they will help students understand it. The assessment, therefore, becomes secondary and learning is strategically planned because every strategy has to support how the big concept is defined. The problematic piece is that it is not done by content. In the content courses the language is coherent. What is examined more particularly is why do we do English in particular and what is English. From that perspective they look specifically at how teaching for understanding is pertinent to the literature and language of English. So it kind of spurts from that core course. Then again, we only teach a foundations course.

Myers: I think we've hit on something, Larry [Wakeford]. You said it first, and I heard some of the same things from the last two speakers. I think the key here is that we inquire into the nature of our discipline or disciplines. And it can be more than one. In my mind they are pretty much the same generic questions, so what we need to do is not so much have interdisciplinary courses in which we say, "here's the stuff you need and here's some more stuff you need"—that somehow we're going to give it to you all in one course. It's not the stuff you need, it's the *questions* you need to learn to ask. I'll lean back one step behind that. It's not the questions you need to learn to ask, it's the fact that you need to learn to ask questions and that they are subject matter bound. Now, how do we say that? I guess I have a higher opinion of the arts and science faculty at my institution than some of you may. I think we do some really fine things in the senior seminar topics. And what usually happens in our case (and it gets back to something that you were saying earlier, Chris [Roellke] is that the arts and sciences folks don't know how much we respect that and how much we expect it. When I begin to talk to them about it, it's like, God, you want that too? And I say not only do I want it, we won't let our people through unless they can demonstrate it! So it gets to that point about being respected across disciplines. Some of it, I think, is just communications. I'll just give you a specific example. We do not have a geography department at Vanderbilt University, but we have competencies in geography that all the social studies people need to meet. So the college of arts and sciences hires a person to teach one geography course a semester. The man who's been doing it for a number of years is retiring, so we've been interviewing a person that we're going to hire. We just decided the other day. I said "we": I helped, but it's obviously the arts and sciences office that hires this guy and so the question was, "Myers, what do you want him to teach? What are the emphases?" And the first thing I said was just the geographical perspective and whatever it is that geographers ask in terms of questions and how they try to frame those questions and what the context of that is and this guy's eyes started lighting up, and he said, "that's the heart of geography." I wish we could get the arts and sciences to know that's exactly what we want. That's only one course, a service course, but it represents what we want arts and science people to realize. We want our students to understand the structure of the discipline they're teaching.

Reollke: I think it can be a useful two-way street. We have a program to enhance teacher effectiveness at Richmond that's interesting because we have new faculty members that meet on a regular basis at the University of Richmond. But my colleagues that have not gone through teacher preparation say that they have nobody to help them learn how to teach and there is nobody on campus that knows how to teach them how to teach. I had to say, "Hey! You know, over here!" Nobody knows that we also have something to offer in terms of professional development, assisting people in college level instruction. I feel like I have to be a cheerleader all the time. I'm saying, "bring it over here!" We finally have a member on this committee from the education department. But, it took a long time to get somebody on it.

Thorne: We had this question come up two years ago in our advisory committee meeting which includes arts and sciences faculty from each of the major fields. We discovered that the arts and sciences faculty were having trouble getting their Ph.D. candidates to understand the real essential questions of their own discipline and because of that they could not teach. They couldn't teach in a liberal arts college, so two professors in the history department devised a course built on a two semester course in American History that has their Ph.D. candidates who are Americanists work with our MAT students in that course participating in teaching. Layered on top of that is a seminar on "How do you teach American History?" "What is American History." So, we have this wonderful congregation of senior faculty at Duke along with Ph.D. candidates and our students who are working together to tackle these problems. So, we are going to try it in biology next year. We think the math department may be a stretch, but we'll see.

Card: At Southern Maine we have a similar program in which there is a blend of what we just heard and what Elaine [Landay] said about Brown. Every candidate is required to create a portfolio as an exit document. In it is a platform that includes beliefs about their content area as well as about teaching. It starts at the beginning of the year with questions about what is the nature of their field. Some of the prompts that are in there include: What are the essential elements that every high school graduate should understand about the field? Should the subject be taught to every high school graduate? To what degree? During the year they refine those as they do their observation and student teaching. They move to strategies for enabling students to learn in ways that are compatible with their belief system about their content area to the actual means to help implement those features. In the spring, the last thing that they do as they build this platform is to write an addenda to that platform that says, "Now that I have been working with kids for a year, this is how I would change everything that I said." The first shot at it is imbedded in the content and the last piece is imbedded in what they find in the classroom and how they will go about blending those two things. Then we require them to distill that into one page that they then use as a document for getting hired when they are asked such questions in an interview. That yearlong piece of writing is the essence of the development of their understanding of what the essential questions are, how it impacts kids, and how they can use that to get work.

Discussion Response

Leslie Quast
Furman University

Think where we were when this session began, where we have moved in terms of the content, and how that all evolved. That is the strongest part of what has occurred, that the conversation has moved to a different level. I want to thank Chris [Roellke] for bringing in the fact that we are bilingual if not multilingual. We have also probed the relationship between teaching and learning in our discipline. We are acknowledging, too, the need to be knowledgeable about the structure of the discipline we teach and that we expect that of our students. We have no apologies to make for that across our campuses; we are proud of this concern. We have talked about our arts and sciences faculties and expressed concern about the way they are teaching—not necessarily what they are teaching but how it has been taught. But we have seen the possibilities for us and our students as we work with arts and sciences colleagues.

I think our challenge is how to have the kinds of conversations that we are now asking our students to engage in with these content specialists. We are giving these experiences to our students and are now asking how we can open these to other colleagues. How can we open them to the larger university community so as to have those conversations across the campus? I think some of you alluded to the beginnings of those things happening, where the teaching and the content and the questions about the disciplines' nature become the process of learning for all of us. If that occurs, we don't have to be concerned about the fact that I am in teacher education faculty and you are in arts and sciences. Bringing high school teachers into that conversation would also offer a great deal to what this whole process is about. I found this whole thing very fascinating because if we, within an hour's time, come to understand so much, we should be able to help that happen across our campuses. That will relieve some of the burden that we feel, because if indeed we have effective methods and philosophies of teaching we can encourage these practices in our arts and sciences faculty and we'll all be the better for it.

Major Strands of the Conversation and Papers

The papers by Baker and Roellke address both the perception of teacher education programs within liberal arts universities and the tension between the liberal arts and professional education. Roellke identifies four common misconceptions that contribute to a "mythology" of teacher preparation, offers a framework for dispelling the myths, and describes how the Teacher Preparation Program and the School of Arts and Sciences at the University of Richmond have developed linkages through interdisciplinary courses and integrated programs. Further, he describes how teacher education faculty members provide professional development for faculty members across the university. Baker portrays how Wake Forest University balances liberal arts and teacher preparation through the provision of financial incentives to attract and retain promising students, close collaboration of students with their area advisors and other fellows in their disciplines, blending of study in the discipline with reflective methodology and pedagogical study and research, teaching rounds modeled after medical internships, and a capstone professional development seminar modeled after the requirements for national certification.

What Heckelman adds to the discussion focuses on how to prepare bright students to enter the teaching profession equipped with knowledge and understanding of the educational system and the students whom they will teach. Teacher preparation at Rice University attempts to instill in its candidates deep commitment to academically challenging each student to do and be her or his best. The program at Rice provides students the opportunity to gain expertise in their discipline, select options to enhance their intellectual growth, and to study the education system. A unique feature is the opportunity to create curriculum that students will actually teach in a summer school experience.

The conversation launched by Roellke's, Baker's, and Heckleman's papers turned to several serious issues along the way:
- the applicationof national standards (National Board, INTASC (Interstate New Teacher Assessment and Support Consortium), NCATE (National Council for the Accreditation of Teacher Education) in the academic program
- the integration of pedagogy and discipline content
- the involvement of students in defining their discipline—identifying the core concepts, theories, and methodologies and then examining how that impacts the teaching of the discipline
- experience in building collaborative relationships between faculty and students in the arts and sciences and teacher education

Chapter Four

Internships

Internships are moving to an ever more significant role in the preparation of teachers. In years gone by student teachers spent only a small part of the day at a secondary school observing and periodically engaging in teaching students. It was more like dipping toes into a cool pool than really diving into the water. Now we have heated discussions about the need to extend our student teaching internships to a full year in the schools. Ten weeks of student teaching that were once considered sufficient by both our students and their mentor teachers in the secondary schools seem no longer sufficient to a faculty aware of the national trend of extended internships as a mark of greater professionalism.

Many teacher education programs have decided that even a semester of student teaching does not suffice and opt for year-long internships. In addition, a number of institutions have moved all or part of their teacher education courses out to the schools and some turn almost exclusively to clinical faculty to deliver the bulk of teacher preparation courses at secondary school sites. These educators believe that practice makes perfect, but the quest for more and more field experience for prospective teachers must be considered in light of the public's equal demand for better educated teachers who have a store of general knowledge that is at least the equivalent of that of other university graduates. In addition to this problem, Wake Forest and some other institutions have raised questions about the appropriateness of an apprenticeship kind of teacher preparation that tends to train prospective teachers by asking them to mimic the technique of their master. An alternative that makes sense is to put more stock in prospective teachers observing a diverse set of good teachers whose pedagogical and philosophical differences can be appraised and sorted through by the students so as to construct a teaching style and philosophical grounding that fits the new teacher rather than one that apes the mentor. Such an education, as distinct from a mere training program, requires that methods courses offer a wide array of classroom-tested teaching strategies that interns can sort through, put into play, and reflect upon in a somewhat secure learning environment developed by an experienced teacher. Using this approach rather than the apprentice student teaching approach allows for fifteen weeks of development as a professional rather than one week of a prescribed regimen of teaching repeated fifteen times in a semester. It is the dynamics of progress and development promoted by reflection and reform that prepares these students to become professional teachers in an amazingly brief time.

The examples of the internships featured in this section of *Developing Teachers* reflect diversity, duration, and intensity. Brown's program was built on a list of ideals for mentors and school settings that could best promote deep learning for its internships. When the ideals were sorted out it became clear that the only way to actualize those ideals was to use clusters of three student interns, three mentor teachers, and three clinical faculty members at selected schools. The process was too successful. It exhausted all of the supporting cast of professionals and could not be realized because of a lack of support from principals at the participating schools.

Trinity found more success in its approach. It extends student teaching for an entire year as does New Hampshire and some other programs. The aspiring teachers see the school year through all of its seasons, but they are pulled away from the daily school experience by two classes that absorb a good part of their mental energy and time. The courses are enlivened by the fact that constant school experiences give the courses a lab tone, but they exact a price in terms of students' time and energy.

Southern Maine also uses the entire year for its internships but that experience is the center of all that is learned. The interns are a part of a Professional Development School where their learning to become outstanding teachers is but one of four goals that focus in addition on student achievement, professional development of the clinical faculty, and creation of research on teaching. Because these goals are so symbiotic, the synergism of the four-tier process produces excellence in all four dimensions of the PDS.

Improving the Student Teaching Experience

Lawrence Wakeford
Brown University

The internship, or student teaching, is usually the most significant experience in the preparation of teachers. Those of us in teacher education often use the internship as the culminating course of our programs. We realize that the internship brings together almost all the elements which novice teachers will face in their own classrooms.

In view of this strong statement at Brown we strive to provide the very best internship experience possible. But, what does this mean? What constitutes the very best experience? This paper will attempt to define the conditions that would provide such an experience, to describe some of our efforts to create those conditions, and to identify some of the problems that hinder our efforts to provide and maintain those conditions.

Conditions that Would Contribute to an Ideal Internship

In finding a placement for student teaching, two elements are most important: the cooperating teacher and the school. Teacher education programs should aim to find the best of both. Let me suggest the qualities for which I look in seeking this.

An ideal cooperating teacher would be:

- highly effective in the classroom
- knowledgeable in the current trends in pedagogy
- reflective of his or her own practice
- positive about the profession of teaching
- interested in being a partner in the development of novice teachers

An ideal school site for student teachers would have the following characteristics:

- a clear vision or purpose
- high expectations for teachers and students
- adequate resources for teachers and students
- a supportive environment for teachers and students
- a faculty and administration that welcome novice teachers
- a commitment to professional development for all staff members

Neither of these lists is meant to be exhaustive. However, these qualities and characteristics are critical. When more of them are present, student teachers are likely to flourish. When many are missing, various problems are created which often lead to a less satisfactory experience for the student teacher.

I have come to realize that finding a teacher and a school with all of the above is very difficult, if not impossible. Schools are not ideal worlds. Even schools acknowledged for being effective may not be the best place for student teachers. Some schools, in spite of limited resources, do remarkable things for their students, but for the majority of schools, inadequate numbers of textbooks, little access to technology, makeshift quarters as classrooms, and similar conditions make it difficult for a student teacher to develop skills that are essential for good teaching.

An Attempt to Create More Ideal Student Teaching Situations

Four years ago, while we at Brown were looking at the sites we were placing student teachers, we began to develop a concept which we thought would improve the quality of the student teaching situation for our students. The core of this concept, which we called "clusters," was to place student teachers in groups and to create a special support system for them.

Each cluster was composed of nine individuals—three student teachers, three cooperating teachers, and three clinical faculty members from the university. Since our program only prepares teachers in three disciplines—English, history/social studies, and biology—each cluster had a representative from each discipline. In the first year we aimed to have three clusters each semester, two at one high school and one at a middle school. For various reasons, the middle school cluster functioned only in the second semester. In approaching schools and teachers about the cluster concept we asked that the three teachers in a cluster have a common planning period. This would allow the cluster to meet once each week during the planning period. We believed from the beginning that common planning time was critical and our experience during the second year confirmed this belief.

Clusters had multiple goals but this paper will only deal with those having to do with the qualities and characteristics of teachers and schools alluded to earlier. It is important to note, however, that the clusters were designed to be beneficial to all three parties—for the students, for the teachers, and for the university faculty. The goal for the university faculty was to accomplish at least two important aims. Clusters provided faculty members increased opportunity to be in the schools and that in turn allowed them to develop a closer relationship with the secondary school faculty.

Our primary goal in creating clusters was to find ways to help teachers develop many of the qualities we listed above. In the case of school conditions, clusters enabled us to create a small learning community that would address the last three conditions we listed.

The literature on school change is very clear about the difficulty in effecting change and the time required. Our experience with clusters over their two years of existence gave ample support to this research.

As with any new initiative we learned some important things in the first year of implementation. Six of them are worth some explaining:

It takes *time to develop trust* needed for such an endeavor. This was especially true for the cooperating teachers and the clinical faculty. The teachers were concerned that the university clinical professors would be coming in and telling how things should be done. It took time to dispel some of this fear, and even then we were not completely successful. Our experience was that it takes at least a full semester of work before a relationship of trust begins to develop.

The actual *work of the cluster needs to be mutually agreed upon* by all three parties. Once again, this takes time, but it is essential work. The agenda cannot be dictated by one party. If clusters are to work, all three constituencies must have the opportunity to have their needs met.

Although there can be many different goals of a cluster, we had the greatest success when *we created a product that could be used in the classrooms* of either the cooperating teachers and/or the student teachers. In our second year, for example, our cluster developed an interdisciplinary unit that has shown great promise.

Administrative support is critical; the lack of it can be disruptive. In the second year, when a common planning period for the three cooperating teachers was not scheduled by the administration as we requested, the need to meet before or after school seriously disrupted the work of the cluster. In the middle school the cluster did not continue for a second year because the administration could not, or would not, deal with the claim that certain teachers were being favored in the placement of student teachers.

Clusters are very *demanding of the university faculty's time*. We had hoped that with time each cluster might not require the involvement of the three university faculty members. We never reached that goal. Perhaps if clusters had operated longer we could have reduced the faculty involvement somewhat, but we realized too that such a change would alter the dynamics of how clusters work.

Having the *university faculty involved in teaching the high school students* is very useful. Both cooperating teachers and student teachers respond differently, and more positively, when they see that university faculty members are willing to put their ideas and skills to the test of the secondary classroom.

We had a total of six clusters over four semesters, all of which were successful to some degree. In looking back at the qualities that are desirable in a cooperating teacher, the clusters showed some success in a number of important areas. Through the work of the clusters cooperating teachers were more open about what they were doing in the classroom

Chapter Four: Internships

and why they elected to do it. This openness to reflection varied from teacher to teacher, but over time most seemed more willing to discuss their own teaching. Many times in the cluster meetings the subject was teaching strategies: Socratic seminar, cooperative learning, and performance-based assessment to name a few. These techniques were new to some of the teachers. Thus, the cluster provided an opportunity for them to learn more about, use, or discuss what they were seeing in the classrooms of the student teachers. Last, since the teachers had agreed to be part of the cluster, they were committed to playing a larger role in bringing novices into the profession.

With respect to creating a more ideal school site, the clusters proved to be successful as well. The cluster certainly provided a more supportive environment for the cooperating teachers and the student teachers. The student teachers got to work more closely with their peers and the other two cooperating teachers. Setting aside a period each week to talk about teaching and learning was a unique and productive experience for most of the teachers. Some seemed to genuinely enjoy the opportunity; others did not, and their attendance fell off.

One of the first steps in creating clusters was to approach the principals. We realized that we needed their support. In general, they were quite enthusiastic about the effort and were helpful in identifying and encouraging teachers to be part of the clusters. In the second year one principal helped solidify the gains of our clusters by scheduling a group of high school students who were taught by all three of the cooperating teachers in one cluster. This structural change allowed the cluster to develop an interdisciplinary strand that was taught across all three disciplines. Unfortunately, this principal was unable, or unwilling, to schedule a common planning time for the three teachers. This seriously hampered the work of the cluster, because cluster meetings could only take place before or after school.

In addition, clusters offered a special vehicle for professional development for all three parties. This was one of the primary goals of clusters and to varying degrees it was successful. Student teachers who rarely see an ongoing exchange between university faculty and secondary school teachers were provided with this opportunity: it gave them an equal place at the professional planning table. In one cluster, members planned a series of topics at their first meeting of the semester, and thereafter. Each meeting was chaired by a different member of the cluster. This was a particularly successful cluster, in part because each person who served as a leader felt responsible for insuring that his or her session was well-prepared and the time well utilized.

Looking Ahead

Our experiment with clusters ended after two years. The major reason was that the administration was unable to schedule a common planning period during which the cluster would meet. I remain baffled why this could not be done, but all parties agreed during the second year that time for planning together was essential for the cluster to function effectively. In order to create clusters we needed to find three interested teachers at the same school, who we thought were qualified to be cooperating teachers, and who taught in three different disciplines. This was more difficult than one might expect. Finally, the need for the university faculty to be at the schools for the weekly meetings was substantial. In the first year, when we had four clusters operating, there were more than fifty meetings. Most were attended by at least two of the three clinical faculty members; more than half were attended by all three. Such an expenditure of time would be worthwhile if clusters were highly successful. Since degree of success varied significantly, however, we chose not to pursue the cluster concept but rather to work with teachers in other schools.

In spite of the failure of clusters to improve the student teaching experience, the attempt was well worth it. My colleagues and I learned some important things. I still believe that the cluster concept is worthy of continued development. But I have come to see that clusters have many of the qualities of professional development schools. Such full partnership is a direction that may better accomplish our goals. For the past year, Brown has been working with the Providence School Department, the Teachers Union, and five other post seminary institutions to develop a plan for a PDS in Providence. As we move ahead I think that our experience with clusters will provide valuable information. In fact, I think that clusters, or something similar, might be used within a PDS. I think that change is easier when one starts small. In a newly established PDS, multiple clusters, operating semi-autonomously, but linking together when appropriate, could provide a scale of involvement that is manageable. A possible PDS cluster might consist of:

- five to six teachers, each having a student teacher
two university faculty members
- three to four pre-practicum students

The cluster would have the following:

- lead teachers working with a group of students
- interdisciplinary work encouraged by the administration
- weekly two-hour blocks for collaborative work
- monthly half-day sessions for long-range planning
- funding to support professional development of the cluster

I know that if our teacher preparation program is to improve, one area in greatest need of attention is the internship or student teaching component. Currently, there is enormous variation in the quality of the experience that students have. Some have a stimulating, challenging semester which provides them with the impetus to move into their professional life with anticipation and enthusiasm. Others finish weary, bruised, and with great anxiety. As a teacher educator, I want all of my students to have a positive experience. That will not happen unless we can make some significant changes in the internship.

Preparing Teachers through Professional Development School Partnerships

Angela Breidenstein
Trinity University

To talk about teacher education reform nationally and teacher education reform in Texas is to talk about two different things. While the national movement in the 1990s has advocated strengthening teacher education programs vis-à-vis program structures, courses, and field experiences, in Texas reforming teacher education has meant cutting down on the requirements for completion of an undergraduate teacher education program (Darling-Hammond, 1997; Grossman, 1990; Ishler, 1992, Tyson, 1992). In 1987, the Texas legislature passed Senate Bill 994, which stipulated that undergraduate students seeking certification could not be required to take more than eighteen hours of education coursework (with exceptions for certification in special education, bilingual education, ESL, and early childhood).

At the same time this legislation was being passed into law, Trinity University was redesigning its teacher education program to incorporate the principles and practices being advocated by the Holmes Group (Holmes Group, 1986; Holmes Group, 1990; Holmes Group, 1995), including internship experiences in professional development schools.

By placing the emphasis of the teacher education program on an extended year of graduate study in a professional development school, Trinity was able to provide for a full-year internship and move this internship from the restricted undergraduate program to the unrestricted graduate program. Therefore, while most programs in Texas met the legislative mandates in undergraduate teacher education by cutting down their program requirements and limiting the field experiences of teacher education students, the Trinity program was expanded with the extended year model, particularly in the area of the full-year internship.

Designing the Trinity Teacher Education Program

The redesign of the teacher education program at Trinity University began in 1987, as Trinity was participating with other schools and colleges of education in the Holmes Group and other national reform networks and simultaneously conducting its own inquiry and reform in San Antonio. In consultation with teachers and administrators in San Antonio schools, faculty in the department of education and across the university, university students, and outside consultants (Boyer, Sizer, Wise, Lanier), this forum of designers created the professional development schools (PDS) network now known as the Trinity University Alliance of Better Schools. Further, a continuum of teacher education experiences was established which begins with undergraduate seminars and practica, continues with coursework in child and adolescent development as well as educational policy and reform, and culminates in a graduate experience which features the full-year internship along with coursework focused on curriculum, pedagogy, leadership, and supervision. The guiding principle for the teacher education program was, and continues to be, an integration of theory, research, and practice. In addition to the construction of the PDS network and the MAT teacher education program construction, this team also created a humanities degree for students going into elementary education; rather than majoring in education, elementary education students receive a bachelor's degree in humanities and secondary education students receive a bachelor's degree in the academic discipline(s) they will teach.

Today the teacher education program at Trinity continues to feature a full-year internship in a professional development school as the central focus of the fifth year as well as the culmination of the undergraduate experience. The extended year master's program serves both continuing undergraduates in a fifth-year graduate program and post-baccalaureate students in a one-year graduate program. The Trinity teacher education program has evolved since the first master's cohort graduated in May 1991, yet the basic theoretical and structural tenets have remained intact. Research, both self-study and outside study, and continued dialogue between the education faculty and the teachers, administrators, and university faculty who created the redesigned program and who participate in the program each year as mentors and students have promoted the continued development and improvement of the program (Center for Educational Leadership, 1994; National Center for Restructuring Education, Schools, and Teaching, in press; Tyson, 1994; Van Zandt, 1996). Additionally, evaluations by the National Council for the Accreditation of Teacher Education and the Texas State Board for Educator Certification have promoted the continued review and refinement of the program.

The Internship

The internship is one of the components of the program that consistently receives the highest ratings from interns, mentors, administrators, and university faculty. In the 1996 program evaluation conducted by the university, Van Zandt concluded that "without argument the most valuable asset of the program is the year-long internship in a PDS, which appears to provide the time and experiences necessary to develop a range of teaching competencies" (p.10). Two statements from graduates of the program emphasize this point:

> The full year teaching experience was the best part. The supportive and visible university faculty every day helped me through many stressful and emotional events that naturally occur during one's internship. I loved finding my philosophy of teaching—I was truly ready for my own classroom.

> Eight months of being in the classroom was the primary strength. It's wonderful to see how a year flows and be able to prepare and expect changes in you and your students as the year progresses. Also, being able to dialogue, reflect with other interns who know the personalities you're dealing with. (Van Zandt, 1996, p.10)

Simply spending time in schools and classrooms is not enough to qualify as an internship. Vital to the success of the internship at Trinity are the structures which underpin the experience: concurrent courses, the guidance of mentors, discussions with other interns and mentors, the support and supervision of faculty, and the professional development school setting.

Pre-internship practicum experiences in the professional development school prepare students for the internship. Undergraduate students complete three practica, with each involving at least thirty hours in a classroom over the course of the semester and accompanying seminars taught by faculty from each of the professional development schools. Each practicum course has a particular focus that guides the seminar discussions and coursework: the school, the teacher, the student. These practica are important not only for their academic and educational content but also for the exposure they give students to the professional development schools, mentors, students, and potential internship experiences.

Internship Organization

While most of the students who participate in the Trinity teacher education program are Trinity students who began their course of study as undergraduates, post-baccalaureate students can apply for admission to the program. Therefore, the Trinity program is both a five-year and a fifth-year program. All students, whether five-year or fifth-year students, must be accepted for admission to the program based on the selection criteria: a cumulative GPA of 3.0, three letters of recommendation, passing scores or exemption from the Texas pre-professional skills test (TASP), approval by department and university committees, and successful completion of undergraduate coursework. Post-baccalaureate students must meet these same requirements as well as a minimum GRE score of 1000 and an interview with education and PDS faculty.

The internship placement process begins in May, when a team at each of the five professional development schools meets to determine the placement of interns with mentor teachers at that school. The placement committee consists of the PDS principal, PDS coordinating faculty (teachers at the school who also coordinate practicum placements and teach practicum seminars), and the university faculty member who works with that school. The size of the intern cohort at each school ranges from eight to eighteen; the average elementary cohort size is ten, and the average secondary cohort size is fifteen.

The graduate program begins with the summer courses in May, and the internship starts on the first day of the teacher in-service in August. As this is a full-year internship, the interns participate in the school from the first day of the in-service to the first day of school until mid-April. Upon successful completion of the internship, graduate courses, and the portfolio, students graduate in May with the Master of Arts in Teaching degree.

Internship Setting: Professional Development Schools

There are five professional development schools with whom the university has established partnerships—two elementary schools, one middle school, and two high schools (both located on the same campus as one is a small magnet high school and the other a large comprehensive high school). The relationships with these schools have been built and strengthened over time, with the school-university partnerships in its ninth year of collaboration. A cohort of interns works at each school where one clinical faculty member serves as a teacher, adviser, and supervisor. Further, the mentors at each school comprise a cohort that works with the same clinical faculty member throughout the year. Clinical faculty are assigned to a professional development school on a long-term basis, so that relationships can be developed and maintained not only with the mentors and interns but with all participants of the school including the administrators.

The students begin their internship in the professional development school in August when all teachers, administrators, and staff begin their academic year. From the first day of the teacher in-service in August to mid-April, the interns participate fully in the PDS; as partners with their mentor teachers, they plan curriculum, teach classes, attend meetings and staff development sessions, conduct research, and participate in school activities. Interns are considered members of the staff and have all of the rights and responsibilities of teachers, although they are not paid a salary or stipend.

Throughout the semester, professional development activities are planned for the interns and mentors of each professional development school. For example, each PDS cohort of mentors, interns, and the clinical faculty member participate in a one- or two-day retreat in the fall. At the PDS and at the university, meetings, seminars, and sessions with special speakers are centered on issues of mentoring, teaching, learning, and curriculum. Mentors, interns, and university faculty also participate in local, regional, and national conferences and networks.

Duration of the Internship

The duration of the internship, a full year, is significant for many reasons. First, the full year allows the intern to experience the beginning of school, as the teacher sets up the classroom and determines the curriculum, behavior management program, expectations, and learning environment; this is a time when many important decisions are made and when the classroom community begins to be established. Because the interns are in the classroom from the first day, not only can they observe the mentor teacher in this phase of establishing the classroom, but they can also be partners in the decision-making that occurs; further, being there on the first day as a partner establishes the role of the intern as a co-teacher in the eyes of the mentor, students, and other PDS participants.

As the school year continues, interns are able to experience the progression over the year in the classroom. They get a feeling for the rhythm of the day as well as the rhythm of the year. They see how curriculum unfolds, grading cycles proceed, and holidays interrupt. Most importantly, they are able to participate in and observe the development of individual students and a class over the course of the year.

Last, in terms of the development of the interns, the full year provides them with time and experiences to more fully develop as teachers, researchers, and leaders. Corcoran and Andrew (1993) describe a progression of five areas of student concern in the full year internship program: immersion, adjustment, expansion, analysis, and autonomy. It is in the context of the full-year internship in a professional development school with a mentor, clinical faculty member, and cohort of peers this development, through time and opportunity, can be more fully fostered.

Teacher Education Coursework

While the focus of the teacher education program is the fifth year of coursework and the internship, students begin their course of study in education as undergraduates. They complete three practica in the Alliance schools, courses in human growth and development, and courses in the foundations of education. The master's program then begins after graduation in May with summer courses where interns engage in curriculum inquiry and teaching inquiry.

Concurrent with their full-year internship in the professional development school, interns participate in graduate courses in the fall and spring semesters. In both semesters, interns meet with their PDS cohort and clinical faculty for Clinical Practice and Advanced Clinical Practice. In the fall, interns also complete a course focused on pedagogy; this course is team taught by the two elementary clinical faculty for the elementary interns and the two secondary crucial faculty for the secondary interns. In the spring semester, a course on educational leadership and supervision is taught by faculty in educational administration.

Two major program components that are completed in the course of the internship are the research project and the portfolio; both of these projects represent the emphasis on praxis, the integration of both theory and practice. In the fall, interns conduct action research in their classroom and/or in the school focused on a pedagogical, curricular, or educational issue; the research paper is submitted as a component of the pedagogics course. This research project is also included in the portfolio, which is the culminating activity for the internship and the graduate program. Interns are responsible for creating a professional teaching portfolio that represents their growth over the year as an intern as well as their potential for growth as a teacher. A portfolio presentation is made at the end of April to faculty, interns, and teachers, and the portfolio notebook is turned in to the clinical faculty upon completion of the presentation.

Internship Mentors

All of the teachers, administrators, staff, and students at the professional development school mentor the intern, with the main mentoring role assumed by the teacher with whom the intern teaches. At the elementary level, the intern has two mentors, a lower grade mentor and an upper grade mentor. Secondary interns usually have only one mentor, although interns with more than one teaching field have a mentor in each teaching field. Mentors are recognized by the university in an appointment ceremony led by the president of Trinity University in the fall. This appointment does not result in monetary or other compensation; rather, it signals in symbol and action the significance of the mentor as a teacher educator. Trinity University mentors participate in the program voluntarily for the professional and personal reward of mentoring a beginning teacher and working with other mentor teachers and the teacher education program.

The significance of the mentor role cannot be overstated. Mentors spend an extraordinary amount of time with the interns daily as the intern's teacher and partner in collaboration. Together interns and mentors write and plan curriculum, teach their students and develop the classroom community. Mentors constantly give interns feedback regarding their teaching in dialogue as well as in journals and observation notes. It is in the mentor's classroom that the intern finds a safe space for protected practice and experimentation to learn from teaching and research.

Clinical faculty discuss and promote mentoring philosophies and practices with the mentors, working with mentors individually and as a group to develop their strengths and to facilitate the intern/mentor relationship. Mentor meetings occur throughout the year, and each year all of the mentors meet in a full-day mentoring retreat at the university to shape the teacher education program. Mentors teach undergraduate practicum seminars, serve on department committees, and participate in departmental programs and projects.

University Faculty

Throughout the program description, the role of the university faculty has been outlined. The Trinity University clinical faculty who work with the interns and mentors wear many hats. To the interns, they are teacher educators, instructors, supervisors, advisers, co-researchers, and cohort leaders. To the mentors, they are colleagues, professional development coordinators, mentoring advisers, and meeting organizers. In the professional development school, they are colleagues working with teachers, students, and administrators on reform issues and initiatives related to issues of teaching and learning. Last , they have roles and responsibilities related to the undergraduate courses and seminars as well as to the greater university arena.

Conclusion

Discontent with the traditional program of teacher education and student teaching which only allowed for limited field experiences in schools with teachers and students, Trinity University and its professional development school partners redesigned and implemented a teacher education program created by teachers, students, faculty from across the university, and colleagues in the field of teacher education. Together, this community has continued to work toward the goal of providing pre-service teachers with the best possible teacher education experience. Salient features of the Trinity teacher education program that have been identified as critical components of the program include a developmental five-year sequence of field experiences and courses; the professional development school setting; a cohort of interns; a cadre of mentor teachers and clinical faculty; and an integration of theory, research, and practice. With these philosophical and structural components as the foundation for teacher education at Trinity, the partnership between the university and schools continues to "tinker toward utopia" to prepare teachers and build professional development school communities which benefit pre-service teachers, in-service teachers, and students (Tyack & Cuban, 1995).

The Internship in a Professional Development School: The Power of Place

Richard H. Card
University of Southern Maine

The "simultaneous" renewal of K–12 schools and teacher preparation programs is dependent upon a rich and full relationship among K–12 and higher education faculties and their institutions. In one Professional Development School model (PDS) such partnership is not an end but a means by which schools and institutions of higher education seek to accomplish four purposes:

- Provide an exemplary education for all students
- Provide a quality clinical setting for pre-service education
- Provide continual professional development for teachers and professors
- Promote and conduct inquiry into teaching and learning

When internships for pre-service teachers are found in programs dedicated to these four purposes, the interns are influenced by the context of the whole school. They not only learn about teaching in a classroom, they learn how to be a faculty member, how the structure of the school affects teaching and learning, about the politics of an organization, about the role of the union, and about the myriad of other influences that shape our schools.

Many Professional Development Schools are not sufficiently evolved to support each of the four stated purposes and thus focus primarily on the creation of high-quality clinical settings for pre-service teachers. Arguably, such a focus is natural and worthy for teacher preparation programs, but it will likely fall far short of the full vision articulated in a Professional Development School model because whole school involvement is essential for simultaneous renewal or reform. The pre-service model where a student teacher is mentored by a single cooperating teacher overseen by a university supervisor cannot create the optimum teacher preparation environment. It is limited to the collective skills and knowledge of those few professionals who are involved. It does not produce the synergistic effect needed in either a school or higher education setting to influence the organizational culture, impact the quality of learning for all students, or contribute much to the teaching/learning knowledge base. For such impact, something more is needed.

Comprehensive Professional Development Schools

The work of John Goodlad, Richard Clark, and the National Council for Accreditation of Teacher Education (NCATE) provide a thorough view of the Professional Development School model. Richard Clark has identified the broadly accepted features of the Professional Development School and has done pioneering work related to the finances and funding of them. In *Educational Renewal: Better Teachers, Better Schools,* John Goodlad (1994) presents nineteen postulates representing the philosophical and programmatic foundations and essential elements to undergird the PDS. NCATE has, in addition, articulated threshold conditions and standards for the PDS. These collective works give informed guidance for those interested in moving the PDS model from a handful of exemplars to the standard for teacher preparation programs.

The Professional Development School Defined

As reported by Richard Clark (1996) in his guide for policy makers, *Professional Development Schools Policy and Financing,* major organizations agree on four basic purposes as defining the work of the

Professional Development Schools. University- and school-based educators collaborate in these schools to accomplish four purposes:

- Provide an exemplary education for some segment of P–12 students
- Provide a clinical setting for pre-service education
- Provide professional development for teachers and professors
- Promote and conduct inquiry that advances knowledge of schooling

The Professional Development School, as envisioned by Goodlad and the National Network for Educational Renewal (NNER), is the setting that serves as the organizational catalyst for the K–16 collaboration necessary to produce the results needed: success for all learners.

The Essence of the Professional Development School

Among John Goodlad's nineteen postulates for designing programs for the education of educators, several specifically relate to and support the Professional Development School model developed by Clark and others. Seven of them are directly related to the four criteria noted above.

1. There must exist a clearly identifiable group of academic and clinical faculty members for whom teacher education is the top priority; the group must be responsible and accountable for selecting diverse groups of students and monitoring their progress, planning and maintaining the full scope and sequence of the curriculum, continuously evaluating and improving programs, and facilitating the entry of graduates into teaching careers. (Provide a quality clinical setting.)
2. The responsible group of faculty and clinical faculty members described above must have a comprehensive understanding of the aims of education and the role of schools in our society and be committed to selecting and preparing teachers to assume the full range of educational responsibilities required. (Provide a quality clinical setting.)
3. Programs for the education of educators must provide extensive opportunities for future teachers to move beyond being students of organized knowledge to becoming teachers who inquire into

both knowledge and its teaching. (Conduct inquiry into teaching and learning/provide professional development.)
4. Programs for the education of educators must be characterized in all respects by the conditions for learning that future teachers are to establish in their own schools and classrooms. (Provide a quality clinical setting.)
5. Programs for the education of educators must be conducted in such a way that future teachers inquire into the nature of teaching and schooling and assume that they will do so as a natural aspect of their careers. (Conduct inquiry into teaching and learning/provide professional development.)
6. Programs for the education of educators must be infused with understanding of and commitment to the moral obligation of teachers to equitable access to and engagement in the best possible K–12 education for all children and youths. (Provide an exemplary education.)
7. Programs for the education of educators must involve future teachers not only in understanding schools as they are, but in alternatives, the assumptions underlying alternatives, and how to effect needed changes in school organization, pupil grouping, curriculum, and more. (Conduct inquiry into teaching and learning/provide professional development.)

Goodlad's postulates provide an excellent directive for planning, formative decision making, and for the evaluation of Professional Development Schools. They provide insight for the PDS as a setting for the pre-service teacher internship; at the same time, they describe desirable qualities and characteristics of academic and clinical faculty, intern candidates, and school settings.

Conditions and Standards

The National Council for Accreditation of Teacher Education (NCATE) has produced a set of draft standards for professional development schools (2/21/97). They acknowledge that many school/university partnerships which call themselves Professional Development Schools are, in fact, in an early stage of development. They do not meet the threshold conditions necessary for being defined as a PDS:

the relationships which are being developed are critical for threshold conditions to be effective. At this pre-threshold stage individuals build relationships, mutual values, and understandings may be worked through and early collaboration between school and university-based educators takes place. Memos of understanding may be transacted about shared expectations and activities which they may participate in together. Agreements, commitments, and working relationships between institutions which are established in the absence of prior collaboration are likely to be weak. Threshold Conditions are measures of the commitment and the understanding of the partnering institutions who are coming together to form this new hybrid institution known as a PDS.

NCATE's draft on these threshold conditions includes five characteristics that PDS participants have indicated must be in place as a foundation for development as a PDS:

1. An agreement that commits school, school district, and university to the basic mission of a PDS: preparation of new teachers, support of children's learning, continuing professional development, and practice-based inquiry.
2. Commitment by partners to the critical attributes of a PDS: there should be tangible commitment from each partner to (a) the support of a learning community for adults and children; (b) standards-based teaching and learning; (c) collaboration; (d) continuous improvement supported by ongoing practice-based research; and (e) equity among students and among teachers.
3. Positive working relationships and a basis for trust between partners.
4. Achievement of quality standards by partner institutions as assessed by regional, state, national, or other review boards.
5. Institutional commitment of resources to the PDS from school and university. This commitment can take many forms including faculty participation, time commitments, financial support, organizational support.

The threshold conditions include a commitment to developing the "critical attributes" of a professional development school and the principles which are embedded within them. NCATE has identified four critical attributes with a standard of quality for each. Indicators, as evidence of those attributes, are also described. The four critical attributes are entitled "Learning Community," "Collaboration Accountability," Quality Assurance," and "Organization Roles and Structures."

The Voice of the Pre-service Teacher Intern

The effect of these important whole school attributes on student interns is dramatic. In a recent seminar, interns discussed these influences on their experiences. Each intern acknowledged the power of the school setting on the internship. The three most significant elements comprising the whole school context were identified to be:

1. *Climate of sharing.* Interns talked at length about the importance of "teacher talk." Interns were excited about teacher discussions that were supportive of one another, students, and families. When teachers were "willing to talk about the way they do things," interns felt connected to a community that was vital and growing. Where teachers readily shared ideas and materials, interns were eager to be involved beyond the classrooms of their mentor teachers.
2. *An environment of respect.* In those schools where respect for all people was the foundation for interaction, interns felt included in a profession. One intern reported, "Even though we are in the learning process, we are seen as and feel like professionals." In schools where discussions were pessimistic, where teachers complained about one another, students, and parents, interns were reluctant to join in any faculty interchange. They were uncomfortable and worried about being judged or ridiculed.
3. *Principal as Leader.* The principal as school leader was most often identified as the single most important link connecting the interns to the whole school. In one school, the principal met weekly with interns to talk about their experiences, school issues, and the profession. In other schools the principals were rarely seen.

A PDS Developmental Continuum

Discussions similar to this one have prompted the creation of a Professional Development School developmental continuum. It is designed to describe specific features that constitute the evolution of a PDS and its four purposes. Attending to the construction of a PDS means acknowledging stages of development. Understanding this continuum allows us to discuss, track, and assess the growth of the setting for pre-service teacher interns. The four purposes of a PDS serve as the components for measuring that development. Additionally, five features for each purpose provide a systemic view of the setting to better ensure that the whole system of schooling is engaged:

1. *Vision/Mission/Goals.* The short-term and long-range plans for moving the setting toward the fully envisioned Professional Development School.
2. *Leadership.* Behavior that moves the evolving Professional Development School toward its vision by considering each of the systemic elements individually and collectively.
3. *Policy and Governance.* The written commitments, procedures and decision-making processes established to direct the Professional Development School.
4. *The Psycho-Social Domain.* The interaction of individuals and groups within the Professional Development School that influence its climate and culture.
5. *Technology and Methodology.* The approaches and systems used to carry out the work of the Professional Development School.

The utility of the continuum is its use as a tool to describe the current state of affairs and a preferred future. When partnership members agree on what now exists and what is desired, written agreements can be drawn, plans can be crafted, and assessment strategies can be created to inform progress. The elements selected for this continuum may not serve every partnership, but they do reinforce four generally accepted purposes of a Professional Development School and they incorporate important features of a systemic approach to organizational change.

Conclusion

Partnerships in PDSs have great potential to support the changes needed in our schools and teacher preparation programs. The realization of a fully formed Professional Development School will require the attention and commitment of K–16 faculty and institutional leaders. A clear vision of a school must be articulated that includes the preparation of future teachers as part of its mission. Guiding principles, such as those found in Goodlad's postulates, must influence the design of the partnerships and the desired qualities of K–16 faculty selected to shape the practice of future teachers. There must be a recognition that the program transformation we desire is a developmental journey. We must measure our progress against a set of standards, such as the ones created by NCATE, using benchmarks, such as those suggested in the developmental continuum. The PDS is not only a powerful place for the development of future teachers, it is an organizational vehicle for the simultaneous renewal of schools and teacher preparation programs called for by Goodlad and desired by thousands of educators. The conditions have been tested, the blueprint has been created, the foundation has been set. It is time for construction.

Response

Alan J. Reiman
N.C. State University

First of all I want to thank the folks that were here today who made the presentations. I think you did an admirable job and certainly in the case of Trinity it was wonderful to have people participate in this conference that are working in schools. I'd also like to say that I continue to be impressed as I listen to educators talk about education. It seems to always resonate with my own experience, at least in situations where the educators care about educating. It usually resonates with both the interpersonal and moral-ethical domains of my work. That certainly has been the case this morning as well as yesterday. I did a little reflecting about what might be the most appropriate way to serve as respondent. I've been involved in teacher education: I've been a mentor myself, I've been a school-based teacher educator, and a clinical educator. Angela [Breidenstein], I've had a chance to be where you stood. So, how do I try to provide some type of a coherent response to the things that I've heard regarding internships and their value in terms of teacher education? What I think I'd like to do is make a few points, and then raise a number of questions. I think the questions I raise will be focused on the internship. But they also will touch upon some of the things that have already been discussed and they may also bridge to some of the things that are going to be discussed later.

I'd like to begin with Barbara Kelley's remarks and just underscore a couple things that she said. There were a few things that really stood out for me. One was when she talked about the need for sustained systemic support. I know that's a catchy little phrase that can mean almost anything, but, it's come up in the conversations today. She talked about the key role that induction plays, and she also talked about the need for universities and public schools to not be separate silos. I had never heard that before, but I really liked that. I think we were also talking about the need for not having separate silos. I've heard in the discussion a need for continuous support, so it connects back to some of Barbara [Kelley]'s comments as well.

I would like to underscore that when Michael [Andrew] and Eleanor [Abrams], from the University of New Hampshire were talking, their conversation touched on internships. I return to you for just a moment, because I was impressed that you had done research, which I do value. I value that enough to let my beliefs go if the research is sound and replicated. It did certainly stand out as significant what the two of you had said that one of the most important attributes of successful internships is the personal qualities those students bring to that internship. I know, too, that you had many descriptions of what those personal qualities are, and I think that's very significant, not only in terms of the internship, but in terms of retention, which many legislators in this country are very worried about. We're not holding onto teachers, and obviously many people in this room are worried about the retention of our good teachers. That's the piece you want to hold onto.

I've been talking with medical faculty, faculty in law, faculty in accounting, faculty in counseling, faculty in social work, faculty in architecture to find out how they prepare their people. I am not prepared today to talk much about that; however, it does strike me that they have all grappled with some of the same tensions we're experiencing in terms of the appropriate duration and intensity of internships and how to best prepare people for the world of practice. It strikes me that perhaps the greatest point of divergence between those professions and ours is what we do in terms of the assignment for the beginner.

I didn't hear a whole lot mentioned about the preparation of clinical educators. You could also add to that the preparation of teacher educators. So I ask, how might we best prepare clinical teachers, mentors, school-based teacher educators, and clinical instructors? Some discussion of that came up in the group from Trinity, but it might be worth a more extensive conversation. I also found myself listening to Scott Baker from Wake Forest University talk and found myself wondering, where, in terms of internships, do we embed the notion of graduated experience? The psychology of learning suggests that graduated learning and spaced practice, rather than a massed experience, is what enhances and accelerates learning and development. So that hasn't been discussed here except tangentially, and I think it's an important issue in light of the research that's going on in terms of child and adult learning and development.

Jerome Bruner would be very pleased by Charles [Myers]'s comments that directed our attention to the structure of the discipline; I was enthralled by that conversation. I have two questions for all of you in light of that dialogue: What about the structure of pedagogy? I don't think Bruner talked about that. And also it seems to me that the folks from Trinity and Southern Maine talked about this in terms of their program. Many people have talked about the unbelievable interpersonal dimension of teaching. So then the other question might be, what is the structure of interaction-pedagogy internships? There may be a different kind of human interaction we need to better understand in terms of its structure and how we help prospective educators understand that.

I have some other questions as well: for Larry [Wakeford] at Brown, we were all wondering, if the wonderful cluster model is no longer going on; perhaps at some point that question could be addressed, because it seemed like a very exciting thing you were doing there, with the clustering of the student teachers and the cooperating teachers and clinical faculty. Richard [Card], I was most appreciative of something that you did when you either intentionally or unintentionally referred to the conceptual theoretical framework for your model. I know Ken Howie at Ohio State University, has spoken , in a very profound way about the importance of having conceptual theoretical frameworks for what we do. I was most appreciative of the fact that it was mentioned by both of you. Kathy and Hilary, thank you for mentioning rewards and posing the big question, "How do we acknowledge our clinical staff?" Obviously some clinical staffers are always dealing with the question of whether they will be tenured or not. So there's a whole set of issues around this. By the way, Kathy [Bieser] also mentioned the term *celebrate*, and I'm finding that we probably don't do a lot of that in the education profession. I'm glad you're doing it at your institution, I think that's most important.

I would like to say to the whole group that I thought I knew what *clinical* means, but I'm not sure I've got it any longer. We may want to make sure we all know what *clinical* means to all of us. I'm also a little unclear about professional development schools. The more I hear, the more I respect the fact that there are lots of different definitions. It might be important for us, however, if we want to be looked at as a profession, that we have very clear definitions of our terms. In terms of actual research, it's a noble idea to work toward! I know that Wake Forest is doing it. Trinity is doing it; it sounds like some other institutions are too. I would draw your attention to some of the research that's been done by Sharon Oja and others who have talked about the collaborative nature of action research that actually accelerates the learning and development of teachers. So putting folks in teams as some of you do could be a really exciting idea.

Does the profession need to more carefully explicate the selection, preparation, roles and responsibilities, and rewards of mentors and clinical faculty? I haven't heard much about preparation, I haven't heard much about some of those other things either. I know that the Association of Teacher Educators has begun to look at that whole issue. Perhaps we need to discuss that a little bit. Richard [Card], thank you for mentioning Alice [Sy]'s comment about the high bar as a metaphor for what we'd like to become, and the need for exemplary practice. I think that also means that we need to be very attentive to whatever research is going on in terms of practice. And in terms of Richard's PDS model, those different overlapping spheres, I really like that and I think that your comments on that were really most additive. Maybe he should consider whether there should be a fifth circle, which is research and evaluation. The 1990 and the 1996 research summaries on professional development schools basically say it's an interesting idea, but there isn't a lot of research that's been done. So, it might be that adding that sphere would not only be helpful to your model, it would be an incredible contribution to the profession, since there's been so little research done there.

I'll finish with this last idea, which is just the whole notion of different sentiments about how you make internships happen. I think Charles [Myers] has offered us an interesting idea when he saw that an intense internship might be one of the best kinds of preparations for those first years. Leslie Heling-Austin spoke about the unrealistic optimism that our graduates have and I think we need to guard against it. On the other hand, I think it would be nice if legislators would actually legislate against unrealistic assignments for beginning teachers. We need to look at that very carefully, because it may chase some of the best teachers out of the profession.

Internships Discussion

Christopher Roellke, University of Richmond; **Kathy Bieser** and **Angela Breidenstein,** Trinity University; **Eleanor Abrams** and **Michael Andrew,** University of New Hampshire; **Robert Evans,** Wake Forest University; **Eileen Landay** and **Lawrence Wakeford,** Brown University; **Ruth Bettandorff,** Agnes Scott College; **Charles Myers,** Vanderbilt University; **Richard Card,** University of Southern Maine; **Vicki Jacobs,** Harvard University; **Margo Figgins,** University of Virginia.

Roellke: Kathy [Bieser], how did it feel to have to take two classes while you were an intern? Could you pull it off? How difficult was it logistically?

Bieser: Logistically it worked out. I had classes at night and was in school during the day. It was very challenging, though. The first couple of weeks of school I was very, very tired. But, after a couple of weeks I became used to it, I got into the routine. At the time, especially after we started writing up our research, going to school all day, going to class at night in addition to completing the research was very challenging. But, looking back on it now, I think it was very beneficial.

Abrams: Along those same lines, as someone who is entitled to critique the process that you are involved in, would you say there might be a way to incorporate the course in the work of your day so that you have a more reasonable schedule?

Bieser: It could be done, but personally it would be very difficult for me to leave the classroom. During the first semester I wanted to go out and observe other interns and other teachers, but if I were out of the classroom more, I would feel pulled in different directions.

Evans: To clarify, are you teaching a full load and going to night classes at the same time or is it a teaming situation so that you are both teaching during the day?

Bieser: When I came to the school at the beginning of August we taught in the class together. Hillary [Barnard] did most of the teaching for the first two weeks. After that we were co-teaching the classes through Christmas. At the same time I was planning and teaching classes when she was out of the classroom. Over Christmas, as our final we wrote a unit. When we came back I taught for nine weeks by myself. Hillary would be in and out of the classroom observing as would Angela [Breidenstein].

Evans: Did you have night classes during that nine-week period when you had the full load and the full responsibility?

Bieser: Tuesday I had a class in school leadership and supervision and Thursdays we had a debriefing where all of the interns came together to talk about what was going on.

Evans: But you didn't have academic courses during that time that you had to study for and read for.

Bieser: One. That nine weeks was the most difficult time.

Roellke: We require that of our students too. I find that they have a very hard time with it. Particularly the reading and papers that may be required in the course. I find the quality is not as strong for those students that are student teaching, but that is understandable.

Landay: My question is, why? We stand back and watch the medical profession being critiqued for what they do with their interns and say, "why should someone be up for 36 hours and treat someone with a heart attack?" In some ways we're guilty of exactly the same thing.

Bettendorf: We have the student teaching block along with our writing component. It is basically writing using technology and is wrapped around the internship. The class stops during the weeks of student teaching time. They meet for two or three weeks before student teaching and then meet at the end of the semester for an additional two or three weeks.

Breidenstein: Let me just say that I'm with him [Roellke]. I know we give our student teachers a lot to digest, but I think if we don't provide it in the first year along with enough time to reflect about teaching, it will be not as rich as the program should be. We're fully cognizant; I know because I teach the course. I supervise the interns and I work with the mentors. I know how everyone is feeling about the stress so that our pedagogic course is much heavier in the fall in terms of the reading, the critical understanding, the conceptional work, and the methods work that we do. It's heavier in the first half of the fall knowing that the interns pick up more responsibility the second half of the fall semester. We know that the interns are completely responsible for teaching the first six to nine weeks of the spring course, so the professor teaching the leadership class structures the appropriate reading so that the debriefing is focused on the issues they are encountering in school. I would disagree that we are overburdening them, that they are not sleeping at night. We try not to do that. It is not a good constructive experience for interns to have so much to do that they are frazzled and are not understanding. Because I'm the only person that coordinates that effort, I'm fully aware of what the stress level is for all of the people who are involved. The mentors are aware as well.

Myers: One of the things that is significant in what we have heard is that we are really talking about creating what I would call learning community schools and your interns function within that. I'm not sure that everyone heard that. This last conversation about the time they spend when they are in the schools as opposed to our courses, that image, which is the typical image, really looks at professional development schools as two parts of something with a big bridge between them. I have two observations about that. In the Trinity program, if the schools are really professional development schools and people get a chance to experience a PDS or are working toward that, that's heavy in terms of experience. My reading of Lynn and Lieberman and all the effort of developing those sites and the relationship with schools is critical in terms of what it is that people are experiencing and how it develops as an ongoing community. The other side of this can be seen in two pieces of writing. Andy Hargreaves has one article and one chapter in a book that I find really important that present the other side of this coin. The article is called "Induction or Seduction," and he says that even if you do all of the wonderful things these programs are doing are you setting up people to be devastated the next year. In my mind it's almost the analogy of how you deal with an adolescent. Do you become really, really protective and then they go off to college and do all of those horrible things, or do you ease them in somehow? Andy's chapter is really good at that. The other one that he wrote is called "The Social Geography of Teacher Education," where he's basically saying what we've been talking about here. You can create these really good things but the people back home who are non-clinical people say that if you go out there and do it, that's fine, but don't dare mess up what we do with the regular program. As long as the clinical faculty are doing their work in the schools, I can do my research. So, what will we really end up doing at the university?

Breidenstein: The answer to that question came from Alice Sy last night in terms of Andy [Hargreave]'s "Seduction and Induction": we should show students like Kathy [Bieser] what's possible. Linda Darling-Hammond and I have talked about this question. If we are not going to prepare student interns for schools the way they should be, then what are we doing? I think that's our answer. We want to show Kathy the way schools should be, the way schooling for children should be, the way professional development for teachers should be, the way that teacher education should be. But, Andy says that these are boutique schools and that we send interns out who will later crash on the rocks on the shore. Well, I hope that our induction will be good enough to carry Kathy through her first year. I think the key is in the preparation she started with. And I thought of Andy's idea about boutique schools when Alice [Sy] spoke, but I think that her testament undercuts it because her thoughtful internship helps her to know now what's possible and how important that ideal situation was to her. And if there's anything I can hope as Kathy's professor and as a leader in our program it's that we show her what's possible out there. We could fall prey to cynicism, but I choose not to do that.

Card: There are other matters I want us to consider. One addresses the question about overload for interns. That balance of maintaining sanity and getting prepared is always on our mind. The thing, though, that keeps us rigorous and honest is talking with our interns one and two years out. Everyone of them says, almost to an intern, that the internship was nothing compared to the first year of teaching. Many of their lessons are the first time they have developed them. And every night they are sitting with papers and new lessons. They are looking at awful curriculum guides, at imposing state standards. They're really heavily loaded down. But they still believe in the rigor of the internship and in building the durability that comes with putting in a lot of hours and hard work that was part of their preparation. So, I think that we need to have a balance, but students also need to know the reality of what they're going to walk into as first-year teachers. And, secondly, to respond to comments about why we develop professional development schools that are more ideal than many of our other schools, I think it's an obligation that we have as teacher educators to be involved in increasing the efficacy of the schools for our nation's children. To say that we're doing a disservice to our interns by having them develop initially in a rich setting, in a rich environment, that it's a disservice to them because they're not going to have that kind of opportunity later on is to fail to acknowledge that schools can become better for all kids. They need to see a model where children are having exciting and enriching activities, where equity is really being concentrated on in school settings, and where there are good parent and community involvement strategies. We want them to see those things so that we can build all schools ultimately to those ideals. And I think training and educating interns in schools that are working hard to achieve that ideal is creating dispositions in our future teachers that there will be a natural interest in working in their schools toward those ideal ends as well.

Abrams: I'd like to return to what Richard [Card] just said. Student teachers and others need to see some of the problems with the school reform efforts so that when something does go wrong they will realize that there are some weaknesses to every school reform, but that this is the best model that we have available now. They need to realize that this is not a perfect world, that there is no perfect world out there, that there are strengths and weaknesses in every approach. Otherwise they won't ever become school reformers. They'll say, "oh it doesn't work; that's what everybody told me." The other point relates to clinical faculty. I really dislike the term clinical faculty. When I say I supervise interns in a cluster site, people always ask me, "Are you tenure track?" That's the first question that I'm always asked and it obviously shows what we value and who we're sending to the schools. At the University of New Hampshire supervisors are full-time tenured faculty members. We choose to develop a relationship with just one school. It goes back to what Larry [Wakeford] was saying: I've worked with one school for four years but I think we are just starting to have real dialogue. They are accepting me as part of the school. If I just went in and said, "okay, this is what we should be doing," they'd laugh. They'd laugh me out of there. But, it was that long-term developing dialogue and that conversation that allows us to start talking back and forth. It also allows my research to be field based and to have my Ph.D. students have open access and honesty in a classroom because my teachers, the teachers that I work with, know that they are not going to be hurt by me, that we are going to work together, that we're going to collaborate together on the research. So, I think having that extended relationship with one school and having a cluster of interns there has been an ideal situation and I think it's really important.

Andrew: I'd just like to speak to the crashing on the shore issue. We have a four-year internship and I wonder about the conflicts that have been described here. One of the things that I've found over the past fifteen years is that all of the studies on interns from sixteen different universities across the country focus on graduate students. There have been five-year MAT-type programs, integrated programs, and four-year programs in the sample. One of the things that I've discovered is that retention is *the* issue of crashing on the shore. The programs with the longest internships have had the highest retention of graduates in teaching and also have had the most positive response to their teacher education programs in retrospect. We visit our former students when they've been out for between one and five years. So, I don't know if that proves the point but at least it offers some data on the argument of crashing or not crashing. I know data sometimes gets in the way of what we believe and so it can be dismissed.

Jacobs: I just want to throw something out that I think is powerful and that's the relationship between the university and the culture of the school and the tension in programs about wanting to support schools as they develop. Roughly half of our interns—we have about 100—are in the Boston public schools and these are not culturally friendly places oftentimes. And, because our interns have mixed feelings about being in those schools, it's harder to find teacher mentors who aren't burned out, who are in it for all the right reasons—not that the same situation doesn't repeat itself in the suburbs. It becomes something of a trial by fire. Our seminars support them in their survival. I just throw this out as one of those dilemmas because we feel a great responsibility to be in those schools but we have a limited number of schools with whom we have partnerships, where we place clusters. So, as we get to know the personalities at the schools, we get to become extended families and some conversations become easier. Our folks definitely know where the rocks are after they go out. But our responsibility toward the interns and wanting them to have the perfect experience clashes with our awareness of the rock business. I think it really extends into our urban responsibility and I just haven't heard that come up so I'd just like to throw that out.

Wakeford: It's obvious we have very strong feelings about this. Let me describe somebody who's a convert. When I came to Brown four-and-a-half years ago, I was told to meet class with our student teachers who never teach more than two classes a day. I said that's crazy, they'll never be ready for teaching; they're not going to be ready for the next year. I've been convinced by both our practice, but also by my colleagues, that we don't have to emulate the insanity of what goes on in the schools to prepare our students for it. They see it. We lose one third of our teachers in the first three to five years of teaching, so what do you want to do; move up that insanity into our teacher education program? Our students teach two periods a day, they observe one class a day. First it's their cooperating teacher and then it's other teachers in the school. They have time to reflect. That's not something that most of us who taught in the schools ever had time to do. We're trying to create a good environment. I've never heard one of our students the following year say you should have made us work harder during that internship. I just think we have to seriously think about what we're doing and how much time we demand. When I looked at Alice [Sy]'s schedule last night, I thought she might survive but I thought that people faced with that workload would probably leave teaching if that were the thing that they had to look forward to year after year.

Figgins: Well, I was thinking about the professional development schools. I don't see it really as an ideal alternative to our regular school environment. I just see it as having different problems that our teachers enter into. I don't see it as a kind of protective environment or something that doesn't reflect the real world. I mean we've certainly had our problems with professional development schools in the sense that they require an enormous amount of maintenance and tending along the way and I'm sort of interested in the trendy experiences of so many professional development schools. I'm wondering what kind of support you get from your dean and your faculty for doing that because when we do that there aren't any rewards in it other than the intensive rewards we get for having that kind of intensive relationship. What we've tried to do, because it's not easy to develop a professional school relationship, is to work on changing the culture of the school and changing our culture to come together into some kind of cooperative and collaborative dialogue and effort. Our approach has become one of going to individual teachers or going to an individual school and saying, "what would be helpful to you? What do we have that we can figure out together?" What we end up doing is providing a lot of different kinds of intern experiences. For instance, in one middle school, they want to see teachers in teams, but they would like to see a team of English teacher interns come to the school, not an interdisciplinary team, but a team of two or three English teachers so that they can get writing going on in all of the content areas. So we had one intern in English who spent her entire internship in the science classroom doing language arts. She said it was absolutely the best experience she could have had because now she knows she can teach anything. But then we'll have one little pocket over here where we'll have an incredible clinical instructor and she's in a really hostile environment of wannabe English professors in her department and she wants to do something really different, a reading/writing workshop, so we'll send a couple of people to team with her because we see that she's doing something that's really consistent with our philosophy. And then we've got one floundering professional school we're trying to develop, one in a high school, but it just seems like we're always looking to see what's the offer we can make that you can't resist in order to get this going. So, anyway, I just want to say that I don't see anyone of them as a kind of nirvana, or being too protective, or being too cruel. I just think each experience is very different. All the assignments are very different, and everybody learns different things. I think our seminar where students come back on a weekly basis to talk about their ongoing experiences is probably the critical link to their being able to see that schooling is not one kind of experience that they're having but a mix of them. It helps them start to make sense of what's happening to them when they start hearing about the different kinds of experiences that other people are having.

Response: Designing Coherent and Effective Teacher Education Internships

Alan J. Reiman
N.C. State University

This section draws from several sources to illustrate attributes of coherent and effective teacher education internships. First the paper examines the major strands of a transcribed discussion of internships and three papers presented by Richard Card (Southern Maine), Angela Breidenstein, (Trinity College), and Larry Wakeford (Brown University). Finally, the paper raises questions and presents concepts that could guide further inquiry and contribute to the development of internships.

The conversation and papers on internships are best understood by seeing them as segmented into four major strands: underlying conceptual frameworks, characteristics of internships, the use of mentors and clinical faculty, and programmatic challenges. They can be most clearly organized by arranging them in a matrix.

Major strands / Source	Conceptual Framework:	Characteristic of internship
Internships discussion	Opaque, not explicit.	Need graduated experience. Exemplary practice should be modeled. Seminars permit reflection on internship. Length of internship associated with retention. Five-year programs have highest retention of graduates.
University of Southern Maine	Developmental/ Contextual plus Goodlad's postulates.	Must meet NCATE conditions: learning community, collaboration, accountability, and clear roles and structures.
Trinity College	Student integration of theory, research, and practice.	Full fifth year in PDS. Place cohort with mentors and one clinical faculty member. Coursework includes clinical practice.
Brown University	Opaque, not explicit.	Cluster placements.

Mentors and Clinical Faculty	Programmatic challenges
Internship needs mentors. Building trust is a key.	Internship plus coursework is demanding. Can be difficult to find mentors who are not burned out in urban settings. PDS sites are energy-intensive. Is optimal internship miseducative in that it does not mirror real school?
Mentors are critical.	Lack of vision and articulated expectations.
Clinical faculty and mentors have two one-day retreats per year. Mentor teaches at university. Primacy given to building trust.	None noted.
Ideal mentor would be a highly effective teacher, knowledgeable about curriculum and pedagogy, reflective, positive about the profession of teaching, and interested in the development of novice teachers.	Ideal mentor is not available. Cluster places extra demands on faculty.

Conceptual Frameworks

A transparent conceptual framework was offered by only two of the four institutions, but its importance at the University of Southern Maine and at Trinity College make it a valuable part of the exploration of internships. In both programs there is an explicit attempt to outline the guiding principle and/or conceptual framework of teacher education programs and the culminating internship experiences. The University of Southern Maine has fashioned a developmental/contextual framework that characterizes its internships. These internships occur in professional development schools that are based on NCATE standards and the propositions outlined by Goodlad. Trinity College's program also rests on a preeminent principle: that students integrate theory, research, and practice into a seamless whole.

Such frameworks are critical; they predict success in designing a coherent and effective internship. After all, program themes can be easily derived from such frameworks and provide continuity and coherence to the program. In the case of the University of Southern Maine, the conceptual framework gives primacy to the internship experience as "the heart of the teacher education program." Card submits that the developmental/contextual framework effectively guides how school settings will promote novice teacher learning and development. It is important to note that a number of universities identify very clear conceptual frameworks that guide their program development. The University of New Hampshire is a case in point. In a national research summary, Howey (1996) points out how development of socialization and educative experiences spring from a defensible conceptual/theoretical framework. Such frameworks "have the power to educate prospective teachers in a more programmatic and potent manner" (p. 143). A series of loosely connected courses in professional education culminating in an even more loosely connected experience called student teaching can no longer serve as the standard for teacher education. To make advances in the quality of internships, teacher educators need to be much clearer about the conceptual frameworks and/or guiding principles that embrace their program. Unfortunately, in too many cases, such frameworks are absent.

Characteristics of Internships

With respect to the process of developing internships, it is important to point out that the three papers and the conversation that followed talk of the need to more carefully conceptualize their teacher education programs and the internships which they support. It also is clear that internships are in a state of evolution. The perfect internship has yet to be designed. Further, the design of internships, in addition to needing the guidance of a conceptual framework, must be developed as well from extensive dialogue among mentor teachers, student interns, school administrators, external consultants, and university educators.

Angela Breidenstein discussed Trinity University's use of professional development schools in her paper:

> In consultation with teachers and administrators in San Antonio schools, faculty in the department of education and across the university, university students, and outside consultants, this forum of designers created the professional development schools network. . . . Further, a continuum of teacher education experiences was established which begins with undergraduate seminars and practica . . . and culminates in a graduate experience which features the full-year internship along with coursework focused on curriculum, pedagogy, leadership, and supervision. (see Breidenstein's essay on page*)

Perhaps such extended conversations and the well designed programs which then emerge are a sign that teacher education is no longer willing to adopt a stance that essentially says, "we know how to solve all the problems of teacher education in America, and we can do it quickly." As Sarason (1990) illustrates, educators made a fateful mistake when they accepted full responsibility for schooling, but, an even more fateful one when they adopted a stance that essentially said we can solve all the problems and solve them soon. In contrast, the medical community has made a virtue of its ignorance by emphasizing the complexity and scope of the challenges and the inadequacies of current conceptions and practices. The MAT program at Wake Forest University is another example of a program that has evolved over a period of ten years, and year by year continues to improve.

Internship Defined

The participants' conversation and the papers that engendered it agree on a number of important characteristics of the internship:

1. Graduated experience needs to be built into the internship so that the internship gradually spirals toward increasingly

complex responsibilities in planning, instruction, and evaluation for the student intern
2. Exemplary practice should be modeled by the mentor or clinical faculty member
3. Greater duration in the internship leads to greater success
4. Opportunities to work in cluster groups at an internship site are preferred
5. Seminars or clinical coursework that complement the internship experience are beneficial because they promote reflection on practice
6. The structure and quality of the internship experience are crucial

All of the conference participants agreed that structures that promote reflection were important but many of them raised concerns about holding classes after an intensive day of interning as the Best Practice Conference exchange attests:

Roellke: Kathy [Bieser], how did it feel to have to take two classes while you were an intern? Could you pull it off? How difficult was it logistically?
Bieser: Logistically it worked out. I had classes at night and was in school during the day. It was very challenging, though. The first couple of weeks of school I was very, very tired. But, after a couple of weeks I became used to it, I got into the routine. At the time, especially after we started writing up our research, going to school all day, going to class at night in addition to completing the research was very challenging. But, looking back on it now, I think it was very beneficial.

Another clinical faculty member's comments support the idea of formal classes after school hours but echoes of the intern's distress can be felt in the statement:

I would disagree that we are overburdening them, that they are not sleeping at night. We try not to do that. It is not a good constructive experience for interns to have so much to do that they are frazzled and are not understanding. Because I'm the only person that coordinates that effort, I'm fully aware of what the stress level is for all of the people who are involved. The mentors are aware as well.

Despite the overwhelming positive feelings about the importance of a well-designed and extended internship, both the papers and conference conversation suggest that what occurs during the internship is far more important that its length. As a part of this discussion Andrew referred to his research with sixteen universities that showed that a five-year program that includes an extended internship is more effective in terms of retention of teachers in their careers than those that do not. But, McIntyre, Byrd and Foxx (1996) found that extended duration of the internship does not necessarily lead to a more effective internship experience. Moreover, Reiman and Parramore (1993) found that carefully structured but not necessarily lengthened experiences that carefully guide reflection and clinical analysis under the supervision of a trained mentor produced more effective and thoughtful student teachers.

A somewhat cynical view of exemplary practice was offered by a colleague who expressed concern that such perfection can lead to unrealistic optimism in the student teacher that can be overwhelmed by the realities of day-to-day first year teaching.

But such cynicism, however, was not the credo of the conference; participating teacher educators argued that strong models and optimal settings were important. They need to see a model where children are having exciting and enriching activities. That equity is really being concentrated upon in school settings, that there are good parent and community involvement strategies. We want them to see those things so that we can build all schools ultimately to those ideals.

Mentors and Clinical Faculty

The papers and conversation transcript underscore the crucial importance of mentors and clinical faculty to a successful internship and quality teacher education. Card, for example, is guided by Goodlad's fourth and fifth postulates (Goodlad 1994). These two postulates describe the need for mentors and clinical faculty and the desirable qualities and characteristics of such individuals. Wakeford suggests very similar qualities of an ideal cooperating teacher or mentor. For him these qualities include teaching effectiveness, knowledge of curriculum and pedagogy, reflective style in practice, positive attitude about the profession of teaching, and an interest in cooperative development of novice teachers. And Breidenstein notes that selection of mentors and clinical faculty for her program depends upon these qualities and other unique contributions.

Most of the teacher educators at these institutions are shaping new types of internships and they are careful in selecting the mentors with whom their students will teach. They are eager to know what teaching behaviors will be emphasized and what theories, philosophies, and practices will be reinforced by the mentor. The placement of student teachers with a mentor appears to be crucial to the internship experience and crucial to the quality of the teacher education program. However, as Wakeford points out, the placement process often becomes an institutional dilemma that hampers teacher development.

Wakeford's frustration, which he attempted to resolve through cluster placements, is mirrored in a national study by Goodlad (1990) that reveals that many universities do not control the placement of student teachers and that placements are too often based on administrative expedience rather than the quality of the experience. In fact, Guyton, Paille, and Rainer (1993) found that some school principals place student teachers with weak teachers so that they could provide support for the weak teacher. This kind of miseducative internship is, regrettably, well documented. As Guyton and McIntyre write, "available research . . . does not present the school context as a positive influence on student teacher development" (1990, p. 518).

Although the question of how to transform the context of internships was only minimally addressed by the conference, the topic will be addressed in my concluding remarks. There was clear consensus among the participants, however, that mentors and clinical faculty members are a vital link to coherent and effective programs. If the internship is the heart of the teacher education program, the caring, skilled, thoughtful interaction and coaching between the student intern and the mentor is the life force of the internship. Given the convergence of opinion, it is all the more striking that so little mention was given to the structures and processes that can cultivate effective mentors and clinical faculty.

Programmatic Challenges

A number of the programmatic challenges of coherent and effective internships already have been discussed, and will not be repeated here. However there are three challenges that warrant elaboration. The first is a concern about the amount of faculty energy required to maintain effective professional development schools as vital learning communities. A number of faculty members commented that such work was energy intensive. Further, the work was not valued by the university. This issue of energy intensiveness with little tangible return in the university culture is well documented. Book (1996) offers a compelling account of this problem. He notes, "Although many . . . articles appear to provide prescriptions for beginning a PDS, caution should be taken. The drawbacks for K–12 educators, as well as for university faculty, coupled with the expense of engaging in such new relationships should not be underestimated" (p.198). And Goodlad (1993) cautions that, in spite of the political climate that celebrates these collaborative relationships, universities should guard against having a PDS just for the sake of having one.

A second issue concerns the energy intensive nature of specialized internships. Wakeford points out that Brown's program encountered a number of challenges as it developed cluster placements for its internship. Among the important lessons learned: it takes time to develop trust, clarity of roles and expectations is required, administrative support is crucial, and the drain on university faculty is substantial. It is worth noting that cluster placements that appeared to show promise at Brown University are no longer in use.

A final challenge regards the time it takes for relationship building. The personnel that make such internships a success are involved in a deeply interpersonal process. Without trust, such internships are not successful. However, trust takes time to develop, sometimes a very long time. Wakeford personalizes this final point: "I've worked with one school for four years and now I think we are just starting to have dialogue. They are now accepting me as part of the school."

These sub-themes—a need for time, trust, and communication—are recurrent in the literature and beg the question, "How are teacher education programs building and sustaining trusting relationships?" The answer to this question may be one essential predictor of a coherent and effective teacher education program and the internships which it supports.

Transforming the Internship: Concluding Remarks

The preceding discussion of major strands of the conversation transcript and papers reinforces a commonly held belief that the internship must be a vital part of the teacher education program. It is clear that the internship can be miseducative, but its many variables can be effectively juggled to make the experience optimal. Accordingly, many questions can be asked:

- How can teacher education programs provide sustained systemic support in PDS sites?

- How do the university and public schools avoid operating as separate silos?
- How might we select prospective teachers and prospective mentors?
- What substantive rewards can be provided for clinical staff?
- How is trust built?
- How might we transform the internship experience?
- What does *clinical* mean?
- What would an ideal preparation program for mentors and clinical educators look like?

None of the above questions are answered simply, but the conference offered a partial response to some of them.

How might we transform the internship experience? The answer to this questions was explored in terms of cluster placements, skilled mentors, rotations in observations, duration of experience and other factors. These attributes have transformed the internship to some degree; however, success may ultimately depend on our definition of transformation. A bold definition might require that the articulated innovation (in this case the internship) must assure that 80 percent of teacher education students will be moderately to highly successful across a broad range of knowledge, skills, and developmental domains (see Sprinthall, Reiman, & Thies-Sprinthall, 1996). Thus, transforming means both the learning and the personal development of the student intern. Such an ambitious goal is amenable to measurement, and will become for some of the programs present at this conference a way to document their successes.

It is likely, however, that such a transformative effort will require new resources and personnel. Moreover, innovations rarely succeed without underlying instructional and curricular technologies to support them (Pogrow, 1996). A large-scale reform like transforming teacher education will require highly specific, systematic, and structural/clinical methodologies of very high quality. Pogrow refers to these structural/clinical methodologies as technologies (i.e., a systemic way of doing something consistently whether training, equipment, or curriculum). Too often, however, we philosophize about the need for better "hands-on" laboratory and field experiences, yet no one bothers to develop the curriculum and training to support them. Examples of current innovations that may have little underlying technology to support them include the internship, mentoring, professional development schools, constructivist approaches to teaching, and a number of others many teacher educators could name.

What does clinical *mean?* In the context of the concepts arising at the conference, *clinical* appears to have a multiplicity of meanings. However the most frequent implied meaning is "in the field," or "field experience." But, clinical experiences could be defined as any school experience that takes place in a "clinical" setting where practitioners are observed at work and where they guide novices into practice. The term *clinical* thus describes a process of professional thought, reflection, and action that has unique problem-finding and problem-solving components. Among these components are the following: evaluating the present state of an environment, person, or situation; generating and assessing alternatives to modify the situation; enacting an alternative that is believed to be most desirable; and evaluating the results of this action. Thus, clinical experience refers not so much to where the experience takes place, but rather to what kind of experience takes place.

What would an ideal preparation program for mentors and clinical educators look like? In the context of an internship, it makes no sense to expect mentors (ideal or otherwise) to develop their own techniques to guide effective learning and development of the novice teacher. It has to be partly the responsibility of the teacher education program itself. In most cases, however, mentors receive no intensive preparation for their roles of guiding the learning of the novice. In rare cases, school systems provide a week of training that all too often models ineffectual rather than effective staff development (see Joyce & Showers, 1995). The same, unfortunately, is also the case for some teacher educators. It is lamentable that such a situation exists. In medicine, if individual practitioners invented their own procedures, it would be called malpractice.

Just as in the earlier question about transforming practice, Progrow's systematic way of doing something consistently is the needed remedy here. Perhaps through conversations with exemplary teachers and National Board-certified teachers, a curriculum could be designed and tested that encourages high quality mentoring, reflection, and coaching. Some exciting developments in this area are reported in Sprinthall, Reiman, and Thies-Sprinthall (1996).

Those who would suggest that a too exclusive focus on structural methodologies and consistencies is misguided, and might lead to rote teaching or mentoring which ignores context, should consider the performing arts. They have survived and flourished because they have been able to systematize the delivery of highly creative performances by achieving the delicate yet necessary balance between highly structured, directive components (e.g., script, choreography) and innovative individual interpretation. The same might be achieved in clinical teacher education and internships.

How rapidly a transformation occurs in teacher education and internships most likely will depend on a plethora of factors. The programs considered in this section have taken an important step toward transformation, and in most cases, represent a dynamic, sustained, and systemic effort. Although this trend is encouraging, quantitative and qualitative research and wise transformations that arise from it have been to date minimal. Research is desperately needed to validate the effectiveness of new approaches to the internship, and to determine whether they are more effective and coherent than their traditional counterparts.

Chapter Five

Research

The three essays on action research form a strong continuum from intense personal inquiry at Brown to robust descriptive research at Wake Forest to concern about the process at Maryland. The project at Brown emphasizes the reflection on the internships and the personal and professional growth that attends that immersion into the school world. The Wake Forest program's descriptive research takes place in four classrooms where the internship begins and ranges from penetrating studies of the influence of particular facets of the teaching art on structural response to broader investigations of more structural matters. Maryland's program has passed through an era of descriptive research that focused on "knowledge of and about teaching," but has experienced an "undertow" of resistance in the schools where a more intuitive response to teaching is emphasized.

The Personal Inquiry: An Example of Teacher Research in a Fifth-Year Teacher Education Program

Eileen Landay
Brown University

As a profession, we appear to have come to agreement about the power and value of "reflective practice." The concept, introduced by Schon (1983) and later explicated by him (Schon, 1987) and many others, has been used well, and is by now perhaps well worn. A related concept, "teacher research," focuses on a specific kind of reflective practice carried out by elementary and secondary school teachers. The idea of practicing teachers being entitled to engage in that lofty and high-status activity called research has been promoted in the professional literature for more than two decades (Britton, 1983; Carini, 1975; Clay, 1982; Myers, 1985). This transformation rests on the foundation provided by ethnographers (Spindler and Spindler, 1987), psychologists and cognitive scientists (Bruner, 1962; Garnder, 1985), and pedagogical theorists (Boomer, 1982; Dewey, 1933; Freire, 1985). The belief that research could be something other than university-sponsored and guided, that it could legitimately be conducted by teachers in classrooms, and that it could produce useful and valid results for teachers, for educational theorists, and for the wider community has gained modest acceptance.

Teacher research has come to be accepted by at least some of those interested in such matters as both legitimate and valuable on several counts. As a means of closely observing classroom interactions, teacher research provides much needed information about the specifics of curriculum and instruction, how students learn, and the nature of classroom interactions. This information is of enormous value to teachers and curriculum developers in planning and revising short- and long-term classroom activities. Second, by promoting teachers' active generation of knowledge about practice that in turn creates significant knowledge about classroom and school learning environments, teacher research increases teachers' status in the educational hierarchy. Finally, by accumulating and analyzing "thick descriptions" of everyday interactions, or detailed case studies of individual students or programs, teacher research can serve as a ground-level agency for institutional change.

As is often the case, however, theory belies the complexities and ambiguities of practice. As a high-status activity, research has the potential to bring substantial benefits to the researcher, and thus issues of definition, method, ownership, standards, and assessment are hotly contested. Traditionally, research has required that the researcher read the professional literature, design studies, collect and review data, and analyze and reflect on the findings. Elementary and secondary school teachers have rarely seen these activities as integral to their basic identity or the roles they play. Nor do they have the many benefits of institutional support so valuable to the work of university-based researchers.

Who precisely is entitled to call him or herself a serious researcher? Are endorsements or institutional affiliations required? What expectations exist in relation to quality control? As we move through the paradigm shift that supports the idea that knowledge is both constructed and personal, that truth is often situational and multi-faceted, that perspectives and positionality matter, these questions grow increasingly complex.

Research and the New Teacher

During the past two decades, teacher educators have often taken the lead in promoting the idea of teachers as researchers and helping elementary and secondary school teachers learn research practices and find resources to support their development as researchers (Berthoff, 1982; Bissex, 1980; Boomer, 1982; Branscombe and others, 1992; Duckworth, 1987; Goswami and Stillman, 1987; Kutz and Roskelly, 1991; Perrone 1991). The National Writing Project and its many offshoots have provided a model of continuing professional development based on the idea of teacher research and collaboration. The North Dakota Teacher Study Group, the Critical Friends Groups of the Coalition for Essential Schools and the Bread Loaf Rural Teachers Network provide yet other models of such support.

The model we present here was designed for teachers enrolled in the Master of Arts in Teaching program at Brown, a program of one year's duration that offers a graduate degree and a beginning teacher license. Its structure is informed by the fact that it enrolls students who have a strong background in their content area. (Brown prepares secondary students in three disciplines: English, social studies/history and science/biology.) Over the course of one summer and one academic year, students complete two practica (each with an accompanying seminar), two education courses, and four graduate courses in the content area. One of the major features of the coursework is the Personal Inquiry which concludes the program.

Personal Inquiry

This assignment began to take shape about four years ago, as faculty members searched for a culminating activity to the student teaching semester which would allow students both to demonstrate and reflect on what they had accomplished and learned, and to place that learning within the context of the literature on teaching and learning. We wished to create an assignment that students could pursue over the course of their student teaching semester. We wanted to promote the practices of inquiry, research, and reflection, the results of which students could present to their fellow student teachers, their cooperating teachers, and university supervisors and, if they wished, to the secondary school students they had taught.

In addition to these goals for students as individuals, we also had goals for the program as an institutional entity. Though ours is a small program, with a clinical professor and a maximum of ten graduate students in each of the three disciplines, over the years these strands had diverged so that they seemed in some ways more like three programs than like one and functioned relatively independently of one another. So, in designing the personal inquiry project, we created parallel assignments, and scheduled the final thirty-minute individual presentations so that the three or four students who presented during one two-hour session would represent more than one discipline. Our intention was to create a final assignment that would help us to unify what had previously been a loose-knit program.

An additional goal was to use the final presentations as a form of professional development for all three constituencies: student teachers, cooperating teachers, and university faculty, and in the process offer opportunities for focused discussion and strengthened professional ties.

At the outset of the student teaching semester, we presented this assignment in the course syllabus for Analysis of Teaching, a weekly seminar that accompanies student teaching:

Personal Inquiry/Final Presentation: Throughout your student teaching, you will be asking and answering many questions about teaching and learning. As a way of focusing your inquiry, you will identify one central question to pursue during the semester. We'll devote several analysis classes to help you shape your question, learn about the questions your peers are asking, and develop an approach to addressing the question. This question and inquiry will serve as the basis of a final presentation made to clinical faculty, cooperating teachers, and peers during the final examination period.

In previous years, Analysis of Teaching seminars in the three disciplines had been held independently of one another. Beginning in 1994, we created a number of joint sessions, several devoted to preparing for the Personal Inquiry. During the first analysis seminar, we handed out and discussed a set of guidelines (Appendix A). We also presented students with a set of assignments and a timeline designed to structure the process of identifying, researching, collecting, and analyzing data. Another handout listed questions addressed in previous years' inquiry projects (Appendix B). This year, we showed a videotape of the first ten minutes of an exemplary presentation from the previous year, and offered examples of the handouts other students had presented during their final presentations.

Four weeks into the semester, student teachers prepare a one-page memo, identifying their inquiry question and describing their plans for addressing the question. In an Analysis of Teaching seminar, they present these memos to small groups of peers across disciplines, and discuss and critique them in preparation for revising them before beginning their research and data collection. During the remainder of the semester, student teachers discuss their inquiry with both their clinical professor and cooperating teacher.

The presentations are the culminating activity of the semester, given in lieu of a final exam or paper. Usually, the school where they have student taught serves as the site, and the presentations are given in groups of three or four per session; they are scheduled after school on a weekday. Students are required to attend at least one session other than their own. Many attend more than one session, to support their peers and learn more about the work they have been doing. Often twenty or more people attend these presentations including Brown clinical faculty members, cooperating teachers, other secondary school faculty and administrators, high school students, and friends and family of the presenters.

In 1997, we created a rubric for responding to and evaluating student presentations (Appendix C). Since both student teaching and the Analysis of Teaching Seminar are pass/fail classes, the purpose of the rubric is not to determine a grade, but to offer explicit feedback from a variety of sources on the form and content of the presentation. The rubric is by no means in its final form; we expect to review and revise it in time for this semester's final presentations.

Discussion

From the perspective of the faculty in our teacher education program, the Personal Inquiry assignment, while still being reshaped and revised, has much to recommend it. It provides student teachers with a structure for documenting their practice, and for creating an ongoing record over time. The very process of becoming an observer, slowing down enough to focus on secondary school students and on their work, and documenting one's practice and student response is an experience that is of great value to many student teachers. The habit of mind of identifying a question, then seeking answers both from the literature and from one's own practice puts student teachers into a different relationship to knowledge, a relationship parallel to the one constructivist teachers wish their own students to experience. As they prepare for their final presentations, student teachers review the records they have made of their work, noting patterns as well as changes over time. This process allows for self-assessment and suggests a process for growth in which assessment is appropriately situated within the larger endeavor of learning.

Not surprisingly, some students seem to make better use of this assignment than others. All students in the program struggle with considerable pressure. Many are teaching in challenging situations and find themselves nearly overwhelmed by the day-to-day requirements of planning and teaching two classes. In addition to the Analysis of Teaching Seminar which accompanies their student teaching, all of the students are taking another academic class, but the links between their student life and their teacher life often seem tenuous.

In addition, some find the assignment irrelevant to their interests, goals or personal inclinations. This negative response may be a result of how the assignment has been presented to them. In writing this paper, I've identified some disparities between my own practices as a teacher and the practices I regularly recommend to student teachers. In conversations or written responses to classroom observations, I often ask, "Have you explained to your students the reasons behind what you are asking them to do?" Frequently, they answer no, and then find that explaining and discussing the purposes behind the work improves the classroom climate. Only recently have I taken note of how inconsistent I am about taking my own advice.

Our students may know far less than I imagine about the background of teacher research presented in the introduction. While they note and voice their appreciation for the unity across disciplines in our teacher education program, it's unlikely they realize how substantively the Personal Inquiry assignment has contributed to that unity. Perhaps most important, they may not understand the ways this assignment reflects the central tenets of the program.

School Context

Ours is a program devoted to school reform. All of the clinical faculty, some mentor teachers and many of the students have been influenced by the ideas of the Coalition for Essential Schools and other reform-minded groups. At the same time, most of us are committed to working in schools as they are in order to help to create the schools of the future. Not everyone in the schools we work with agrees with us. These schools vary widely in their attitude toward and implementation of the principles or practices of school reform. We work hard to develop mutual respect between school and university and to acknowledge and address inevitable tensions between the two institutions.

In *The Fifth Discipline: The Art and Practice of the Learning Organization,* Peter Senge writes about the creative tension between vision and reality: "The most effective people are those who can 'hold' their vision while remaining committed to seeing current reality clearly" (p.226). It is this dual vision that we hope to produce by asking students to become teacher-researchers. We believe this dual vision is a crucial component of school reform. The Personal Inquiry assignment is designed to contribute to both goals.

It is clear that the Personal Inquiry assignment has succeeded in unifying the strands of the teacher education program. Similarly the assignment accomplishes the goal of introducing our students to the concept of teacher research. As they complete our program, they are by no means confirmed teacher-researchers; but they have been introduced to the process with the hope that, as they take their place in the teaching profession, they will meet it again and find it familiar and valuable.

It is much less clear that we have been explicit enough with our students in explaining the goals behind the Personal Inquiry assignment. Nor have we investigated whether exposure to and involvement with this assignment has had any effect at all on the cooperating teachers and the schools in which our student teachers are placed. In the four years that this project has been developing, we have done very little to ascertain the school faculty's response. Neither have we taken serious steps to link our students and their work with ongoing university-based researchers and research. All of these limitations help us to see directions for the future and ways that the assignment and the program can be strengthened.

Appendix A

Some Notes on Designing a Personal Inquiry

1. *Identify the question:*

   - The question should be one that is of genuine interest to you.
   - It should be directly related to teaching and learning in your classroom.
   - It should be answerable by descriptions and observations.
   - The key words are most often *how* and *what*.
   - The question should be modest, in that you should be able to make some headway on it during the time of your student teaching. it should lend itself to developing subquestions.

2. *Develop subquestions.*

   - These should help you explore and understand what your question is really about and what assumptions underlie it.

3. *Make a list of the kinds of data you'll collect.*

   - Don't be intimidated by the fancy word *data*.
   - Your journal observations are data. So are student work and student words. So are interviews, surveys, audio and videotapes.

4. *Make a list of the kinds of readings you will do to provide context for addressing your questions.*

   - Talk to your clinical professors, your cooperating teachers, and other faculty. Search bibliographies, the Brown catalog, ERIC.

5. *Think about the final form your presentation might take.*

   - It's the old "plan backwards" idea.
   - What kinds of representations will you compile for your presentation?
   - How can you present your conclusions vividly and concisely?

Appendix B

Question from Previous Years' Personal Inquiries

How can I structure the "reporting back" aspect of group work so that the audience is engaged with and responsible for what they are hearing?

How can I make talk a tool in my classroom that allows ALL students to practice inquiry skills and deepen their thinking about texts—that encourages them to be "active participants in articulating [their own] responses" to literature?

How can I empower my students to take more ownership over their own learning?

How is participation in a "fishbowl" evaluated? What are the implications of this evaluation process for girls?

What are some of the strategies for designing and implementing an effective unit on essay writing for eighth-grade students?

How can I establish a classroom in which students take responsibility for their work?

How can I develop strategies to aid students in constructive reading?

How can I combine the use of non-traditional forms of instruction with traditional forms of assessment?

How does a teacher's behavior (misbehavior) affect the classroom environment?

How can I promote writing in a history class?

What happens when individualized reading becomes the center of an English class?

How can I individualize teaching and learning in large classes?

How can multiple intelligence theory aid me in teaching in a classroom where students are heterogeneously grouped?

Appendix C

Feedback for final Student Teacher Exhibition.

Strengths   Needs Work   Comments

Content

1. Question
   - Can the question be reasonably researched?
   - Does the question generate appropriate sub-questions?

2. Quality of Research
   - Have a variety of sources been searched?
   - Is there evidence of data collection?
   - Is analysis of data apparent?
   - Are terms clarified (if necessary)?
   - Are the conclusions interesting/thoughtful?
   - Do the findings push past the obvious?
   - Are the conclusions clear?

Strengths   Needs Work   Comments

Presentation

1. Performance
   - Is the audience appropriately engaged?
   - Is appropriate eye contact and body language employed?
   - Is speaking clearly audible and appropriately paced?
   - Are audio-visuals used (if appropriate)?
   - Is the presentation brought to an appropriate close?

2. Process
   - Is the student well-prepared?
   - Has the student clearly reflected on his/her work and presentation?

Research Times Two: A Model of Formal Research and Personal Reflection

Leah P. McCoy and Robert H. Evans
Wake Forest University

The Wake Forest University Master Teacher Fellows program includes a two-component research requirement: a traditional formal research study and a reflective teaching portfolio. Both parts are rigorous and are designed to immerse the student in a problem-solving orientation to educational research. The entire program is rooted in a constructivist model and attends to both process and product outcomes as students experience the many dimensions of teacher research.

Formal Research

The formal research part of the program is completed during the first summer and fall semesters. The first course is Educational Research. This is a basic course where students learn the fundamentals of research methods. The course includes the full range of methods, from an introduction to ethnographic narrative reports to computer software for descriptive and inferential statistics. It fully integrates both quantitative and qualitative methodologies, and students are encouraged to become familiar and comfortable with both approaches.

The second course, Seminar in Curriculum and Instruction, requires students to conduct a broad review of the literature in their particular content area following a specific four-part set of guidelines developed by each of the five content-area advisors. Students present each of the four dimensions of the research in their discipline on successive weeks to the entire group. This activity deepens and broadens the research foundation knowledge both within and across disciplines.

The Methodology and Research/Teaching Rounds course during the fall semester contributes to the annual research forum by requiring regular observations in master teachers' classrooms where most research projects are based. Students observe master teachers at work and try to isolate features of their practice and understand their effect on student performance.

The final research course, Descriptive Research, is also taken in the fall semester. In this course, each student selects a research topic, prepares a literature review, and conducts an original research study. Faculty members assist each fellow in conceptualizing, designing, executing, and reporting their research. Issues of literature review, statistical analysis, and presentation that were introduced in the first summer of the program are refined and applied in the fall. Students are encouraged to follow their own interests within the broad domain of instruction. Some of the Master Teacher Fellows develop collaborative research projects with master teachers. The course includes weekly meetings with the area advisor, and group seminars throughout the semester. At the end of the semester each student reports his or her study in three products: a full paper of fifteen to thirty pages that is submitted to the advisor, an abstract of five pages that is included in the "Studies of Teaching" proceedings which is also published in the ERIC database, and a poster presentation that is given at the annual research forum held each December.

As the time for the annual research forum approaches, the Master Teacher Fellows are oriented to its protocols. Each prepares a standard trifold poster (48"x36"), which will stand upright on a table, as well as copies of their five page abstracts to hand out to interested attendees. The goal of the posters is to explain the essence of a student's research to a viewer the explicit narrative of the abstract. Students must make their titles readable from a distance (using headline-generating computer software) and design the posters so that they are both informative and engaging. They are encouraged through the use of examples

Chapter Five: Research

from previous students' work to avoid distracting clutter in their posters, to guide viewers sequentially through their projects from hypotheses to conclusions and to provide relevant and useful graphics.

The Research Forum proceedings are modeled after those at professional conferences. Students are grouped in a large room by content area so that all of the second language projects, for example, are set up together. To provide a diverse and stimulating forum, different groups of interested educators are invited to attend. Master teachers, education department faculty, relevant content area Wake Forest faculty, and university administrators are all encouraged to come and participate. The goal of the session is not to merely passively display results, but to actively engage attendees in the process and content of each study. To accomplish this, the following agenda is followed.

- fifteen minutes—Guests take a quick look at each content affinity group's posters and decide which of the five subject groups they would like to join for the afternoon.
- thirty minutes—Graduate students present their research to their affinity group in five minutes, using their trifold poster as a visual aid.
- thirty minutes—Guests take a close look at the posters and abstracts in other affinity groups and talk with students about their research.
- thirty minutes—The affinity groups reassemble to participate in a discussion of the group's projects, led by the area advisors for the group. An effort is made to find threads of commonality, when they exist, among the projects and to create a productive discussion based on both the presented research and the experience of the participants.
- fifteen minutes—Guests are invited to once again explore other posters in any group and to interact with students about their work.

Each year, to facilitate dissemination of the forum's contents to an even wider audience, all of the project abstracts are accumulated in a bound volume which is made available both in printed and electronic forms as well as through the ERIC resources. Typical projects from this past year included the following.

- English: To Sprint or Crawl? The Effect of Classroom Activities on Student Behavior
- Foreign Language: Testing What You Teach: Speaking Skills in the Foreign Language Classroom
- Mathematics: Facing the Hurdles: Perspectives of First-Year Mathematics Teachers
- Science: The Effect of Database Use on Secondary Science Achievement and Attitude
- Social Studies: The Role of Current Events in the Social Studies: An Assessment of Student Attitudes and Lesson Composition

Personal Reflection

The second research component is undertaken during the second summer of the program. The Professional Development Seminar is intended to facilitate students' reflection on their student teaching experiences and to assist them in defining their personal philosophy of teaching. This reflection is structured in terms of the propositions of the National Board for Professional Teaching Standards.

The five propositions of the National Board Standards are
1. Students and Their Learning
    - Recognize individual differences in students
    - Understand how students develop and learn
    - Treat students equitably
    - Extend beyond developing cognitive capacity of students
2. Subjects and How to Teach
    - Appreciate how knowledge in subject is created, organized and linked
    - Command specialized knowledge of how to convey subject
    - Generate multiple paths to knowledge
3. Managing and Monitoring Student Learning
    - Call on multiple methods
    - Orchestrate learning in group settings
    - Place a premium on student engagement
    - Regularly assess student progress
    - Be mindful of principal objectives
    - Seek advice and draw on educational research and scholarship

Chapter Five: Research

4. Members of Learning Communities
   - Collaborate with other professionals
   - Work collaboratively with parents
   - Take advantage of community resources

While beginning teachers are not eligible to apply for National Board Certification, this framework is ideal for examining one's beliefs and practice. We expect that many of our students will apply for National Board Certification after they have the three years required teaching experience. Preparation of the Professional Portfolio in this course should improve their familiarity with this process.

This portfolio provides an opportunity for students to think systematically about their teaching practice, and to present their personal beliefs along with supporting documents to provide a representation of their professional development as a teacher. The two-part portfolio is both paper and electronic. The electronic portfolio is formally presented in an exit interview with a committee consisting of two faculty members from the education department and one administrator from the public schools. The exit interview includes a good discussion about teaching as the student describes his or her beliefs about teaching and then interacts with the members of the committee. The paper portfolio is also submitted at this time.

The contents of the paper portfolio are as follows:

- Title Page
- Résumé
- Introduction, a one-page overview of the student's philosophy of education
- Propositions, a one-to-three page reflection for each of the five general areas
- Appendix, which includes artifacts (lesson plans, student handouts, an assessment instruments) and attestations (observation reports from the student teaching supervisor, and recommendations from cooperating teacher and university supervisor)

The electronic portfolio is a CD presentation, which presents the same information as the paper portfolio in a multimedia format. It includes a title page, introduction of the candidate's philosophy, reactions to the National Board propositions, and a conclusion which is a personal description of the candidate as a teacher.

The technical requirements of the CD presentation are that it must contain twenty to thirty slides, with at least three video clips from tapes of the candidate's student teaching. It must also contain at least three graphics, preferably photos of the teacher, which are either scanned images, images from a digital camera, or images captured from a video clip. The presentation is burned on a CD, and is presented as an automated slide show with narration and timed slide advances. By this point in the program, students are skilled computer users and can complete this technology project with minimal supervision and assistance.

Summary

Our plans for the future include efforts to strengthen the links between our students' research projects and their own spring semester student teaching experiences. Currently we integrate their findings into our content methods courses, which are held in the months immediately following the research forum. In addition, we would like to facilitate the application and implementation of the results of the students' fall studies during their ten weeks of student teaching and then have them reflect on this process. Our goal is to demonstrate for them through experience the value of not only their own research on teaching, but also that of the educational research community at large.

Another modification we have considered is incorporating the Council of Chief State School Officers' INTASC (Interstate New Teacher Assessment and Support Consortium) Standards into our portfolio process. These standards are in use in our local school systems, and we may incorporate them either as an alternative or additional structure for the portfolio.

We believe that the two-component approach gives our students a solid foundation in educational research. In the first half of the program, they have extensive experience as consumers, producers, and disseminators of formal educational research. Additionally, the Professional Portfolio Seminar requires that they reflect extensively on their experiences and beliefs about teaching. This blending of the formal research and personal reflection gives students a remarkable opportunity to learn and grow as teachers.

An Evolution in Action Research from Improving Practice to Personal Authority

Joseph McCaleb and Jeremy Price
University of Maryland

The Maryland Master's Certification Program was designed about fifteen years ago as a model fifth-year graduate teacher preparation program in part to try out and study innovations in teacher education. One of the key innovations was to use action research to promote reflective activity. In the early 1980s, the idea of teacher as researcher was coming into the literature but it had not been implemented in our initial teacher certification programs nor had it been sufficiently field tested elsewhere. The dominant notion was that the business of initial teacher preparation was about developing teachers with competent instructional practice; it was not designed to prepare them to do research. The two activities, research and teaching, were mostly considered to be separate endeavors. Given this context, we found it an innovative idea to try to prepare teachers as reflective professionals with doing research as a keynote in their preparation. This innovation would mean that prospective teachers would be well informed of the burgeoning research on teaching and learning and that they could make sensitive applications and interpretations of these findings in their specific contexts. Conducting an action research project would also function as the equivalent of a master's thesis and would carry similar status. In this paper, by discussing how reflection and action research have evolved through the twelve years of the Maryland Master's Certification Program, we point out four significant challenges that have emerged.

The First Challenge: To Construct a Knowledge Base on Teaching

Sometimes persons preparing to teach (as well as experienced teachers) just want to be given a cookbook technology: the ditto-sheet mentality. The first challenge is to get teachers past the idea that teaching can be satisfactorily done as a prescriptive, technical activity. This is an old problem that Dewey (1933) referred to as "routine action" which is "guided primarily by impulse, tradition, and authority" (Zeichner & Liston, 1996, p. 9). Preparing teachers is also complicated because even if persons accept that they want to be thoughtful professionals rather than non-reflective technicians, sometimes they believe they already have sufficient knowledge out of their personal experience acquired from having been in schools. Sometimes the presumption of sufficient knowledge resides in their content knowledge. To counteract these presumptions, we designed the program around a particular knowledge base:

> Teachers must become knowledgeable about the processes of educational change (Fullan, 1991). . . . The program faculty observed that, unless convinced there is a body of knowledge that they need to acquire, prospective teachers often act as if they already know enough about what happens in schools. . . . A crucial characteristic of the professional teacher is the quality of being reflective and that being reflective as a professional involves referencing a special knowledge base. This knowledge base and associated technical language enables the professional teacher to observe instructional events and episodes, to explain them with principles from learning and from pedagogy, and to see how instructional events relate to numerous contextual variables. Teachers also use the knowledge base in considering moral and ethical aspects of what they and others are doing. (McCaleb, Borko, & Arends, 1992, p. 46)

Looking back, it appears that we were invoking an emphasis on the external authority of published research to counteract what we feared teachers might do when left to their own resources. As we will discuss later, this emphasis on the knowledge base led to one kind of success and to another kind of problem.

Since the second year of the program, we have enjoyed the luxury of a large applicant pool from which we have been able to fill our twenty-five-member cohort with persons having strong academic backgrounds and often with career experience. Given their credentials, we assumed they could be reflective or thoughtful, but that they were probably uninformed about the findings from research. As we reported in an account of the program, "most scholar-teachers already had habits of reflection; therefore, a major task of the program was to instill a common knowledge base as the formulation of plans and as a primary consideration in the analysis and evaluation of action" (McCaleb, Borko, & Arends, 1992, p. 51). We defined this knowledge base as the findings from five areas of inquiry: theory-based studies of classroom methods; research on effective teaching; studies of learners, learning, and learning strategies; school effects studies; and learning-to-teach studies. One example of how this knowledge base was considered essential was that it contains findings that contradict commonly held practices or beliefs such as what the appropriate success rate should be (Berliner, 1987).

We set an overall objective concerning the development of reflection:

A reflective teacher who has command of the knowledge base on teaching can: 1. Explain the core ideas emanating from the knowledge base and cite appropriate best practices associated with them. 2. Cite key pieces of research associated with the knowledge base and provide a thoughtful critique of this research. 3. Execute effectively (at a novice level) selected best practices which grow out of the research in simulated and laboratory settings and in real classrooms. 4. Engage in critical reflection and intellectual dialogue about the knowledge base and understand how the various ideas are connected and how they interact to inform (situationally) a particular teaching/school event or episode. (McCaleb, Borko, & Arends, 1992, p. 57-58)

As the program was translated into a curriculum, reflection was operationally defined especially through the structure of four required classes (Models of Teaching, Cognitive Bases of Instruction, Research on Effective Teaching, and Conducting Research on Teaching). Through these classes, reflection was conceptualized in terms of knowledge and use of research related to teaching and learning (then termed "technical reflection") and consideration of social and cultural values ("critical reflection"). The primary activity for applying this reflective ability was the action research project. We explained the purpose for doing action research in an early article on the program this way:

> The relationship between the research on teaching and teachers must be reconstructed to promote the active role of the teacher. A possible way to make this change is found in Fenstermacher's (1986) practical arguments where teachers actively apply research findings to their decisions about teaching. Teachers construct the arguments for their actions often drawing their premises from research findings. (McCaleb, Borko, Arends, Garner, & Mauro, 1987, p. 58)

The research project was initially seen, not surprisingly, as being similar to what is done by university scholars:

> Two major research projects were required for all scholar teachers. The first was a library-based project requiring them to gain mastery of a particular field of knowledge by doing an extensive search of the literature and a careful synthesis of the knowledge base on a particular topic drawn from their studies in learning and teaching. For their second project, the scholar teachers identified a researchable problem and conducted a classroom-based action research project. (McCaleb, Borko, Arends, Garner, & Mauro, 1987, p. 62).

Evidence of how reflection and action research were understood by prospective teachers in the program can be indicated through samples from early action research reports. We excerpted passages that showed how the writer indicated the purpose of the report and how the writer concluded the report. These components were found to be particularly revealing about their perceptions regarding action research and their relationship to it.

> P [purpose]: The present study examines the relationship between homework and learning and whether an accountability intervention causes a greater percentage of students to do homework. Also it examines whether this intervention results in a higher accuracy rate in homework.
> C [conclusion]: Further study is needed to determine the relationship between homework and learning. After all, homework assignments are on the increase, and if there is no correlation between homework and learning, why assign it? (JR, 1986)

> P: The original purpose of the dialogue journal investigation was to study the effects of dialogue journals on writing performance and attitude toward writing.

Chapter Five: Research 181

C: The results of my study, although minor on an academic level, yielded student pride, creativity, and change of attitude. It is for these reasons I highly recommend the use of the dialogue journal. (MJ, 1988)

Note the apology in MJ, "although minor on an academic level," which suggests the higher status granted to published researchers in contrast with her own findings which concerned matters more personal and subjective: pride, creativity, and attitude.

Our attainment of the goal of preparing teachers who are competent with technical reflection using their action research projects as a criterion appears to have been overwhelmingly successful. We selected eighteen projects to be representative over the twelve-year period and studied them for changes in the ways action research was interpreted in their studies. The selection of reports intentionally included several from certain years in order to make comparisons within a cohort as well as across cohorts. The titles of their reports suggest the topics they selected and methods that were emphasized:

- "Does Homework Facilitate Learning?" JR, 1986
- "Dialogue Journals in the English Classroom" MJ, 1988
- "Beyond the Red Pencil: Teaching Writing Through Response" DF, 1988
- "Teacher Clarity: Improving the Quality of Clarity in the Classroom" CL, 1989
- "A Study of Teacher Reactions to Off-Task Behavior: How Effective Are They?" MB, 1990
- "Performance Assessment for Secondary Science Activities" DD, 1992
- "The Art of Writing/Writing as Art: Using Landscape Paintings to Teach Descriptive Writing" SS, 1992
- "Wait-Time: Effects on Classroom Disruptions" AA, 1992
- "Using Affective Education Activities and Conflict Resolution Strategies with Third-Grade Students" AR, 1993
- "Relationship of Student Perception of Grading Processes to Classroom Behaviors and Personal Factors" BG, 1993
- "A Struggle for Understanding: The Case Study of Kevin" LF, 1993
- "Through the Students' Eyes: Using Student Feedback to Improve Teaching" JV, 1994

- "Modern World History: The Dilemma of Curriculum Development" MM, 1994
- "Personalizing Mathematics Word Problems" DM, 1997
- "Does Reinforcement Based on the Multiple Intelligences Theory Promote a Comprehensive Understanding of Short Stories Read?" AG, 1997
- "What Does It Mean to Create and Enact a Feminist Curriculum in an 11th-Grade Honors English Class?" MD, 1997
- "'They're Not Empty Vessels': Issues of Reciprocity Between My Students, the Curriculum, and Me" AP, 1997
- "Teaching for a Relational Understanding of Mathematics: Pedagogical Challenges and Dilemmas of a Student Teacher" TB, 1997

The titles show the focus on themes such as teacher clarity, performance assessment, wait-time, and multiple intelligence theory that have characterized the research literature. Dominant methods such as process-product approaches are also reflected in the titles. The reference lists in the reports show consideration of leading scholars in the knowledge base we set as the target for the program. The action research projects confirmed what was quite evident in class discussions and exams. Through the experience of the Maryland Master's Certification Program the participants became thoroughly versed in research on teaching and learning.

The Second Challenge: To Promote Critical Reflection through Action Research

As shown in documents already cited, technical reflection had never been our only goal. While the program has been very successful with regard to that goal, we have found critical reflection to be more difficult to accomplish. Perhaps in the beginning of the program, we were more focused on solving the immediate classroom problems. Our review written in the early years of the program showed this approach to reflection:

Operationalized it means: 1) taking action (sometimes routine), 2) reflecting (thinking back, analyzing) upon that action (what happened, why, what it meant), 3) if resolution is not reached, moving on to a higher level of reflective or critical thought (multiple causes, conflicting goals, larger moral or ethical conflicts), and 4) coming up with alternative actions and thus continuing the cycle (McCaleb, Borko, & Arends, 1992, p. 51).

Notice that the consideration of moral and ethical concerns is recommended when "resolution is not reached." Moral and ethical concerns are often what breaks down a resolution which until exposed to their lens remains unconscious of the larger issues.

We have found that our construction of action research may have unintentionally functioned to develop technical reflection more than it has provoked critical reflection. This construction is probably representative of most approaches still taken in programs that use action research. By examining the way we set it up, we may be able to suggest how the notion of action research needs to be elaborated if critical reflection is to be approached. Here's the way we viewed it:

> The definition of action research that guides this assignment is that it should be research conducted in a 'field setting,' by participants in that setting, to help them improve their teaching. The focus is on a 'problem of practice' identified by the teacher/researcher and the goal is to discover possible solutions to that problem. Implicit in this notion of action research is the premise that teachers are autonomous, thinking professionals who can and should take an active role in making their own histories and directing and improving their own teaching [Hopkins, 1982, 1985 was cited for reference]. (McCaleb, Borko, & Arends, 1992, p. 52–53)

The assignment seems to be appropriately worded, but this has not been sufficient to push critical reflection. Some of the projects have moved into critical reflection while others seem to stay at the technical level. The excerpts cited earlier showed the writers were working primarily at the technical level. The next two excerpts indicate how others were attempting to apply personal concerns and social issues that extended outside the narrow constraints of the research task. DF tries to reflect on her ultimate purposes; MM struggles with the role of the community in which the school is located.

> P: This review of the research on response, while not exhaustive, suggests among other things that to maximize the effectiveness of response teachers must collaborate with their student writers in helping them ultimately to become independent. In an attempt to accomplish this goal while student teaching, I embarked upon a study of my own response and an assessment of the concerns and needs of my student writers. My interest in the response phase of the writing process led me to explore my own responses

to students' writings as well as my students' perceptions toward various modes of response.

C: Certainly, it is flattering to feel needed, to be assured that one's responses to students' writings are appreciated. But, ultimately, knowing when to let go is the kindest, most rewarding response of all. (DF, 1988)

P: The focus of my action research evolved out of necessity . . . . The focus of my action research became an analysis of the decision making process I went through in developing and executing the units I taught. I began a study of the way in which I made decisions, what impact different circumstances had on my decisions and how my ultimate goals shifted as different needs had to be attended to in my development of the curriculum.

C: Going back and forth on this issue I find no easy solution. I found the experience of deciding on my own to be exciting and intimidating because I knew that I was new and I was supposed to be making mistakes, but in the future I would want the freedom I had to make many of the same decisions. It ultimately comes down to where the control of the classroom should be: with the community or with the teachers, and in a democracy, as hard as that can sometimes be, it is probably safest with the community. (MM, 1994)

In our conclusion to the review of the program in Linda Valli's *Reflective Teacher Education* (1992), we suggested an issue with the way reflection and action research had been utilized:

> Reflection is not easily evaluated, and the ways it can be evaluated may not provide the most useful information toward program improvement. For example, scholar-teachers can be measured on the use of conceptual language from models of teaching or on their references to research literature; however, it is much more difficult to evaluate the blending of personal knowledge with critical perspectives in order to break open significant problems in their classrooms or in the broader educational enterprise. So it appears problematic to continue or expand evaluation of the technical reflection and by so doing to potentially restrict growth in critical reflection. (McCaleb, Borko, & Arends, 1992, p. 63)

Zeichner and Liston (1996) critique what we are calling technical reflection especially at the end of their book in the section called "Reflective Teaching and the Illusion of Teacher Empowerment":

> First, one of the most common ways the concept of reflective teaching is used in this restrictive way involves helping teachers reflect about their teaching with the primary aim of encouraging them to replicate in their practice the findings of educational research conducted by others, research

that has allegedly been "proven to be associated with effective teaching." (p. 74)

They assert that this "denies teachers the use of the wisdom and expertise embedded in their own practice" (p. 75). Their critique seems to circle back to what was identified as the first challenge in this paper where we stated that prospective teachers sometimes claim to know about teaching based on their experience and set about replicating traditional, unexamined practices. However, we suspect that Zeichner and Liston are referring to another kind of experience, an examined experience, which can come to be known as an internal authority within the teacher. We even believe that action research can be a ground for coming to authenticate that internal authority in addition to the "expert" external authority.

Recent action research reports show how this struggle to find this inner authority can be worked on:

> P: This paper will examine the struggles—with myself, with my classes and with certain individuals, that I had while trying to create and enact a Feminist curriculum in two 11th-grade Honors English classes. . . . My ultimate goal in my teaching, as in my research, is to help students and myself become more critically literate persons. I feel that pursuing issues such as those raised in this paper will help both my students and myself better understand who we are as gendered persons and how the world around us shapes that reality. (MD, 1997)

> P: It is hard to know how to begin explaining where my research question came from, or what exactly it is. Put the simplest way possible, I ultimately wanted to examine the relationship between the curriculum in its different versions (including my students' and my own), the students comprising two larger classroom collectives, and me. Tied into all of this, for both of those larger groups, are issues of connection, ownership, and validation. . . One of the larger goals I've set for myself as a teacher is to establish a classroom community where going out on a limb artistically, intellectually, and emotionally is a safe and encouraged activity for both my students and myself. . . Making art a relevant and broadening experience requires that students engage, and engagement with the discipline, buying in to it, requires, on some levels, that they buy in to me, too (or my program), and that we buy into each other. This paper is about my struggle with two groups of students who "bought in" to varying degrees. (AP, 1997)

In order to help these prospective teachers hold the tension of claiming their inner authority while still incorporating the findings from scholarly literature, the action research projects are guided so that attention is given to understanding students, understanding pedagogical content knowledge, and understanding the social and political issues embedded in classrooms and schools. But most importantly, what prospective teachers come to study emerges from their interests, concerns, and experiences in ways that deepen and broaden their understandings of teaching, all the while being mindful of the relationships among power, knowledge, and the lives of students. Student teachers are encouraged to ensure that they are part of the research, that it is about their relationship with students, with curriculum, and that their emerging pedagogies are the focus of the research.

In classroom conversations we explore questions such as: Whose knowledge is represented in the curriculum? What does it mean to respect and affirm the lives of students? What does it mean to know and understand in the context of particular subject areas? We also explore tensions such as attending to the needs of individual students and the needs of the classroom community. These questions and tensions are integral to the ebb and flow of the conversations about teaching. Through encouraging student teachers to develop their own research questions, and through the critical discourse in our classroom community, the action research project no longer narrowly focuses on external authority; rather, prospective teachers themselves expand what counts as knowledge of and about teaching.

The potential for growth as a teacher is perhaps evident in the following statement about action research that MD made during a presentation to our current cohort of student teachers about six months after she completed the program:

> You have to find something that is close to your heart. It won't be something from the outside that you are tacking on. I probably wouldn't have done what I did on Feminist issues in the 11th-grade English class if it hadn't been for action research. It actually pushed my teaching forward. It helped me validate where I was coming from. Just because nobody else was doing feminist literature, or literature from a feminist perspective didn't mean it didn't have a place. It didn't mean that I shouldn't be the one to make a place for it in the classroom. And I did that despite initial groaning from my students; it was beneficial to the students and myself. And I think that is how you have to approach action research. It isn't some kind of outside experience that once you've done it, it's over. You are going to carry it with you, what you have learned. (2/12/98)

The approach to action research that MD describes is not about ownership of a topic, nor about writing a project report; it is about the process of inquiry, reflection, and action in the moments of teaching that enhance her understanding of herself and her teaching. This process tends to strengthen internal authority in ways that foster personal and professional growth. Internal authority emerges in relation to and not as a substitute for external authority in the making of her professional identity.

The Third Challenge: To Connect Reflection (Action Research) to Community

Zeichner and Liston critique Schon's conception of reflection: "reflection is portrayed by Schon as largely a solitary process involving a teacher and his or her situation, and not as a social process taking place within a leaning community" (p. 18). The tendency for action research to be an isolating experience is a persistent challenge. We feel that we have been quite successful in reducing the isolating tendency in action research on one level and have made little progress on another level.

The success story has been the way that we develop a sense of community among the cohort of persons in the program. We intentionally provide experiences (including storytelling and outdoor adventure activities) so that the persons come to perceive each other as important resources and that norms of mutual respect and trust are established. Acceptance of differences is strongly advocated and modeled. We try to practice learning how to challenge one another in ways that promote lively yet healthy conversations and relationships. Within this sense of community, the ideas for action research are explored and the process is shared. Persons often have a partner with whom they are in frequent dialogue about their project. Results of the projects have typically been presented in small conference-style settings, often to the incoming cohort. So it is clear that our construction of the action research project has not been entirely a solitary activity.

Unfortunately this sense of community has not extended outside the cohort. We have found it difficult to engage the action research projects in the community of the teachers where the projects are being conducted. These schools have School Improvement Plans, and connections are seldom made between the action research projects and these plans. We have given considerable thought to this but have not found a satisfactory response. One concern is that the School Improvement Plan might function as another external authority that inhibits the development of the internal authority that has been the focus of the second challenge. Our current thinking is to work with the teachers in the schools so that they are doing more of their own action research. This year we plan to hold a forum in which both the teachers and the prospective teachers can present reports. We hope that this will provoke dialogue which may lead to better connections. Is it possible for prospective teachers to continue to inquire about issues that are close to them and to also find linkages with the concerns of the school? Perhaps the concerns of the school may be expanded beyond the usual focus on improving students' performances on statewide testing to other topics that are reflected in prospective teachers' inquiries. This dialogue promises to be a significant part of expanding what it means to be a professional development school.

The Fourth Challenge: To Make Action Research Friendly to All Knowings

While pre-service teachers in the MCP generally accept the action research project as a reasonable component of a master's degree, and they typically conduct impressive projects, at least on some occasions they treat doing the project as a necessary evil rather than as a vital part of their professional lives. This undertow is sometimes reinforced in the "real world" of the schools where we have found continuing resistance and resentment from many of the cooperating teachers toward the action research projects. They perceive action research as an intrusion into the student teaching internship. Are we imposing our own university culture in ways that are not appropriate for some or all of the involved parties: beginning teachers, experienced (cooperating) teachers, learners? If the persons in our program are influenced by these resistances to doing action research, then it may be that action research will not be incorporated into their professional life. Because we view the persons coming into and completing this program as one of the best hopes for revitalizing schooling, we are concerned with carefully examining the way action research is being experienced by these beginning teachers.

Central to the resistance from the experienced teachers is their concern for time. How, they ask, can the extensive time spent on this action research be justified, particularly given the pressing demands of students, grading, and parents, to say nothing about preserving fragments of a personal life? And we respond, when we can take time away from our research agendas, that the time spent is an investment in developing a way of thinking which will surely make teaching more efficient. And that the research process can, with practice, be integrated into the everyday, minute-by-minute decision making that teaching requires. That taking time to do action research should become part of the ecology of schools because it is integral to being a professional. And, of course, the curriculum and teaching practice will be improved and learners will benefit. The experienced teachers nod, their ivory tower impressions confirmed.

We feel the real concern from the cooperating teachers has not been clearly articulated. Perhaps even deeper in their concern about time is a suspicion that thinking like a researcher is not the key to their successes in teaching. It's not that they are unfamiliar with the findings of research: many of them have completed research projects, so they are familiar with the process and the way of thinking. It is more that the way they know what to do and when to do it in the classroom, at their best, comes from something other than, or in addition to, that scientific, logical way of knowing. Their knowing, which they defer naming and probably with adequate reason, may be more of an intuitive sort. It's more of the way an animal senses the environment and can act instantly. It's the way an artist, a Georgia O'Keefe, opens a rose, coming deep from inside her perceptual sensors and imaginations. Eisner (1979) may have been trying to tell us about this. If they were more direct, the experienced teachers might tell us that even if a teacher had time to think like a researcher, the outcome of such thinking-based teaching is going to be flawed.

Maybe we're using the experienced teachers as a cover for our own barely-articulated fears about the possible implications of our investment in action research. Are the experiences with action research producing teachers who are more or less oriented to being change agents? More or less effective and artistic in their teaching? Is their thoughtfulness about what they are doing enhanced and does this improve their teaching? Is their intuitive knowing blocked or expanded by action research? Have we sponsored action research in ways that are friendly to intuitive knowings? Have these teachers learned through action research how to combine being thoughtful with being intuitive?

We don't claim to be experts on intuitive knowing but will offer some speculations on what action research that is friendly to it might look like. First of all, the writer would show a high level of ownership of the project:

> C: Through the length of this study, it has become increasingly apparent to me that my most important personal definition as a teacher is that of a person who facilitates student empowerment and the strengthening of student internal motivation for success. In fact, student empowerment has become the metaphor for my journey through the Master's Certification Program at the University of Maryland. While one of my principal goals as a foreign language teacher will always be to open a window to the Hispanic world for my students, their success in assuming responsibility for their own learning and their own lives will be the most important goal I can help them to achieve. (BG, 1993)

The selection of the topic would be personalized rather than accepted from outside authority:

> P: I am interested in the learning benefits of presenting mathematics word problems in a personalized, familiar context. . . . I hypothesized that the child street vendors develop schemata for familiar mathematics procedures that relate to their individual circumstances. It seemed logical that this self-taught knowledge (a) was fostered as a result of its arising in the course of the children's personal experience and (b) could, if channeled appropriately, be a natural first step towards a more complete mathematical understanding. The objective of the action research project described in this paper was to investigate the extent to which these benefits can be realized in an ordinary classroom setting, using only the techniques and equipment that are reasonably available to teachers generally and that are neither unduly burdensome to the teacher nor disruptive of classroom routines.
> C: The study, together with previous educational research, suggests that personalizing word problems' context is one important way in which teachers can facilitate students' translation of mathematics word problems into the forms necessary to solve the problems. With the use of modern word-processing software, I found it both simple and relatively speedy to implement the personalization techniques described in this study. Will I continue to explore the benefits of personalizing instruction? Based on the results of this initial inquiry, my answer is a definite "Yes!" (DM, 1997)

The language structures would show the syntactical complexities needed to situate meaning in the writer's frame. For one thing, it is likely to require more space, more words, to explain the meaning of central themes. The author cannot rely on generally accepted terminology or on conventional definitions because they are insufficient for unique meanings:

> P: When I began my student teaching I had a general purpose for my action research, but no idea of what in particular I wanted to examine in my own teaching. As a student teacher, there are so many areas of teaching which I would like to hold up for closer inspection; however, I recognized that there was a common link running through all of my concerns about teaching—namely, how would I translate my philosophy of teaching mathematics into actual practice. (TB, 1997)

The writer is likely to find the unexpected, perhaps something outside the conventions that have been discovered by the scientific frame:

> C: Finally, I learned that the action research process yields a great number of unexpected ideas. I also began to get a deeper understanding of the intricacies of the learning environment I had become a part of. In this way, I discovered that classroom research can itself be a form of communication with students. (JV, 1994)

Findings are likely to include both discoveries about the "what" of the inquiry, typically about a content and/or a method of teaching and/or some artifact of the learners and something about the person doing the inquiry. Another way of saying this is that findings are both objectivized (reflecting the scientific method) and subjectivized (respecting personal intuitive knowing).

As we meet this challenge we will accompany teachers in their most significant growth. Zeichner & Liston (1996, p. 27) quote Dewey: "Unless a teacher is . . . a student [of education] he may continue to improve in the mechanics of school management, but he cannot grow as a teacher, an inspirer and director of soul life" (Dewey, 1904/1965, p. 151).

Research Discussion

William Palmer, University of North Carolina at Chapel Hill; **Leah McCoy** and **Joseph Milner,** Wake Forest University; **Richard Card,** University of Southern Maine; **Leslie Ann Quast,** Furman University; **Susie Slack,** Cornell University; **Margo Figgins,** University of Virginia; **Eileen Landay,** Brown University; **Vicki Jacobs,** Harvard University; **Greg Smith,** Lewis and Clark College.

Palmer: This set of papers spoke to me in a powerful way. It was so different in its perspective. We had to be amorphously natured, yet with a tendency to capture reflective thinking as it was promoted at Brown. The deliberate emphasis at Wake was to do classroom research where there's a professor involved with each of the articles written, so that there's a collaborative kind of emphasis on reflectivity. And in yours at Maryland it almost moved me to tears because we don't honor in ourselves or give our students the opportunities to develop what you call "internal authority," to trust research that grows out of our own ways of knowing. That's the feeling part of it all, why I liked it; but what we have to do, if we're going to include research as part of the MAT component, I think, is to ask ourselves these questions: Why are we asking these questions for research in the first place? And, what paradigms are the best to use to get at the answers to those questions? It may be that the one that worked well for Wake Forest won't work at Brown or at Maryland. It's either going to be qualitative or quantitative—critical, or intuitive, or a combination of those. If we do that, what questions are we answering, which paradigms best answer them, and how do we know that? We gain a great respect for programs where they are blended as they are at Brown. When they can not be blended, we need to know why it would be better to use a particular perspective rather than the one at Wake Forest. We could have a richer array of approaches to a wide range of questions and we could frame them from the point of view of what we do best to get at answers in education. Even at the doctoral level we do not do that well. We don't frame studies in theoretical constructs and don't honor blended studies. We start paradigm wars. I think in teacher education what I heard today was more colorful because it was asking us to look at the rich array of approaches to answer a wide range of questions. This argues for putting on the web what teacher educators are doing at both the undergraduate and master's level to get at research in education as part of training. I was wondering if Wake Forest had a web page or if you were interested in doing anything with Learn North Carolina or if there is a national movement to say, "here are research efforts in teacher training." If there is not, I don't think we are making information available to the multiple populations. It seems to me that it would be a wonderful outcome to have a web page for best practices that deals with such research.

McCoy: If Joe [Milner] will give me next semester off, I will do that.

Palmer: We probably could get funding from the Governor through Learn North Carolina.

Card: I am impressed by the action research orientation. It is something that is relatively new in the area of teacher preparation. The power of it, for me, is when we say to our interns, "You can think through your practice, identify those areas which you puzzle about or you have a question, and come up with some interventions that you can try to see if you can make a difference in your own practice. The resources that you need are all around you. You can use master teachers, you can review the literature." The idea here, and one of the things I like about the Wake Forest action research is that it doesn't have to be long. It represents the systematic investigation of your own practice and you can master that. The follow-up power is when you go to your own classroom you can remember that inquiry and think about how to improve your practice. The collaborative aspect of it is something worth promoting. It would be terrific if we could have our mentor teachers collaborate with our interns in thinking about and narrowing the scope of the investigation so that there's something you can really make some progress with in the course of a semester or two. Then they can collaboratively collect baseline data. The mentor teachers can work with counting student responses or whatever focal point; to do that together would inject that model into the professional development school, so that their school-wide collaborative action research would be something that the university could really help with in terms of school improvement and school culture development. I think it's really powerful.

Milner: I want to make a quick point, to add to what Richard [Card] said about how students bring their research ideas into their practice when they start teaching. The research we do takes place before our students begin teaching; it takes place in the classroom they're going to teach in, but it's not done while they are teaching. What we have done is to ask young teachers in our graduate program who are supervising our student teachers to see how the student pre-teaching affects their teaching. We want to know if a student who completed a research project (on asking questions or how you construct a discussion or how you teach fractions in mathematics, for example) puts that knowledge into play in their own classroom. We are trying to find out if they honor that learning and if they give it emphasis in their teaching. In other words, does the research matter or is it just something they do to complete an assignment. I think that is important. So far, we have found it does matter, it does have an effect, and that's gratifying.

Quast: Just a comment about what Eileen [Landay] and Joe [Milner] have shared with us: the effect research has had on students and their teaching. To me our old model may need to go; we learn something new and then we use that because it's a great idea, but how has that changed us? How has that renewed us and our own teaching? I think what you both have shared is that you and your students have been transformed in some way by what you have been doing. I dare say you've shared with your students, "Gosh I wrote this paper and I can't believe that all this time this is what I've been doing." That is a profound learning opportunity for the people who are with you. But the fact that you can share that with me is the kind of thing that we would like to have our students do with their students and be willing to share. I am also a learner, and sometimes I have these "aha" moments; sometimes I think about what I'm doing and I realize that what I've been doing is not really anything unusual but now I'm changing that. So I appreciate that challenge and I think such a moment really calls us all to be very self-renewing and reflective about who we are and how we teach.

Slack: One of the things that we see through classroom supervision of our student teachers is that we talk a lot about what we call shared vulnerability, in other words the three of us—the cooperating teacher, our student and the university supervisor—are all in this thing together. And none of us has all the answers, no one necessarily knows anything more than somebody else does about what's the right thing to do in a certain situation. But, I like what I've heard here too about using the approach and that we also use that collaborative approach when we think about our student teaching semester. It's kind of gratifying for your students to know that you also feel sort of vulnerable in the situation, and don't have all the answers.

Figgins: A question that's arisen for me, which is not directly related to the research, but keeps bubbling up for me in each of the different segments of this session, is that it sounds to me like there is, in most cases, a pretty strong interface among the different people and the different disciplines. And that's not true with my institution. There are pretty radically different experiences for the science students as opposed to the English students as opposed to the social studies and math students. I was reflecting a lot during Joseph McCaleb's presentation. One of the strands that I do in English is an autobiographical strand that starts in the very first semester that I have my students and runs all the way through. It gets carried forward through a variety of artistic presentations and transformations of information. And I kind of hide out on that part of what I do because it's pretty clear to me, at least for a couple of colleagues, that they just wouldn't even consider that as an important part of what they do with students. It's just pretty impressive to me that there is this communication, for instance, between Larry [Wakeford] and Eileen [Landay] and what it is that you are all doing together. A question for myself that I am taking away from this is, "How can those of us who don't have such a strong interface become more unified, not carbon copies of each other, but perhaps more unified in the reflective activities that we have for our students in the different disciplines?"

Milner: One of the unintended consequences of this research is that three of my students did excellent pieces of research that they presented at the National Council of Teachers of English three years ago. Bob Probst, who is a star in the field, asked them out for drinks with him. They were thrilled because he is the king of reader response. It has solidified and deepened their sense of belonging to a profession and having commitment to teaching English well. And one of our big problems in teacher education is the lack of staying power by new teachers.

Landay: If I could just respond to the question about the reason for this kind of inquiry. The personal inquiry is the process and that's in the paper that we've written. One of the factors of the personal inquiry was to bring together the disciplines. And one of the reasons that we embarked on it collaboratively, even though they might look different in the different disciplines is to present them together. It has become a feature that has allowed us to unify our work. One thing you might suggest to your peers is that you embark on some such piece of work even though what your students do might look very different in the way that Joe [Milner] and Bill [Wakeford] suggested. They might look very different coming from the very different disciplines, but if they present to one another they will probably learn a great deal. And that's been an important factor in bringing our work together. It hasn't always been like that. That's one of the primary reasons for our doing the program-wide personal inquiry.

Figgins: We have a final semester that is a field-based research inquiry that does get presented to the members of the cohort, but again, the way those experiences get defined are so different that the students end up sort of looking at each other and going, "Gee, what happened over there? That's really different from what I did." And there's a kind of dissonance that's uncomfortable. But I think this is an interesting unifying model that might be brought across disciplines.

Jacobs: I'm just thinking that in the fall term when we do our science teaching and English teaching, the science guide asks for one thing and the English another. What we have in common is a language and an articulated understanding of the philosophy, purposes, and intentions of the programs. And I think that's another way to bring all those folks together. In fact, everyone does classroom research. And in fact our students are mixed up by content toward those ends. The expectations and a constant need to revisit our purposes come alive as I think about my spring course because it's an analytic seminar. It's one that everyone just wants the answers for, and wants me to be really clear about its purposes. I think that is consistent across all sections and classes. And I'm thinking that this is something that I'm just now realizing in listening, that it is maybe what saves us.

Smith: I've got a question that may be too late to get answered, but if people have answers to the question, please share them with me. One of the things that I've found in teaching a research course that seems most valuable for research teachers is that we're trying to help the students realize that they are hypothesis-making creatures; all the time they're constantly doing research. The difficulty is that they need to scrutinize the answers and to realize that the questions raised in the hypotheses are often considerably faulty and that one of the values in developing a research prospective is that it asks them to look for data that will give them a clear picture of what is actually happening out there. So I'm just curious as to how other people are drawing other students into the kind of thinking that requires close examination of the assumptions that may lead them to those faulty conclusions. If you have any advice about that, I'm all ears.

Jacobs: I have to laugh because in that spring term course, what we are going to do the next two weeks is data analysis, and the honing of the question is the hardest thing. It is in the honing of the question that we really work on. It has almost gotten to be a joke. It is like they bring the questions to me and they say, "How do I engage students?" and I'll say, "Well, how do you define engage? And what are you assuming? Do I have to explain what I mean by the word 'The'"? It is all wrapped up in the defining of the questions.

Palmer: We don't do well with the idea of challenging our own assumptions and our own hypotheses. I think that the reason we don't do a good job is because when we do an analysis and test our assumptions, we find that we are functioning amidst a series of contradictions. So, we add a little of this and take away that from our stance; we live with our heads half in the sand. Because that is the case, we have to be sure that what we ask of our students is really based on reliable tenets and clear methodology. It really warrants that much if we are pure in our research.

Response Paper

Charles B. Myers
Vanderbilt University

I would like to thank everybody including all of the people who responded to these three presentations. Many of your responses have already expressed ideas that I might have said. I will try to build on them.

Research at Brown University

Eileen Landay provided in her presentation her own criticisms and analysis. She not only reflected on her practice, but she reflected on her process of reflecting on her practice—she described her meta-cognitve reflections. I very strongly support this approach to teacher education, but I must say that I am biased on this point because I come to reflection as a tool of intellectual inquiry in relatively recent years as a convert. (My graduate students cannot even approach their classes with me without knowing that they will be writing reflective journals and inquiring into the ideas that they record in their journals.) Landay described her program's use of what I call personal reflective practice, or inquiring into practice, and she noted that she gets her MAT students involved early in this process.

Although I think there are many educators who would say that what Landay described is not really research, I think it is very important research for professionals. She asks her students to address questions about their own teaching early, which means that they are looking at what comes out of their practice. By doing this, I assume they can use that questioning as a frame of reference for further inquiry. In her reflection on her program, Landay asks, "Is this a real research experience? Does our program really need to create a reflective practice in the long run with these students?" And I guess my response to the latter question, would be, I think it must. The one question I have though, and it applies directly to the Wake Forest presentation as well as Landay's, is, Why are you so concerned with external validation? Why put so much stake into the student presentations?

Two writers whose thinking has influenced me significantly on this point say that teachers get their rewarding feedback from the students they teach, from knowing that those students have achieved what they had hoped for them, and from knowing that they were successful with the students they taught. Dan Lortie (1975), in *School Teacher: A Sociological Study*, notes that the most important validating experiences for teachers occurs when a student who has graduated comes back and tells a teacher how important he or she was to him or her. Michael Eraut (1994), in *Developing Professional Knowledge and Competence* points out that there are very big differences among the types of validation that professional educators get based, on whom they are educating and what their roles are. As he describes the situation, college and university educators get validated when they make presentations, talk at AERAA, and have their writings published in journals. Policy people and school administrators get validated when someone important says they have a good school or good schools. Teachers, however, get validated when what they do in the classroom works with students. And that kind of validation is harder and more demanding than all other kinds of validation because it makes success and perceptions of success different from those of others. With this line of thinking, I would suggest that MAT student presentations are less important than their questions about how well they succeeded with their students and how well their personal experiences as MAT prospective teachers make them better teachers for the future. For me, the issue for any MAT experience is, How does it make each MAT participant a better teacher? An MAT student could find this out through personal inquiry and reporting on it rather privately in a personal journal. How he or she feels about the value of the experience, how he or she has learned from it are more important than how others react to a presentation about it.

Research at Wake Forest University

I wonder how much the Wake Forest MAT program is still driven by a traditional idea of a discipline-based master's degree and by its own history. Leah McCoy and Bob Evans talked about how the program had been a thesis-based degree, and that it is not anymore, but I still see what they describe as a study among separate subjects, all of which come before a student gets into practice. I wonder, if they were to totally redesign the program, if they would keep the separation and the sequence. If I were to redesign it, I think I would break down both the separation and the sequence. I do realize, however, that the experience with "rounds" probably mediates the separation a bit. But the program as they describe it seems to emphasize external validation and recognition by outsiders of student-developed presentations. (Here my reaction is similar to what I said concerning the Brown program.)

McCoy and Evans mentioned that the students say that the presentations seem to "drag out" the experience, and I think that they might really be pointing out something that needs attention. It might be that those presentations are just too demanding and detract from the important work the interns are doing in their classrooms. Even the web page they suggest could be a distraction unless, of course, it serves as a means for showing and sharing teaching success and children's work rather than as a medium for presentations or for showing off traditional-type research.

In the discussion, Eileen Landay referred negatively to the medical-school overload model of graduate, professional education. That comparison and the description of the Wake Forest program leads me to ask theoretically how much do we want to squeeze into a little more than a year's life of these people? Why should we force them to do so much in this getting-starting phase of their professional careers? How important is a research component in their program? What should that component emphasize? I assume that the students in all of our MAT programs enroll in them primarily because they want to be teachers, not because they want to be professional researchers. They want to learn what they need to start a career in teaching. In that context, the research they need to learn about is research that will help them inform their practice, as they begin as MAT interns and as they move into their early years as full-scale teachers. If the research is more discipline-bound, more traditional, and in place primarily because of the historical nature of most degrees, we may have an "overload model" of professional education much like old-fashioned medical schools. Frankly, I think having MAT experiences that are self-fulfilling, energizing experiences for our students is critically important and that overloading them with non-essential burdens—and research that is not tied directly to informing their practice can be non-essential—can drive good potential teachers away.

Once we get our MAT students started with positive experiences with their students, and show them the importance of inquiring into their practice in a scholarly way, they will develop their own research and inquiry agendas in their early years of their careers. They do not need to learn traditional research in the first MAT year: they do not need to engage in research that they see as a burden that is added on to their work with students: but they do need to see teaching as a scholarly activity that they can do well, enjoy, and continuously get better at doing so.

Joseph McCaleb's Reflections on His Experiences with the Maryland Program

I did not label my responses as "The University of Maryland Program" because McCaleb spoke more about his experiences and reflections about those experiences as a participant in The University of Maryland MAT program than describing the program apart from his reflecting on it. In my notes, I subtitled his talk, "A participating professor's reflections on his personal, intellectual, and professional struggles." Because of the nature of his comments, instead of reacting to several of his specific points, I want to react to his comments more generally. In short, he reflected upon and inquired into what his participation in the Maryland program has meant for him intellectually and professionally—what questions it has caused him to ponder and rethink. McCaleb's questioning represented for me the primary reasons why we are all here: to inquire into our own practice as teacher educators and to use our thinking to improve our programs and our individual work within them.

So, I want to finish my responses with two general comments that were prompted by what McCaleb said but that apply to this conference as a whole. First, I wonder what the people who developed the original MAT programs decades ago would have thought about his, and all of our, reflections. They might have thought, as they listened to us, that they were at the wrong conference. The programs that we have been describing are much more than that old MAT format of content courses with add-on teaching applications—strong subject matter preparation and little pedagogy so the interns can teach the content accurately. I know that I am distorting that old idea of the MAT somewhat, but clearly we are engaged in discussions that I do not remember from when I started with my MAT efforts nearly thirty years ago. Our comments at this conference show that all of us know that teaching is much more than infusing content into students and that we are teaching our MAT prospective teachers and ourselves who will replicate the artisan-level work of their masters.

And finally, I have a suggestion for the next conference of this group. (I sincerely hope there is a next conference.) Let's extend the "best practice" focus of this session into a focus that might be called "reflecting on our best practice envisioning future MAT programs." Let's step beyond telling each other what we do back home. Let's use our collective experiences and our collective ideas about what we do to dig more deeply intellectually into our work and to probe for and with questions that we have just begun to raise. Let's do more of what Joseph McCaleb just did for us.

Chapter Six

Induction

The induction section of this book is the most problematic because we have not been as effective in this endeavor as we have in any of the other areas of our exploration. We have been slow to develop effective internships and are still trying to determine the importance of diversity and duration as we place our students in the rigorous settings of real classrooms. We are also just beginning to learn about the power of teacher inquiry and action research and are wondering how quickly and how vigorously our students need to engage in this activity as they begin their internships. But, we are far more woefully inadequate in helping our students enter the teaching profession. We are not fully engaged in the school world, so we do not like to acknowledge that to ourselves and want to hide it from our students. Some feel that preparation is our mission, not help in entering the profession. For some educators this is a matter of principle that calls for independence rather than prolonged dependence on university advisors.

We can do more to develop job fairs, seek recruiter visits to our campuses, and make calls to clinical faculty we know well and principals and superintendents who might be interested in hiring our students. Principles like this need to be examined. Sometimes such principles are espoused as a way to cover an unwillingness to be helpful and at times because teacher educators are not willing to warranty their products. Even greater than our reluctance to help our students enter the teaching profession is our failure to support them in their first year in teaching. When they have left behind the security and academic purity of the university where their idealism is bolstered by cohort members and engaging professors they are all the more vulnerable to the pressures of socialization that can dampen their hopes and make them question their expectations. They especially need support as beginning teachers because they are typically given extremely difficult teaching assignments both in terms of number of students and difficulty of preparation, and the burden of extracurricular duties. They need support for their high standards and inventiveness so that they will search for best practice rather than being subdued into standard practice. That can include university functions to pleasantly getting together with other members of their cohort and helpful university people. It means, for example, in the ABC program at Wake Forest a chance to easily apply for small grants that support travel to special professional development events, registration for state and regional professional meetings, or materials and equipment for special projects in their classrooms.

The two sections of this chapter speak in different ways about how this transfer to the world of work can be made more certain. The first essay seeks to convince readers that professional development school (PDS) involvement makes all the difference at Ohio State's Science, Math and Technology program. The author makes us feel that such an enriched context for student teachers will surely steer these fine students into satisfying teaching careers. The final essay takes a very honest look at the Duke program and how it re-formed itself as a way to select, prepare, and support outstanding students who would eventually enter teaching.

Professional Development Schools and their Influence on Developing Teachers in an Integrated Program

John R. Mascazine, Ph.D.
The Ohio State University—Columbus

The purpose of this paper shall be to explain the significant changes and benefits that a major university has realized since the development of Professional Development Schools (PDS). The PDS model will be considered in light of the Mathematics, Science, and Technology education (MSAT) program of Ohio State University. Of greatest importance is the impact such an integrated program and Professional Development Schools have had upon the development of capable and confident middle and secondary teachers.

The Ohio State University College of Education has adopted the Holmes model recommendations as set forth in the report *Tomorrow's Schools of Education: A Report of the Holmes Group* (1995). This report was the culminating work of professors and deans of colleges of education across the nation. It set forth five primary goals:

- To make teaching intellectually sound
- To recognize differences in teacher's knowledge, skill, and commitment
- To create relevant and intellectually defensible standards of entry into teaching
- To connect schools of education to local schools
- To make schools better places for practicing teachers to work and learn

The last three goals are addressed and confronted regularly in Professional Development Schools. The purpose of PDS–university partnerships is to create opportunities for professional growth and development through the sharing of time, talent, and resources. Prior to the establishment of PDS designated settings, such collaboration was limited and often deemed sporadic.

Professional Development Schools is the phrase commonly used by the Holmes Group. Other organizations refer to such collaborative partnerships as Professional Practice Schools (American Federation of Teachers), Clinical Schools (Carnegie Report), or Partner Schools (National Network for Educational Renewal). All of these partnership arrangements espouse common program goals and characteristics.

Four common goals of these partnership efforts include: 1) To improve and maximize student performance and achievement; 2) To prepare beginning teachers and school personnel; 3) To promote professional development of novice and veteran teachers; and, 4) To apply research and methods that will improve instruction and teacher practice (*Professional Development Schools at a Glance*—AACTE, [1998]).

Collaborative efforts between colleges of education and local school districts share common commitments and characteristics as cited by the American Association of Colleges of Teacher Education. These tenets include efforts to promote equity policies and practices, and efforts to create parity among collaborating partners. Such partnerships also show commitment to improve schools and teacher education programs, and the application of knowledge and proven practices to educational settings.

Professional Development Schools and partnerships require a great deal of commitment and effort from both the school (and school district) and the university or college. Such partnerships are not developed easily or over short periods of time. However, when such PDS arrangements are in place and have had time to mature, they are the greatest benefit to teachers, university professors of education, and beginning teacher interns.

PDS sites prove especially helpful for the induction of new teachers into the profession. The mentoring and continual opportunities for professional skill development are pivotal in supporting new teachers. As reported in *Learning the Ropes: Urban Teacher Induction Programs and Practices in the United States,* many large urban districts are able to meet the needs of beginning teachers with such collaborative mentoring relationships. There are many instances when I have been able to follow up with OSU teacher graduates who have been employed by our PDS colleagues. Such communication revealed they received helpful attention, mentoring, and support in PDS sites on a continual basis. Many novice teachers at PDS sites have also chosen to attend ongoing workshops and training sessions offered by the university professors as a way of maintaining those contacts. Some have chosen to update or upgrade their teaching certificates through programs and courses offered through university–PDS partnerships.

Established PDS relationships offer benefits to administrators and teachers who are seeking to fill vacancies within their schools with beginning teachers who may share their vision and possess specific skills. The awareness of the specific needs and philosophies of specific PDS sites allows university partners to make informed recommendations of interns for specific positions. Likewise, such relationships allow district personnel to gain an understanding of programs and resources offered by the university partner. Such input may be pivotal and extremely helpful to school districts and interns as they strive to achieve a smooth transition into teaching. As reported by the National Commission on Teaching and America's Future (September, 1996) many beginning teachers enter the profession lacking the necessary skills and training. Novice teachers need the continued professional support and development that PDS relationships provide. Such formal and informal PDS support mechanisms may be just as beneficial to veteran teachers as well.

Many of the greatest benefits of working PDS relationships are not immediately visible to those unfamiliar with the partners. Such benefits include the support and understanding that has taken years to develop and that frequently appears to have always existed among the partners. These elements were recently singled out and reported as extremely beneficial by a group of OSU interns over the course of their initial field experiences at a PDS site. They cited the unique ways in which OSU faculty, district administrators, and teachers acted collaboratively for the maximum benefit of their students. The interns remarked favorably that university personnel understood and worked with the specific needs of teachers and the district. They came to see the district as a community of professionals deeply concerned with their own development, as well as the development and success of the students they taught. The interns reported that such a community of professionals created an accepting environment for themselves as developing teachers. Finally, the interns reported that the mentor teachers at their respective PDS sites were facilitators of change in their own right, rather than complacent professionals. These interns expressed their observations and positive comments in a registered letter to the district's board of education.

In another urban district, a PDS partner of OSU produced similar results. Many high school teachers working collaboratively with the college of education partners have been able to suggest and volunteer innovative strategies that helped university professors improve methodology courses for interns. Some district teachers have also co-taught workshops at the university and at local public schools and have lectured on topics such as authentic assessment, innovative pedagogy, effective classroom management, and district inclusion policies. Many of the benefits of strong PDS and College of Education partnerships were highlighted in the book *Collaborative Reform and Other Improbable Dreams: The Challenges of Professional Development Schools,* which describes explicitly the changes and benefits realized by Ohio State University, local schools, partnership school districts, and community organizations.

Ohio State's Integrated Program of Mathematics, Science, and Technology (MSAT) Education

The principle advantages and benefits of Ohio State's integrated Mathematics, Science, and Technology (MSAT) Education program fall into three areas: 1) quality and selection of pre-service teacher interns; 2) content integration and preparation; 3) professional cohesiveness and collaboration. These will be discussed briefly as they relate to the training of future mathematics, science, and technology teachers at the middle and secondary school levels. Previously, pre-service teachers were trained by separate divisions in the department of educational studies in the College of Education. However, at present it is an integrated program which seeks to emphasize the sharing of resources and the interdisciplinary nature of these content areas. The methods and pedagogy courses in the MSAT program are lead by the faculty members who often team teach such courses. Often one mathematics education professor will be paired with either a science education or a technology education professor. Doctoral students collaborate with faculty members in conducting field experience seminars. Such arrangements allow for much collaboration and the sharing of resources.

Quality of Interns and Applicants to the Graduate MSAT Teacher Program

One of the most significant changes that has occurred with the implementation of the graduate teacher education program at Ohio State University is the quality of applicants. The interns accepted into the graduate program usually have accumulated work experience and are generally more mature than those entering previous undergraduate programs. Many of the interns have informal teaching experience and are well accustomed to working with students. Thus, interns are entering the MSAT program with a greater awareness of the demands and expectations placed on teachers. Some of our interns have made informed choices to work with special populations of students and many are intent on developing skills that will enable them to be effective with these populations.

The MSAT interns exhibit a commitment to research. Although it is emphasized as part of the graduate program, interns often exceed the required course assignments to discover resources that will benefit them personally and professionally. They have a clearer vision of what they need to be prepared and comfortable in teaching specific content. Many of our interns work collaboratively with each other, as well as with their mentor teachers, even after they have graduated from the program.

The interns are more likely to take greater responsibility for their own professional development in the context of a graduate program. Many exceed the required number of hours of field experience, choosing to gain additional practice interacting with veteran teachers and working with students. Many volunteer their expertise from previous employment in science, mathematics, or technology related fields. School and district administrators enthusiastically embrace our interns, who willingly share their practical work experiences. To many interns, teaching is a profession they have chosen only after having discovered their own talents and personal strengths in previous work experiences. One challenge for our interns is that of balancing time for work and family commitments with those of a demanding graduate program. This becomes more problematic as the field experience requires more time, leading up to student teaching in the third quarter. Although many of our interns are encouraged not to work other jobs or take other courses during their student teaching, some still attempt to do so. This was a similar problem for the undergraduate program as well.

Content Integration and Preparation

A second positive change noted among interns in the MSAT graduate program is their level of content preparation. Many enter the program with the undergraduate content course work completed and are thus able to concentrate on the education rudiments and research components of the program. Those who do take content courses are often trying to diversify their skills and pick up additional certifications, which may require only a few courses to be completed over the five quarter program. Many interns also enter the program with research or laboratory experiences that can directly aid in the teaching of secondary school science and mathematics. Such experiences increase the intern's employability, since many districts prefer to hire science and math educators with practical work experience.

The Ohio State University teacher education program in mathematics, science, and technology is an integrated program. Every intern in the program is instructed in ways to integrate these content areas into their core concentration specialty. Such emphasis on integration gives interns a greater appreciation of other disciplines, as well as facility in designing integrated lesson and unit plans. There is an emphasis on the use of technology across the areas of mathematics, science, and technology instruction, as well.

An integrated approach enables interns to adapt more easily to PDS sites and extend their skills there. Interns are able to practice and share what they have learned from collaborative and integrated experiences with their mentor teachers in PDS placements. Mentor teachers have commented on the ways MSAT interns have helped them discover and develop new teaching strategies through an integration of content.

Professional Cohesiveness and Collaboration

The MSAT program promotes cohesiveness among the faculty and interns of formerly separated disciplines. Math, science, and technology education interns collaborate on projects in many of their education core courses. Many also choose to collaborate on research with professors of other disciplines. Professional cohesiveness is also evident among many of the faculty members of the college of education. It is not uncommon to have mathematics education professors and science education professors collaborating on research and coordinating in-service programs for school districts and local teachers. Technical education professors may collaborate with their math and colleagues to apply for grants, to update curricula, or plan teaching assignments. The sharing of different approaches to content can be an enriching experience for instructors who become professionally involved.

Although it has taken some time and considerable effort to begin thinking of the MSAT program as a truly integrated program, as the quarters have progressed there has been an increasing level of acceptance and willingness to function as one. As with most restructuring and organizational changes the struggle has been ongoing. However, most faculty, graduate students, staff, and MSAT interns have been open and supportive of the overarching spirit and intent of integration.

Some MSAT faculty members are also forming collaborative partnerships with professors in other colleges on the OSU campus; for example, the School of Natural Resources and the Department of Geological Sciences have cooperated with the College of Education in such ventures. These partnerships offer insights to non-education faculty about the condition and concerns of local schools. Such arrangements often bring local schools and community organizations in contact with research projects and content that may otherwise be inaccessible through the College of Education alone. Another benefit is that of encouraging other professors and departments outside the College of Education to form their own partnerships with teachers, school districts, and community groups in an effort to support and improve student learning. The bottom line, reaching out and working collegially with individuals and organizations, is being realized and appreciated by those who believe in integration and the PDS philosophy. The PDS organization is one of the most concrete ways to emphasize integration and collaboration.

Preparing Teachers with Staying Power

Rosemary Thorne
Duke University

Most universities have not, historically, been involved in the induction process. Duke is no exception. Therefore, we have not had a great deal of experience in the optimum ways that induction occurs. At Duke we have relied on our close relationship with the local school system to help us determine ways to provide graduates with a seamless transition from graduate study to what we hope will be a long and fruitful career. We looked at two areas: what we can do during pre-service so that our graduates survive their first year of teaching and become career teachers, and how we can support our graduates once they are teaching. What follows is a brief history of the program and the ways we tried to address these two concerns.

Duke reinstituted the Master of Arts in Teaching Program in 1989. From the outset, the program was a close collaboration among university faculty, Durham's two school systems, and a cohort of highly skilled teachers who serve as our mentor teachers. Our aims were the same as most other MAT programs: to attract very well-prepared graduates of liberal arts colleges into the profession and to provide those individuals with the knowledge, skills, and attitudes needed to be outstanding secondary school teachers. Our philosophy was then as it remains today, to build an attitude of reflection in the teachers that we prepare.

The development of the new MAT program occurred against the backdrop of a politically charged merger of Durham's two school systems: Durham County Schools, a mostly suburban, racially and socioeconomically diverse school system, and Durham City Schools, an urban, mostly poor, mostly African-American school system.

For the nine talented, eager students in the first class, the MAT program focused on making sure those future teachers were well prepared in their teaching field and had the benefit of a full-year (albeit parttime) internship under the guidance of a strong mentor. We were very pleased with this group of students: the mentor teachers praised their dedication and skill; and, with no help from any Duke faculty or staff, they easily found teaching positions after graduation. Of the nine, seven entered the profession. By December, only four remained. Now, eight years later, only one of the original nine is still teaching at the secondary level. That early failure caused us to think carefully about preparing students for real classrooms and supporting them once they arrived there.

We first considered admissions. It was clear that some of the students in that first class, while academically talented, were better suited to a life in academia than in the secondary classroom. We wondered if their failure in the real world of teaching in secondary schools might have been predicted and, if so, on what basis?

We believed that our education curriculum was appropriate for preparing teachers, but in light of the difficulties encountered by our initial graduates, we decided we were demanding more of our students than could be effectively mastered. Our program's pedagogy was too crowded into the time allotted and too directed to provide students with the time to develop a reflective perspective on and critique of their own practice.

We next looked at the internship. The high school students encountered by our interns in their first teaching practicum were typically far better than the high school students they taught in the first year of their teaching after completing the program. We contracted with the best teachers in the local school systems to mentor our students, and, typically, these teachers taught the best students in the system. That is not the experience of most first year teachers. Our graduates were prepared to deconstruct Milton in English classrooms or explain implicit differentiation in math; the students they encountered in their real world first jobs were often reading well below grade level and struggling to plow through consumer math.

Finally, we looked at our graduates and discovered that they were professionally naive. They were brilliant, dedicated, and enthusiastic, but they tended to rely too exclusively on the secondary experience gained through their own schooling or that of these high-powered placements in the local public schools. They were such an elite group that they were totally unfamiliar with the real experiences and the real struggles of the vast majority of high school students. After having considered all aspects of the program, from admissions through the exit interview, we made subtle, but significant, changes.

We began by requiring an interview in addition to the substantial application packet. In that interview we asked applicants to talk about their own experiences in school and to describe the kind of teachers they expected to be. We asked them to predict their futures as teachers and to reflect on the skills they would need to acquire in order to become the teachers they wanted to be. We put less weight on the caliber of the undergraduate institutions, GRE scores and undergraduate grade point averages, and more weight on letters of recommendation and attitudes toward children and schooling. We horrified our colleagues in other departments by rejecting students who could be (and sometimes were) admitted to our doctoral programs in their academic discipline.

We revisited our coursework. We cut out some theory and added practical applications. We instituted a seminar, meeting over the course of the internship, where interns from different schools reflected upon and shared their experiences, ensuring that all interns would think broadly about issues of adolescents and schooling, regardless of their own personal experiences. We required a journal so that interns would develop the habit of reflecting critically on their own teaching practice. We instituted a portfolio requirement, formative rather than summative in nature, with required artifacts building on the foundation that our students brought with them. We regularly required students to explain to us how their attitudes had changed, what they had learned, and what they still needed to know.

Of the nine mentor teachers who worked with us during our first year, six continue to work with us today, providing us with valuable ongoing collaboration. Those mentors, and the others whom we have recruited over the past eight years, serve on our advisory and admissions committees, and they have a strong and central voice in all facets of the program.

The politically painful merger of the two Durham school systems actually provided a benefit to our students. Prior to merger, it had been possible for a good teacher to spend an entire career without coming into very close contact with a needy adolescent. But the mentor teachers we selected early in the program's history accepted the challenge of a student reassignment plan that brought large numbers of poorly prepared, disadvantaged students into schools that, prior to reassignment, had sent 85 percent of their graduates on to four year colleges. One of our mentors, who was part of the initial cohort group, developed a skills-level course in American Studies for high school students who were ill prepared for productive citizenship. He teaches that course in addition to Advanced Placement American History, ensuring that our MAT students who intern with him will be teaching a diverse group of students. Two of our mentor teachers, one of whom had served on the initial committee that designed the MAT program, developed a bridge course for ninth graders who do not yet possess the skills to be successful in high school. These teachers team-teach the bridge course in addition to teaching Advanced Placement English, ninth-grade English for both regular and academically gifted students, sophomore English for both remedial and academically gifted students, and a host of electives from Young Adult Fiction to Mass Communications. The MAT students who intern with these teachers are prepared to teach a very wide range of adolescents. We no longer allow our interns to teach only those students who are headed for the most prestigious colleges and universities, or even for graduation from high school. While we insist that our mentor teachers are truly skilled at both teaching and coaching beginning teachers, we also insist that our students teach as broad a group of students as possible.

Throughout their internship, MAT students are asked to review their original thoughts and attitudes about teaching and future careers by considering the kind of teaching position they intend to seek upon graduation. We provide guidance toward an appropriate post-graduate placement: we share with our students early on our thoughts about the best fit for their developing skills, abilities, and inclinations. If their vision of the future does not match ours, we provide guidance on the things that must be done to meet their own expectations. For example, this year we have an extremely talented student, who, in addition to being a Woodrow Wilson Fellow, is also a Marshall Fellow and hopes to return to teach in an inner-city after he completes his two years at Oxford. His own private high school and Ivy League undergraduate experience are not experiences which have well prepared him for life in the inner-city. His mentor, in conjunction with school system employees and the MAT faculty and staff, has structured experiences in his internship that approximate those which he will find in the inner-city. We ask him to reflect on his experiences teaching advantaged and disadvantaged youth and to assess the ways in which he will need to modify his practice. We talk with him about the differences in administrative structure, and perhaps administrators' skills, between impoverished schools and the school in which he is completing his internship. In other words, we hold him to his own intentions.

We are proactive in our placement. After we have consulted with students and have helped them determine the location and kind of school in which they would like to teach, we make phone calls for them. We contact principals and superintendents and tell them about our candidate. We tell them why they would be a good fit. We are fairly aggressive in describing the kind of teaching schedule that would best suit a particular candidate. This year we have one student who completed high school one year early and completed a double major at a rigorous liberal arts college in three years. He will graduate this spring as a twenty-year-old who, unfortunately, looks like a fourteen-year-old. Although we have provided him experiences teaching a broad range of students, it is not realistic to believe that he will be successful in an inner-city school. He will, however, be very successful teaching bright, motivated, and capable students. We have secured for him interviews at three magnet high schools that serve those populations.

We are also candid enough to tell our students when we think they are better suited to a different kind of career. For example, over the course of the last nine months in the teaching internship, it has become clear that one of our interns simply does not have the combination of skills he will need to be successful in a high school classroom for any length of time. He is applying to doctoral programs in his academic field. All of us involved with his preparation agree that is the best choice for him.

Our approach does not always work, of course. Sometimes we are just wrong. And sometimes our students do not listen to us as well as we would like. But by carefully considering the outcomes, placement, and staying power of our graduates (that is, by practicing what we preach: an attitude of reflection about our own practice) we have made changes that have improved every facet of our program.

Once our graduates are placed it becomes much more difficult to help them. Like many programs that attract students from all over the world, our graduates tend to spread out. We have always known that providing support for those people once they have left North Carolina would be difficult, if not impossible. We do what we can. Electronic communication has helped us enormously. We regularly communicate with all of our graduates and we encourage them to communicate with each other. When we cannot provide advice on problems they encounter, we try to find someone who can. We stay in touch. We help those graduates who are interested return to Duke during the summer where they can either teach, or, sometimes, conduct research while they live on campus. When we have them back for a few months it is much easier to help them with the problems they are encountering in teaching. Those graduates who remain in the area are put to work by the program on advisory committees and as peer advisors to new students. When they are interested, we help them link up with Duke faculty members to explore continuing research in their teaching field.

Our record is much better. All but two graduates of the class of 1998 plan to teach. Of the two who will not, one will pursue a Ph.D.; the other will come back to the U.S. to teach in the Washington, D.C. area after he completes two years of study at Oxford under the conditions of his Marshall Fellowship. We are confident that all of them will be able to handle the problems they encounter in their first teaching assignment.

All of our graduates from 1997 tell us that they will be back in the classroom in the fall of 1998. All but one of the 1996 graduates who entered teaching remain; that same number holds true for the class of 1995. Five graduates from 1994 are no longer teaching. Only one of the graduates of 1993 and two from the class of 1992 have left the classroom. In contrast, only six teachers from our 1991 class remain teaching today.

A graduate of our first class who remains in his first teaching assignment will come back this summer, as he does every few years, to tell the new crop of MATs how he has managed to survive in the classroom.

Induction Discussion

Greg Smith, Lewis and Clark College; **Angela Breidenstein,** Trinity University; **Lawrence Wakeford,** Brown University; **Joseph Milner** and **Leah McCoy,** Wake Forest University; **Richard Card,** University of Southern Maine; **Alice Sy,** high school teacher.

Smith: One of the things that we've thought about doing but haven't yet accomplished for teacher education is to create an opportunity for graduates who are out of our program one to four years to come together periodically over the course of the year for dinner and a book discussion. I'm curious about whether other people have done this. We are now developing such a forum for people we admit into the program. We think it will be positive and seems like one good way to stay in touch. It not only will provide support but it will also encourage useful conversation. It will be a one semester course that will include a monthly dinner. Eight or nine times over the course of the year there will be a reading list that folks come up with on their own during the first session and then just commit to having the dinner and having the conversation once every four or five weeks.

Breidenstein: One of our elementary specialty centers has done a similar thing. We invite graduates back once a year for an alumni day with a luncheon, round tables, discussions. We bring in a national teacher of the year to do the speech. We also honor teachers of the year, so everybody knows that in April there's a date to come back for extensive conversations, adding on more teachers each year. And we're trying some things like an email network, a Teacher Center, and other ways to stay in contact with beginning teachers. The other thing I would like to say is that in our last semester we focus on finding support networks in your new school, your setting. It goes all the way from, if you have a great setting to what if you're the only person in your school, what are you going to do? They really brainstorm the first year of teaching and come up with the strategies that they'll take into their schools as first year teachers so that they continue to rely on new cohorts. They come back to us, but they also look to the resources of their teaching community.

Wakeford: What are some other ways that our programs support new teachers?

Milner: Some of our faculty have mixed feelings about a new way we support teachers. Every year we award a $20,000 Waddill prize to the best elementary and best secondary teacher who has graduated from Wake Forest. That sizeable award says a lot to young teachers who are in our program about their future in teaching. An alumnus who wanted to celebrate his father's fine teaching gave us the money that supports the award. Two faculty members, two members of the donor's family, and two most recent winners select the winners each year. It is a fine tribute to career teachers.

Card: Is that helpful, or does it create animosity in the school district?

Milner: We worried about the problem of competitiveness. We also worried about how to select the best teacher. That is very hard to decide. But the award honors teaching, so we make the award and try to diminish the competitiveness in every way we can.

Smith: Is the winner a graduate of the previous year?

McCoy: No, nominees must have taught three years. We wanted to award and encourage long-term teaching. So, most of the winners have taught more than three years.

Card: We don't have a lot of the informal work at the University of Southern Maine; the heart of our induction support is the completion of the master's degree. Our internship year is thirty-three credit hours. The following year is the thirteen-credit-hour experience that is designed to support, to be the induction year for our first-year teachers. At the heart of it is one full Saturday each month, September through May; it's all day with a luncheon for the cohort group. You join that group and stay for the year. Right now the focus is on some required coursework for the master's degree as an assessment teacher. The heart of the Saturday work involves the cohort members identifying issues that they're facing in their first year of teaching and the creation of partners and triads of people who give one another support. On those Saturdays and at other times throughout the year, they read articles together, write together, and present together. The intention is to provide a full year of support as induction. The only requirement for it is you have to have gone through our year of internship and you have to have a teaching position. You have to have a job somewhere so that you bring that as the context for our year together.

Sy: I think the key player that we're missing in this discussion is the school systems themselves. I know that they're difficult to work with but whoever trains the administrators, and the principals should make sure that they understand that when they bring teachers to their school, they have a big responsibility for retention as well. I think that some of the issues that have been brought up are related to, "What could faculty members offer me if I call them and say I'm having this problem in Atlanta?" But some of the universities, maybe those in the cities, like Wake Forest, can also do something for first year teachers in Winston-Salem, even if the teachers didn't actually attend Wake Forest for their training. But principals must realize that their first year teachers can be some of their most valuable assets and that they need to hang onto them. No matter what universities do in terms of setting up an infrastructure to help them, and no matter how much faculty reach out, if that's only taking place in the academic setting and not in the school world setting of "this is my job and these are the people I work with," it's still not going to be nearly as effective. I don't know how that will happen other than sitting a superintendent down and saying, "you know, this is what you've got to do or you're going to have an incredible turnover rate." I think that's what we're missing.

Induction Response

Michael Andrew
University of New Hampshire

I think that there's some dirty little secret is out here. A very large number of our graduates leave the profession in the first few years and I think John [Mascazine] cited 60 to 85 percent and we had only one person left from the class that you [Rosemary Thorne] mentioned at Duke. So, this is an issue that we need to attend to and it's interesting to me that a state is taking us on as a mission. I think it's hard for me from New Hampshire to comprehend this possibility but I do think that what Beverly [Carter] described to us is something that holds a lot of promise; just by having that dialogue will be hopefully among the better ways to handle this problem. I heard a few suggestions in the last part of this discussion about things that we can do institutionally and there seem to be several categories of that. What I call informal, semi-formal, and formal. The informal were things like the e-mail idea which I think is something that is not only very easy to do, but with a little organization we could set up some kind of a system through Internet and email were we could put ourselves in contact with graduates and graduates can contact with each others. That ought to be something that holds a lot of promise. Now, the semi-formal category, I think that students think back to conferences or informal workshops and dinners, and

I know some schools have done that with quite a bit of success That's an idea which has some potential. The formal category we've just heard from: programs that build into the master's where students finish the degree with what is an induction.

But I don't want to go left unnoticed. What strikes me as the most fertile ground to make a difference here is the first presentation that we heard about what has been done at Duke. Too many of its students were not staying in the schools, so Duke looked at what could be done to repair the program to address this issue and it seems to me that that's wide-open for us and all the things that they did, starting out with admissions, doing an overhaul of their coursework, diversifying the student population, doing a better job of advising in particular with regard to job possibilities and environments, proactive work and placement, all of these things have paid off.

I think we can look right at our own programs and think of ways in which we can enhance the success of our graduates so that they won't leave the profession. Most of those who leave because they weren't very successful at it, it wasn't much fun, and they didn't do very well, leave in the first few years. That's our fault for who we picked and how we prepared them and how well prepared they were. I'm not saying that it isn't part of the school's responsibility, but I think that the last point that was made is that we've got to do a better job with the principals in sensitizing them to the need to provide programs for beginning teachers. But, still, we're always trying to float these faults off on somebody else when the real issue is right in front of us and I think Duke and Ohio State have shown that and I think that's something we all ought to take to heart. There are things that we can do in our own programs to address the attrition of teachers.

Chapter Seven

Program Profiles

Wake Forest University Master Teaching Fellows Program

Representative: Joseph Milner

Program length: thirteen months, from the beginning of June to the beginning of July.
Financial assistance available: All students are awarded a Master Teaching Fellowship, which includes a full tuition scholarship and a $4,000 stipend. There are four minority student fellowships available, which include a full tuition scholarship and an $8,000 stipend.
Number of students admitted per year and their demographic makeup: Typically, there are roughly twenty-five graduate students in five disciplines. The cohort is predominantly white, with between zero and two minority students.

Disciplines included in the program: Secondary English, social studies, math, biology, chemistry, physics, K–12 Spanish, and K–12 French.

Number of education faculty members teaching in the program: six full time professors and adjunct faculty as needed for specific courses.

Admissions criteria and procedures: Applicants are asked to submit an application, GRE scores, recommendations, and a one-page personal statement. Education faculty, master teachers, faculty in the particular disciplines, and current students in the program are involved in the selection process. Finalists are asked to find someone who can conduct a video interview of them. Questions for the interview are sent to the applicant and must be opened by the chosen interviewer on camera.

Number of courses taken in the concentration area/academic discipline: three courses—two in the spring, and an additional course in the second summer. Students have an option of participating in an AP Institute in place of a traditional content course the second summer.

Number of research courses and a brief description: one research methods course, one educational research course. Students review a vast amount of educational research regarding various aspects of their discipline. They summarize and reflect upon the research in a journal. One educational research project (one semester).

Type of research project developed by students: In a semester-long course, students conduct educational research of interest to them. They work closely with a master teacher and their advisors to design and implement their research. The semester culminates in a paper, a five-page abstract, and a formal poster session and presentation open to all master teachers, education faculty, and the public. Education faculty and master teachers evaluate the students' work and the abstracts are published.

Teachers of the concentration area methods courses: Education faculty who have strong knowledge of the subject matter, solid pedagogical understanding, and experience in secondary teaching.

Duration of methods course: eighty hours within the five-week intensive "January block."

Required field work prior to student teaching: one semester class which entails approximately forty hours of classroom observations. Students rotate through all possible future teaching sites.

Student teacher supervisors: methods course professors.
Frequency of student teacher observations: once per week.
Others involved in supervision: Education graduate students sometimes methods course professors, where the number of student teachers exceeds five.
Duration of student teaching: ten weeks.
University teaching roles, titles, or compensation provided to secondary classroom teachers who serve as mentors to student teachers: Cooperating teachers are considered "Master Teachers" and are compensated with $1,500 for their input regarding the program's design.
Decision-making roles of secondary teachers: Master Teachers help with selection of candidates for the program. The department also asks for their input regarding the program's design.
Assistance to students in gaining employment: Job fairs and job openings are posted and announced. Students are also provided with web site addresses that could aid their search process. Career Services runs a workshop on the teacher job search and provides free dossier services. Advisors also work closely with students to help them secure a teaching position.
Percentages of students who enter teaching and who remain in the profession after five years: Virtually 100 percent of students entering teaching, and 60 to 70 percent remain after five years.

◆◆◆◆◆

Vanderbilt University

Representative: Charles B. Myers

Program length: Two years
Financial assistance available: Two one-half tuition scholarships per year, need-based aid, and possible teaching assistantships.
Number of students admitted per year and their demographic makeup: Two to five, no real pattern except from U.S.
Disciplines included in the program: English, history, mathematics, sciences, social studies, foreign language, Latin, classics.

Number of education faculty members teaching in the program: Many, depending on the courses the students take (potentially all graduate faculty in the disciplines listed above plus education).

Admissions criteria and procedures: Normal master's level admissions criteria—generally 3.00+ undergraduate GPA, GRE scores of 1100 or more, three strong letters of recommendation.

Number of courses taken in the concentration area/academic discipline: At least eighteen semester hours. (It is a thirty-six-hour degree program.)

Number of research courses and a brief description: No specific minimum is required; the actual number varies among the students.

Type of research project developed by students: No specific research project is required but many students register to do one.

Teachers of the concentration area methods courses: A professor of education in the field of concentration.

Duration of methods course: Three semester hours, one semester.

Required field work prior to student teaching: Various practica attached to education courses.

Student teacher supervisors: Professors of education and doctoral students in the field of concentration.

Frequency of student teacher observations: A minimum of one time per week.

Duration of student teaching: Fifteen weeks of full time in schools (in two sites).

University teaching roles, titles, or compensation provided to secondary classroom teachers who serve as mentors to student teachers: No official title. We call them "cooperating teachers." $100 per semester.

Decision-making roles of secondary teachers: They choose to accept the student teacher or not, and share in the evaluation, the assigning of the final grade, and the recommendation for state licensure.

Assistance to students in gaining employment: We make recommendations if asked, we watch for openings and make "connections." The University Career Center does most of this work.

Percentages of students who enter teaching and who remain in the profession after five years: Nearly all who complete the program with positive recommendations enter teaching. (And nearly all do finish with a positive recommendation.) Most remain for five years or more (I do not have exact figures. We do not separate the MAT students from education students on this question.)

University of Virginia
Curry School of Education

Representative: Margo A. Figgins

Program length: 5 years for the BA MT program; two years for the Postgraduate MT program.
Financial assistance available: UVA loans and work study grant aid and scholarships—a very small amount divided among program areas.
Number of students admitted per year and their demographic makeup: one male for every seventy-five females; 14 percent minority students; approximately 115 graduates per year.
Disciplines included in the program: Elementary, special education, secondary English, social studies, science, math, and foreign language, physical education.
Number of education faculty members teaching in the program: twenty-five.
Number of courses taken in the concentration area/academic discipline: Full academic majors plus graduate courses in the discipline from thirty-two to forty or more upper division credits, ten to fourteen courses.
Number of research courses and a brief description: Most of the teacher education courses are research-related.
Type of research project developed by students: A field project in he final semester.
Teachers of the concentration area methods courses: Specialists in the teaching areas, not generalists, in the Curry School.
Duration of methods course: Three semester-long courses per discipline.
Required field work prior to student teaching: two to four semesters of tutoring and practice teaching.
Student teacher supervisors: Tenured faculty and advanced graduate specialists in the teaching area.

Frequency of student teacher observations: six to ten times per semester.
Duration of student teaching: fifteen weeks
University teaching roles, titles, or compensation provided to secondary classroom teachers who serve as mentors to student teachers: Supervising teachers are titled "Clinical Instructors," paid $500 per student teacher, and receive some prerequisites like library and internet privileges. Some teach parts of the methods classes.
Decision-making roles of secondary teachers: They help with the Student Teaching Handbook, evaluate our students and supervisors, and serve on policy/program advisory boards
Assistance to students in gaining employment: We have a superior placement office. We write effective letters of recommendations, critique resumes, and network with colleagues and alumni for info on job openings.
Percentages of students who enter teaching and who remain in the profession after five years: 98 percent enter teaching; retention rates are unknown.

◆◆◆◆◆

University of Southern Maine

Representative: Richard H. Card, Extended Teacher Education Program (ETEP)

Program length: Nine months
Financial assistance available: The same assistance available to all graduate students is available to ETEP interns.
Number of students admitted per year and their demographic makeup: Ninety to ninety-five students are admitted annually. More than 95 percent are from Maine. The average age of the ETEP intern is approximately twenty-seven years old. Most have had some type of work experience outside of education, yet have had some experience working with children.
Disciplines included in the program: Interns come into the program with a BS, with a major in an academic area. The thirty-three credit hours comprising the program include discipline/content methods.

State certification requirements in the content areas must be met prior to admissions. Certification areas include: elementary (K–8), foreign languages (K–12), fine arts (K–12), and secondary (7–12) English, social studies, mathematics, life science, and physical science.

Number of education faculty members teaching in the program: eleven (six FTE).

Admissions criteria and procedures: There is a two-tiered admissions process. The candidates are accepted into the graduate program of the university in a traditional way by providing transcripts, references, GRE scores, etc. This makes candidates eligible for the program. In the second tier of the process candidates meet and are interviewed by teams of K–12 teachers and university faculty. If the K–12 teachers are unwilling to work with the candidates in their classrooms as a result of an unsatisfactory interview or file review, candidates have no school placement and are not admitted to the program.

Number of courses taken in the concentration area/academic discipline: Candidates must meet all state certification requirements regarding content/concentrations.

Number of research courses and a brief description: It varies by concentration and such courses are taught in the content or discipline undergraduate work. In the Extended Teacher Education Program itself, interns are required to complete an action research project related to a classroom dilemma they are facing.

Type of research project developed by students: Students are expected to become reflective in their practice of teaching. This is reinforced through an action research project in which interns select a puzzle to explore related to a dilemma each is facing in the classroom. An action research cycle is used to provide a systematic approach to the inquiry. Topics range from the exploration of discipline procedures, to homework completion strategies, to parent involvement, student engagement, or impacting disaffected youth. It is the expectation of the program that the graduates will develop and maintain a disposition for inquiring into the nature of teaching and learning.

Teachers of the concentration area methods courses: They are taught by a combination of university faculty and adjunct faculty who are our most insightful K–12 professional development school partners/practitioners.

Duration of methods course: Six credits (three fall, three spring).

Required field work prior to student teaching: A full semester of classroom internship in one of the program's partner professional development schools is required prior to the student teaching experience.

Student teacher supervisors: Student teachers are supervised by a team of ETEP coordinators and mentor teachers.

Frequency of student teacher observations: In a typical school site, the interns engage in twelve to fifteen full clinical supervisory cycles during a minimum of six weeks of full time teaching. The mentor teacher observes the intern on a daily basis.

Others involved in supervision: The team described above has at least two university faculty members. One is the site coordinator for the university. The other is the partner coordinator from the K–12 site. He or she works at least half time for the university in the ETEP position dedicated to the preparation of future teachers.

Duration of student teaching: A minimum of six weeks of full time teaching is required where the intern is responsible for all of the planning, instruction, assessment, parent conferencing, grading, etc. Much more time is spent preparing for the full-time load. Interns participate in mentor teacher classrooms at least half of the days during the fall semester and all day, every day, from January through May of the second semester.

University teaching roles, titles, or compensation provided to secondary classroom teachers who serve as mentors to student teachers: Secondary, middle school, and elementary teachers have the same role opportunities and compensation. Mentor teachers are paid $500 for a year of service as a mentor teacher. Teachers who co-teach university courses receive up to $500 depending on the nature of the instructional role. Teachers who are the primary faculty for coursework are considered "instructors" of the university and receive, depending upon credentials, up to $2,200 per course. All mentors have full access to the university facilities as adjunct faculty.

Decision-making roles of secondary teachers: As team members, teachers decide who is admitted to the program, and with which interns they will work. As team members they decide whether or not the intern with whom they work will become certified. Some school sites have faculty representatives on a steering committee which serves as a policy making body for the program. Decisions such as approval of mentor teachers, job descriptions, and site coordinator hiring are part of the steering committee responsibility.

Assistance to students in gaining employment: The program provides seminars in resume writing, interviewing, and portfolio development for the hiring process. In many sites mock interviews are held. Site coordinators and mentor teachers alike write letters of reference for any intern who asks. Hundreds of phone calls are made each year on behalf of the interns seeking employment.

Percentages of students who enter teaching and who remain in the profession after five years: Approximately 87 percent of the graduates enter teaching. We are in the process of gathering data regarding those who remain in or leave the profession.

◆◆◆◆◆

University of Richmond

Representative: Christopher Roellke

Program length: University of Richmond students: two semesters plus one summer session. Bachelor's Degree holders from other universities: four semesters plus one summer session.

Financial assistance available: two to three graduate assistantships per year for secondary M.T. students.

Number of students admitted per year and their demographic makeup: five to ten secondary M.T. students per year. Demographics reflect the student population at the university and the graduate School—91 percent white, 6 percent black, 2 percent Asian, 1 percent Hispanic.

Disciplines included in the program: Art, English, modern languages, mathematics, biology, chemistry, physics, social studies, health and physical education.

Number of education faculty members teaching in the program: Five full-time tenured or tenure-track faculty.

Admissions criteria and procedures: Undergraduate major in the liberal arts or equivalent, 3.0 grade point average, Graduate Record Examination.

Number of courses taken in the concentration area/academic discipline: Varies by endorsement area—students must satisfy licensure requirements in order to obtain the M.T. degree.

Number of research courses and a brief description: One research and analysis of teaching course is required. One research course in statistics and design is optional.
Type of research project developed by students: Curriculum analysis project, research report in educational policy/practice.
Teachers of the concentration area methods courses: Education faculty with the exception of modern languages.
Duration of methods course: A semester-long three- or four- credit course.
Required field work prior to student teaching: one observation laboratory in introductory course, one directed observation in educational psychology course, four weeks of intensive observation in student teaching context.
Student teacher supervisors: 90 percent adjunct faculty members, 10 percent full-time tenured or tenure-track faculty
Frequency of student teacher observations: At least seven separate visits during the ten-week student teaching experience.
Duration of student teaching: four weeks of observation, ten weeks of teaching.
University teaching roles, titles, or compensation provided to secondary classroom teachers who serve as mentors to student teachers: Cooperating teachers have no university teaching roles or titles. Cooperating teachers receive a $75 honorarium.
Assistance to students in gaining employment: Participation in early decision program, seminars with our Career Development Center.
Percentages of students who enter teaching and who remain in the profession after five years: Over 90 percent enter teaching and over 90 percent remain.

◆◆◆◆◆

University of North Carolina at Chapel Hill

Representative: William Palmer

Program length: one full year, starting second summer session.
Financial assistance available: none.

Chapter Seven: Program Profiles 237

Number of students admitted per year and their demographic makeup: Up to 120; 70 percent in state; 30 percent out of state.

Disciplines included in the program: Math, science, social studies, English (9–12), foreign languages and music (K–12).

Number of education faculty members teaching in the program: thirteen.

Admissions criteria and procedures: GRE scores, GPA scores, Purpose-of-intent statement, non-certified applicants only, and sometimes personal interviews.

Number of courses taken in the concentration area/academic discipline: We have a fifth-year program; hence, up to two maximum.

Number of research courses and a brief description: Some action research; no specific course (in progress).

Type of research project developed by students: Action research across these strands: context of learning, the learner and learning, and teaching methods.

Teachers of the concentration area methods courses: Different faculty in that particular area.

Duration of methods course: One course each semester, plus year-long clinical component.

Required field work prior to student teaching: Good to have, but none required.

Student teacher supervisors: Faculty in the specialty area.

Frequency of student teacher observations: Once a week.

Others involved in supervision: Some clinical appointments in content area with large student enrollment.

Duration of student teaching: Year-long graduated student teaching.

University teaching roles, titles, or compensation provided to secondary classroom teachers who serve as mentors to student teachers: We call our cooperating teachers clinical instructors and we appoint them to clinical status at UNC-CH. Minimum compensation at present.

Decision-making roles of secondary teachers: A lot. Most are members of our PDS sites and staff. They attend new MAT meetings and we attend their meetings to make our joint efforts a partnership.

Assistance to students in gaining employment: We try to arrange meetings and interviews with school personnel officers. Job fairs.

Percentages of students who enter teaching and who remain in the profession after five years: We do not know this data. I would venture this guess: 95 percent get jobs, 50 percent are in teaching after five years.

University of New Hampshire

Representative: Michael Andrew

Program length: There are two types of students entering the University of New Hampshire's Department of Education post-baccalaureate program. The first is the UNH undergraduates who have completed most of the six core education courses required for teacher licensure as part of their undergraduate education. These students can complete the thirty-credit master's program and the requirements for teacher certification in an academic year and one or two summers. The other type of student is either deciding to become a teacher in his or her undergraduate program or entering UNH from another university's undergraduate program. These students must complete the six core education courses, a full-year internship, and eight graduate credits. Usually these students take two years to complete the program.

Financial assistance available: Need- and merit-based aid is available to graduate students through the graduate school in the form of assistantships and tuition scholarships; and through the UNH financial aid office in the form of loans and the college work-study program. Several Excellence in Teaching Scholarships are awarded by the Department of Education each year to students who display potential for excellence as classroom graduate interns. Financial assistance may be available through paid internships, which represent a minority of the intern placement sites that are available. While stipends are not equal to full salaries, they often are enough to defray the costs of tuition and fees.

Number of students admitted per year and their demographic makeup: About 120 students are admitted each year to both secondary and elementary master's programs. About 85 of these represent 21–23 year olds who have just finished their undergraduate education. About twenty of these are from liberal arts institutions across the United States. The remainder are from UNH. About thirty-five are career change people, most of them are in the secondary level program.

Disciplines included in the program: Our program offers teacher certification at the secondary level in art, biology, chemistry, earth sciences, English, English as a second language, French, general science, general special education, German, Latin, mathematics, music, physical education, physics, Russian, social studies, and Spanish. At the elementary level, we require a subject discipline major other than education.

Number of education faculty members teaching in the program: Fourteen full-time faculty and a number of adjunct faculty serve as teachers in the program.

Admissions criteria and procedures: see essay detailing our program in this text for complete details.

Number of courses taken in the concentration area/academic discipline: Twelve credits, equaling three or four courses, are required in a graduate concentration area.

Number of research courses and a brief description: No research-related courses are required unless a student chooses a research thesis as a concluding experience.

Type of research project developed by students: The capstone experience for our fifth-year teacher education program consists of a concluding experience designed to involve a personal synthesis of course work, field experiences, and related literature and entail some form of research. The type of concluding experience is chosen in consultation with the student's advisor from among three choices: (1) development of a set of professional theses, followed by an oral examination; (2) a research thesis; (3) a project. All concluding experiences are initiated with a proposal, including a time line, which is approved by the student's official program advisor. Students working on concluding experiences can take advantage of group orientation and support group meetings sponsored by the teacher education faculty.

Teachers of the concentration area methods courses: Most of the methods courses are taught by the faculty members with an expertise in the particular subject area.

Duration of methods course: The secondary methods courses are one academic semester. Five methods courses are required for elementary teachers. Three of these are full-semester courses, two of these are half-semester courses.

Required field work prior to student teaching: The first education class in which students enroll, usually in their sophomore year or at the beginning of their post-BA experience, is called Exploring Teaching. The students are assigned a class that corresponds with their future certification. Students in Exploring Teaching spend sixty-five hours in local classrooms or in a university-run summer school to obtain realistic views of current classroom practices. These views provide a backdrop for students to explore what excellence in teaching means to them and edging the process of deciding whether or not to pursue a career in education. An important component of Exploring Teaching is assessment based on classroom performance: students reflect on their strengths, weaknesses, and predispositions with respect to teaching, and teachers and seminar leaders provide feedback to the students about their effectiveness in the classroom and in the seminar. The other field work students receive is in their methods courses. This experience usually entails observing a class, interviewing a teacher, and teaching a lesson.

Student teacher supervisors: Tenure-track faculty from the education department, adjunct faculty, graduate assistants, and teachers supervise the student teachers called interns.

Frequency of student teacher observations: Interns are observed a minimum of six times per semester by the university supervisor and several times a week by the cooperating teacher.

Others involved in supervision: Tenure-track faculty from other departments such as English, mathematics, and music also participate in supervision.

Duration of student teaching: Two semesters of full-time attendance, or thirty to thirty-two weeks, are required. Paid interns teach for the full school year.

University teaching roles, titles, or compensation provided to secondary classroom teachers who serve as mentors to student teachers: Elementary and secondary teachers who are called cooperating teachers receive $300 per year and a course tuition waiver to be used within the University of New Hampshire system. These experienced cooperating teachers often become part-time faculty within the education department and teach courses. The education department also hires one teacher each year to be our teacher-in-residence. This teacher teaches a full load and takes part in relevant committee meetings. This person's suggestions and comments from the field are taken seriously by the department faculty. Cooperating teachers who regularly teach within the teacher education program are also listed in the official teacher education program brochure.

Decision-making roles of secondary teachers: Some may serve on a "Unit Coordinating Board" which oversees teacher education at the university. Some serve on a school-university advisory group and most are involved in decisions about intern placement.

Assistance to students in gaining employment: Since the five-year program's inception in 1974 and in the MAT program begun in the 1960s, nearly 85 to 92 percent of our intern graduates have secured positions in teaching or a closely related field. As part of the weekly intern seminar in the spring, students are mentored in constructing resumes, writing cover letters, and interviewing techniques. These seminars form a job sharing informational network and the supervisors share job openings in their biweekly Supe Group meetings. Services of the career services office include an on-campus recruiting program of 250-plus corporate, government, and social service organizations. Individual career counseling, group career planning, testing, and a computerized career decision-making program are available for those involved in career planning. UNH is a member of a statewide consortium which sponsors a job bulletin newsletter for educators, the Teacher Information Service (TIS). The TIS is produced throughout the prime job search period of May through August. This consortium also hosts an educator's job fair each spring.

Percentages of students who enter teaching and who remain in the profession after five years: Eighty-five to 92 percent of our graduates enter teaching and about 80 to 85 percent of all graduates are still teaching in five years.

University of Maryland

Representative: Joseph L. McCaleb

Program length: One calendar year consisting of two regular terms and two summer terms. The program begins mid-July and finishes mid-July the following year.

Financial assistance available: We have no financial aid from the department or from the college. Our students compete, often very successfully, with other graduate students in the university for fellowships and grants. Many also secure loans with assistance from the campus financial aid office.

Number of students admitted per year and their demographic makeup: We prefer to limit the cohort size to about twenty-four students each year. Typically a number of persons to whom we offer admission do not end up in the cohort: some applicants are unable to secure the financial support they need, others do not satisfy the conditions of our offer (which may require them to complete prerequisite course work), and some have other reasons for a change of plans. We typically admit about thirty-five persons in order to have twenty-four who accept the admission offer and show up for classes in July. The demographics vary from year to year depending on the applicant pool. The average age is about twenty-eight and about 75 percent of the cohort is female. Minority representation has varied widely from one member of the cohort to as many as ten, averaging 24 percent over the past five years. 18 percent of the cohort members from the last five years have been African-American.

Disciplines included in the program: Roughly half of each cohort is preparing for elementary certification and the other half is split among these secondary certification areas: art, English, foreign language, math, science, social studies.

Number of education faculty members teaching in the program: Almost all of the classes are staffed by faculty from the College of Education. Persons being certified in secondary education may be taking one or two classes to complete their content preparation and these classes are taught by faulty in other colleges. About twenty-one faculty members are involved in teaching the thirty classes that are taken through the College of Education by one or more of the cohort members. In the approximately twelve classes that a particular cohort member will take during the year, he or she is likely to have ten different instructors.

Admissions criteria and procedures: Applicants are considered under the criteria used by the College of Education graduate programs which include: minimum undergraduate G.P.A. of 3.0, Graduate Record Examination or Miller's Analogy Test score average in the fortieth percentile, three letters of recommendation, and a statement of purpose written by the applicant. In addition to considering these, we conduct an interview with applicants who are considered finalists. Particular attention is given to the applicant's life experience for evidence of successful work with children. The applicant's transcripts are reviewed by content specialists to see if the appropriate subject matter has been completed. Based on these considerations top candidates are selected in each area and then program faculty decide on an appropriate balance of elementary and secondary, and on the six areas in secondary certification.

Number of courses taken in the concentration area/academic discipline: Persons admitted to the program are expected to have completed an undergraduate degree with a major in a relevant academic discipline. The Master's Certification Program only has allowance for one or two classes outside the College of Education.

Number of research courses and a brief description: All classes include study of appropriate theory and research and require scholarly projects and papers from the students. The program includes a class in quantitative methods and statistics, a class that reviews researching education, and an action research class. Through the program students complete at least one major review of literature, several structured analyses of teaching, and at least one seminar paper which reports their major action research project focused upon their own teaching.

Type of research project developed by students: The action research project is designed by the student with direction from professors in two or more classes and with assistance from field personnel. The student conducts the inquiry in his or her field placement with continuous reporting in an action research class, and culminating in a presentation to peers and school personnel. Attempts continue to connect these studies to the action research that is being done by teachers in the schools where field placements are done.

Teachers of the concentration area methods courses: For secondary teachers the cohort members enroll in the same special methods class that is taken by undergraduates and in a reading/writing across the curriculum class. Both are taught by regular members of the Department of Curriculum and Instruction. For elementary cohort members, the methods courses are taught by regular members of the Department of Curriculum and Instruction.

Duration of methods course: Methods courses are three-credit courses with the same time allowance as other courses (approximately three hours of class time each week for the sixteen-week semester).

Required field work prior to student teaching: Cohort members have a variety of field experiences prior to student teaching. In their first term which takes place during the summer session, students visit professional development centers for the school system where they will be teaching. They are placed with the person with whom they will probably be doing their student teaching prior to the beginning of the school year and participate with that teacher in the preparation for their first day of class. During the first week of school, the cohort member observes most or all of each day in order to collect information and to gain experience in this critical time in the life of classrooms. After the first week, the cohort member continues to observe and participate one day each week, first in the same school and later in a different school. Usually a provision is made for the cohort member to attend the field placement for a series of days in order to provide some continuous instruction which may range from three days to two weeks. The second placement is made to broaden the cohort member's range of experiences and grade levels. Usually he or she goes to a different school system and continues to do observations related to assignments given in the methods and research classes. Some university classes are offered in school setting and/or feature special trips to exemplary classrooms and schools.

Student teacher supervisors: Most supervision is done by the director of the professional development center in which the student teachers are placed. The director is affiliated with the school system and with the university. Often other university faculty members, particularly the director of the Master's Certification Program, observe during field experiences.

Frequency of student teacher observations: Student teachers are typically observed each week.

Others involved in supervision: The director of the Master's Certification Program typically visits most of the cohort during their field experiences.

Duration of student teaching: During the spring term, cohort members are in their full-time student teaching placement for about twelve weeks. They then have a shorter two- to three-week experience depending on their individual needs and interests which may involve additional teaching.

University teaching roles, titles, or compensation provided to secondary classroom teachers who serve as mentors to student teachers: Mentors are given compensation for the field experiences as negotiated by the College of Education's Office of Field Experiences. Also, during the summer terms of the Master's Certification Program, teachers who mentor cohort members during the regular terms are often asked to participate in the instruction. Compensation is negotiated depending on the number of presentations that are made. Major leadership in the summer terms has been done by classroom teachers who are also graduates of this program for about the past six years.

Decision-making roles of secondary teachers: Public school teachers participate in the governance committee for the PDS. Issues related to the structure of field experiences are presented and determined by this group. Mentor teachers participate in the placement and evaluation decisions regarding field experiences. Mentor teachers who provide instruction during the summer terms participate in decisions about that instruction and evaluation relative to the scope of their involvement. For example, when a mentor teacher has full responsibility for a class, he or she makes decisions comparable to those of a regular faculty member.

Assistance to students in gaining employment: Virtually all graduates of the program are employed as teachers. We assist them by requiring and assisting the preparation of a portfolio. We also bring in principals and other school personnel who employ teachers to brief them on interviewing. We arrange for some interviews and the university provides job fairs where they are able to make other contacts. In addition, we have available a very influential informal network of supervisors and administrators who promote graduates of this program. Teachers who have graduated from the program are also contacted and they offer consultation and sometimes leads for jobs.

Percentages of students who enter teaching and who remain in the profession after five years: Our data indicate that 95 percent of our graduates enter teaching. After five years we have less complete data but it appears that over 80 percent of them are still teaching.

Lewis and Clark College

Representative Gregory Smith

Program length: 14 to 15 months: two summer terms, fall and spring semesters.

Financial assistance available: Most students take out government loans to finance their participation in the program. We currently have five to six endowed scholarships, a handful of paid internships, and an arrangement with a national multicultural alliance and a private school to provide support for a small number of minority students.

Number of students admitted per year and their demographic makeup: If we were fully enrolled, forty students would be participating in our two elementary cohorts, and sixty students in our three secondary cohorts. The elementary program is almost always filled; the secondary program generally is short five or six students. We added a third cohort three years ago with the intention of focusing on middle school preparation, and the secondary program has not been fully enrolled since that time. We often have a waiting list of approximately ten to fifteen students to fill slots made vacant by successful applicants who choose to go elsewhere. This number, of course, varies from year to year. Most of our applicants are white, middle class, and in their mid-twenties to mid-thirties. For the first eleven years of the program, more than half of the applicants tended to be career changers in their thirties to fifties, with less than half being recent college graduates or people in their late-twenties. On average, we enroll approximately ten minority students each year across all cohorts.

Disciplines included in the program: In the secondary program, we offer licensure in language arts, social studies, mathematics, science, foreign languages (Spanish, German, French), art, and music. One of the elementary cohorts focuses on language and literature; the other, on science and technology.

Number of education faculty members teaching in the program: Sixteen full-time faculty members (eight tenure track, eight contract) and approximately a half dozen adjunct faculty members who teach one or two courses for us each year. A larger number of adjuncts teach subject area (six semester-hour requirement) or CORE (addresses issues that are relevant to all graduate school programs; four semester-hour requirement) courses, as well.

Admissions criteria and procedures: All applicants must possess a B.A. or B.S. in liberal arts or science. The elementary program requires its applicants to have experience working in schools as well as a strong and varied course of study as undergraduates. The secondary program favors applicants with extensive experience working with youth as well as experience with people from other cultural backgrounds. A strong subject-area background is essential for admission into the secondary program.

Number of courses taken in the concentration area/academic discipline: In the elementary program, required education courses focus on mathematics, language arts and reading, science, creative arts, social studies, and thematic inquiry. In the secondary program, students must take three courses in their concentration area/academic discipline at the master's level totaling six semester hours or more. More course work may be required on gaps in a candidate's undergraduate education.

Number of research courses and a brief description: In the secondary program, research activities are embedded in five classes: Literacy, Culture and Learning (fall); Teaching [specific subject area] to Adolescents (fall); Curriculum and Inquiry (spring, first eight weeks); Classroom Teaching and Learning II (spring); and Experience and Meaning (second summer). In the fall students write a case study about a student who is struggling with literacy issues using methodologies associated with qualitative research. In the spring, students must complete two inquiries into student learning to fulfill state of Oregon requirements for licensure (called work samples). These inquiries involve assessing student learning during a unit of two to five weeks in length, analyzing the link between this learning and what was taught, and proposing changes in curriculum and instruction aimed at enhancing achievement the next time the unit is taught. A final exercise in self-assessment is part of students' last education class, Experience and Meaning. In this inquiry, they must review their unit and lesson plans for the spring semester and reflect on their own decisions as novice teachers. Students in the elementary cohorts must write two work samples over the course of the program, take a course on assessment, and another on real world problem solving.

Teachers of the concentration area methods courses: These courses are taught by full-time faculty (language arts, social studies, science, music) and adjunct professors (art, foreign language, math). We work with adjuncts in disciplinary areas where enrollment numbers are small and vary significantly from year to year.

Duration of methods course: These are four-semester-hour courses that are taught in the fall semester. It is not uncommon for professors who teach these courses to meet informally with interns during the spring semester.

Required field work prior to student teaching: As part of the Adolescent Development class taught in the secondary program during the first summer, interns are required to spend a morning a week in an educational site that works with youth. In the fall, secondary interns are expected to spend six to eight hours a week at the placement site where they will eventually student teach.

Student teacher supervisors: Regular and adjunct faculty. We hire retired teachers and administrators to help with the task of supervision. In the secondary program, interns are matched with supervisors with extensive experience teaching in their subject area.

Frequency of student teacher observations: Supervisors are required to make six visits to the placement site from December to May; more visits are expected if the intern is experiencing problems.

Duration of student teaching: The state of Oregon requires fifteen weeks of student teaching. During nine of these, the intern must be in the school full-time. Secondary interns at Lewis & Clark are in the schools for a total of thirty-six weeks. Intensive student teaching begins in December when interns take responsibility for teaching a two to three week unit to one or two classes. In late January, they take responsibility for teaching one class for the remainder of the academic year. In mid-March, once two eight-week courses are completed on campus, interns are expected to spend the same amount of time as a contract teacher in their school site, taking on two and then three classes through the end of the academic year in mid-June. If interns work in schools where block classes (90 minutes in length) meet on a daily basis, they take on no more than two class assignments.

University teaching roles, titles, or compensation provided to secondary classroom teachers who serve as mentors to student teachers: Mentor teachers receive a $350 honorarium, one semester hour of continuing education credit for participation in mentor seminars (six scheduled over the academic year), a Lewis & Clark library card and e-mail account, and a voucher for a two to three semester-hour course at Lewis & Clark. A number of mentors over the years have taught content area classes during the summer.

Decision-making roles of secondary teachers: Participating teachers evaluate the program on an annual basis and make suggestions about a variety of domains: curriculum, scheduling, program emphasis. Their input is also actively sought throughout the year during mentor meetings.

Assistance to students in gaining employment: Lewis & Clark supports an educational placement service that provides information about available openings, résumé development, interview skills, etc. Nearly all of our graduates who seek employment are successful in their job searches.

Percentages of students who enter teaching and who remain in the profession after five years: Approximately 95 percent of our students enter teaching. After five years, approximately 75 percent remain in the profession.

Harvard Graduate School of Education/ Teacher Education Programs

Representative Vicki A. Jacobs

Program length: The length of our fifth-year Programs—the Teaching and Curriculum Program (TAC) and the MidCareer Math and Science Program (MCMS)—is nine and one-half months (beginning in the middle of August and ending during the third week of May).

Financial assistance available: The Harvard Graduate School of Education offers candidates financial aid in the form of grants, loans, and work study.

Number of students admitted per year and their demographic makeup: The Teaching and Curriculum program enrolls about 80 to 85 candidates annually, and the MidCareer Math and Science Program enrolls about ten to fifteen candidates annually. The Programs' minority enrollment is generally 35-45 percent. The average age of TAC candidates is about twenty-five; the average age of MCMS candidates is about thirty-five.

Disciplines included in the program: The TAC Program prepares candidates to teach in grades 9 through 12 in the fields of biology, chemistry, earth science, English, general sciences, history, mathematics, physics, and social studies. Preparation is also available at the grade 5 through 9 level in the fields of biology, earth science, English, general sciences, history mathematics, and social studies. Preparation at the grade 5 through 12 level is available in Latin and classical humanities and in world languages (Chinese, French, German, Hebrew, Italian, Japanese, Russian, and Spanish). The MidCareer Math and Science Program prepares candidates to teach in grades 9 through 12 in the fields of biology, chemistry, earth sciences, mathematics, and physics—and at the grade 5 through 9 level in the fields of geology, earth sciences, and mathematics.

Number of education faculty members teaching in the program: During the 1997-1998 academic year, ten different faculty members teach a total of ten required Programs' courses. Candidates are also required to take at least two electives—one of which must be a graduate-level course directly related to their teaching subject areas. These electives may or may not be taught by Programs' faculty.

Admissions criteria and procedures: The TAC Program emphasizes that candidates who have an intense interest in their subject matter make more enthusiastic, more creative, and more stimulating teachers. TAC candidates typically are recent liberal arts graduates who already possess in-depth knowledge of the subject they wish to teach. TAC applicants also include midcareer professionals (from such fields as law, publishing, media, and business) who wish to enter the teaching profession. Candidates who enroll in either the TAC or the MCMS Programs must hold a bachelor's degree with a liberal arts and sciences or interdisciplinary major. In addition, they must show evidence of having completed post-secondary course work or other experiences relevant to their teaching field as identified in the subject-matter knowledge requirements established by the Commonwealth of Massachusetts. The Harvard Graduate School of Education requires all applicants to submit an application, a personal statement, letters of recommendation, official transcripts from previous degree and other course work, and scores on either the MAT or the GRE. Applicants to the Teacher Education Programs fashion their personal statements in response to specific questions concerning teaching and learning that have been developed particularly for them.

Number of courses taken in the concentration area/academic discipline: Programs' candidates enroll in at least two courses related to the subject-areas of their certifications. One is a required Programs' course (i.e., Teaching English, Teaching History/Social Studies, Teaching Mathematics, Teaching Science, or Teaching World Languages). In addition, one of candidates' two electives must be a graduate-level course related to their teaching subject areas; most candidates enroll in a course offered by the Harvard faculty of arts and sciences.

Number of research courses and a brief description: All students enroll in "Teaching and Curriculum, II"—a course designed to support the Clinical Experience. One of the three central activities of this course is conducting a semester-long classroom-research project which is presented at a mini-research-conference at the end of the term. In addition, most candidates are engaged in ongoing research/study groups in their required Programs' subject-specific course. In research/study groups, candidates typically identify an aspect of teaching their subject area about which they would like to become more expert, develop extensive annotated bibliographies related to the topic, compile resources and commendable practices related to the topic, and design and conduct an in-service session with their colleagues to demonstrate and share their understanding.

Teachers of the concentration area methods courses: Currently, faculty with full-time and part-time appointments teach required Programs' courses. All are subject-matter specialists with appointments in the Graduate School of Education. Also, secondary-level practitioners can serve as "Associates in Education," co-teaching some of the courses. It should be noted that all of the required Programs' courses examine the translation of subject-matter knowledge into curriculum and practice.

Duration of methods course: All required Programs' courses meet for a full semester with the exception of the Summer Component which is an intensive, four-week course. One course is the equivalent of one-third of a full-time teaching position at Harvard.

Required field work prior to student teaching: The Commonwealth of Massachusetts requires a seventy-five-hour pre-practicum experience which Harvard candidates complete by observing, assisting, and/or co-teaching with their assigned teacher mentors. TAC and MCMS candidates complete their field work (as well as their practicum and clinical experience) with public high school or middle school, state-certified, experienced teachers who work in schools in the greater Boston area that belong to the Harvard School Partnership Network. This network includes about fifteen schools in seven urban and suburban school districts that vary in size, location, and ethnic and social distribution. Candidates have an opportunity to observe at least one school site different from the one to which they are otherwise assigned.

Student teacher supervisors: Practica and clinical experiences are supervised jointly by teacher mentors and university supervisors. university supervisors, hired by the Harvard Teacher Education Programs, are usually Harvard doctoral candidates (who have had teaching and/or supervisory experience); experienced classroom teachers (who, for various reasons, are not presently teaching full-time); or currently practicing teachers who are participating in the Programs' on-site supervisory effort. The criteria for selection of these individuals includes experience with clinical supervision, direct knowledge of teaching with experience in particular subject areas at particular grade levels, the ability to fulfill requirements of site visitations and attend various meetings, and the interpersonal skills to perform the supervisory role.

Frequency of student teacher observations: University supervisors are expected to have eleven contacts with each of the interns during the academic year; eight of these are observations. Most generally, the university supervisor's primary responsibility is to be a resource and support for interns during their fall-term practicum and spring-term clinical experience. Because supervisors meet with their interns only about once a month, the supervisor's role is meant to be supplementary to that of the teacher mentor. Interns should expect the most support and guidance from their teacher mentors.

Others involved in supervision: Each Harvard partnership school is paired with a Programs' representative (administrator and/or faculty member) who visits each of his or her schools about once a month as a "liaison." Liaisons serve as official links between the schools and the Programs—soliciting schools' concerns and needs in an effort to strengthening the Harvard/School Partnership Network. While the role of liaison does not include the formal observation of interns, liaisons usually check in with interns during their visits. Further, faculty who teach the course that accompanies the clinical experience are usually the liaisons at the schools in which their students are completing their field work.

Duration of student teaching: During the 1997-1998 academic year, during the fall term, TAC and MCMS candidates fulfilled the Commonwealth of Massachusetts' requirements for a 75-hour pre-practicum and 150-hour practicum by spending two full days, per week (from September 4 through January 16) and every day (January 20 through January 26). In the spring, candidates fulfill requirements for a 408-hour clinical experience over 13.5 weeks (from January 27 through May 15).

University teaching roles, titles, or compensation provided to secondary classroom teachers who serve as mentors to student teachers: The Harvard Teacher Education Programs provide each full-time teacher mentor with a voucher (which can be used to enroll in most Harvard courses); library privileges at the Graduate School of Education's Gutman Library; Professional Development points, and an honorarium of $250. The Programs also encourage teacher mentors to participate in On-site Seminars (as described below). In addition, practitioners from Partnership schools can play other central roles. For example, practitioners provide (and are remunerated for providing) professional assistance as "Associates in Education," guest lecturers, and curricular resource in course, required programs' course work; school-based practitioners teach or co-teach some of the Programs' required course work; and school-based faculty lead focus groups on middle-grade and urban education. On-site, school based faculty serve as university supervisors (as well as teacher mentors) and as On-site Seminar leaders (developing and implementing a series of sessions for interns to focus on the nature of their particular school and the community in which it resides).

Decision-making roles of secondary teachers: Faculty and staff from the Harvard Programs and from partnership schools meet together several times a year. For example, the Programs annually host a series of teacher mentor dinners to review the Programs' and the partnerships' hopes and work and to examine relevant educational issues; Programs' administrators and school liaisons, department heads, and school contacts meet similarly; the Programs sponsor a half-day conference and reception for faculty in partnership schools to examine an issue of current educational interest (with a nationally recognized speaker); and partnership leaders meet annually to consider with each other and with national leaders facets of educational reform which they would like to inform the partnership. Finally, practitioners are represented on the Teacher Education Programs' Advisory Board.

Assistance to students in gaining employment: Candidates can seek employment through the Graduate School of Education's Career Services Office (which offers candidates workshops—in part, in coordination with the Programs) and through direct referrals from the Programs in response to inquiries from our partnership schools and from schools which have previously hired our graduates (which, since 1985, number well over 1,000). Candidates also develop professional portfolios in required Programs' course work which they are encouraged to use during interviews.

Percentages of students who enter teaching and who remain in the profession after five years: Roughly 80 to 90 percent of each year's graduates enter teaching; virtually all who want to teach are able to procure jobs. Roughly 80 percent of our graduates at any one time are teaching. In previous studies, we have found that patterns of employment vary for our graduates. Some candidates enter teaching and remain teaching; others wait to teach and then enter and remain in teaching; others teach, leave teaching, then return. Those who leave teaching often enter doctoral work in education or engage in other education-related work.

Cornell University

Representative Susie Slack

Program length: Master of Arts in Teaching is a combined undergraduate/graduate program five years. As a graduate program for students earning degrees at other institutions it is three or four semesters.

Financial assistance available: Limited tuition for students who are under-represented in teaching

Number of students admitted per year and their demographic makeup: Each student teaching cohort is twenty-five students—preference is given first to CU undergrads and then remaining slots are filled with graduate students.

Disciplines included in the program: chemistry, physics, biology, earth science, mathematics, agriculture.

Number of education faculty members teaching in the program: eight not including foundations professors.

Admissions criteria and procedures: Prior teaching experience, formal or informal, around a three point average, an essay on how they might teach a certain concept, and an interview.

Number of courses taken in the concentration area/academic discipline: a major.

Number of research courses and a brief description: portfolio for student teaching, curriculum analysis course.

Type of research project developed by students: some are teaching assistants in other departments.

Teachers of the concentration area methods courses: education faculty.

Duration of methods course: fifteen credits. It meets for two weeks full days and two hours each Thursday during the student teaching semester.

Required field work prior to student teaching: four to six hours in two core courses—Knowing and Learning in Science, Math and Agriscience, Observing and Teaching Science, Math, and Agriscience.

Student teacher supervisors: Faculty, extension associate, and a senior lecturer all full-time employees.

Frequency of student teacher observations: six visits with four detailed write ups on observations.

Others involved in supervision: One TA assigned to the program as a Ph.D. student.

Duration of student teaching: Ten to twelve weeks.

University teaching roles, titles, or compensation provided to secondary classroom teachers who serve as mentors to student teachers: Teachers are provided a $300 honorarium.

Decision-making roles of secondary teachers: We depend on them heavily for day-to-day decisions with our student teachers. Invited to campus during the two week session prior to student teaching.

Assistance to students in gaining employment: We belong to a consortium of thirteen colleges and universities in central New York that hosts a two day job fair in the spring, the college maintains a JOBTRAK, we keep descriptions of the districts that have attended the last three job fairs, include a seminar on résumé writing and conducting a good interview.

Percentages of students who enter teaching and who remain in the profession after five years: 100 percent enter. In our short history of ten years approximately 70 percent. Some have gone on to Ph.D. programs.

◆◆◆◆◆

Duke University

Representative Rosemary Thorne

Program length: One full year, from July 1 until June 30.

Financial assistance available: Varies from none to full tuition. Most students who demonstrate financial need receive scholarships equivalent to fifteen units of tuition (in a thirty-six-unit program).

Number of students admitted per year and their demographic makeup: The MAT program at Duke is limited by the Board of Trustees to a class size of twenty-five. Our typical class size is eighteen. The typical MAT student is a twenty-three-year-old year old white female. We have under-representation of minority groups, and a slight under-representation of males. In this year's class there are two African-Americans and one Asian student.

Disciplines included in the program: Biology, English, mathematics, mathematics/physics, general science, social studies. We also offer a joint degree program with Duke's Nicholas School of the Environment (Master of Arts in Teaching/Masters of Environmental Management) and, in rare circumstances, an MAT en route to the Ph.D.

Number of education faculty members teaching in the program: No tenured Duke education faculty serve as teachers in the program. Since Duke's efforts in education are small, most of our faculty are adjunct. Regular rank arts and sciences faculty serve as disciplinary advisors to students, and also serve as members of students' masters' committee.

Admissions criteria and procedures: In addition to the PRAXIS exams required by the state, the university requires GRE scores (general only), transcripts, three letters of recommendation, a statement, and an interview with the director and the member of the faculty advisory committee in the student's major field. The interview committee makes recommendations to the faculty advisory committee, which in turn makes recommendations to the dean of the graduate school. The dean reviews the files of all applicant recommended for admission.

Number of courses taken in the concentration area/academic discipline: Six.

Number of research courses and a brief description: No research courses in education are required. Most students do independent research which combines pedagogy and their teaching discipline as part of the six courses in their major field of study. For example, this semester one student is investigating North Carolina environmental policy and the ways in which that policy can be presented in the AP Biology curriculum; another student is exploring mathematical problem solving as it is taught at the university level and its implication for using a process approach in high school mathematics instruction; a group of English and History MAT students are analyzing appropriate texts and appropriate strategies for teaching world literature and world history through an interdisciplinary approach; another student, working across the Departments of Cultural Anthropology, Sociology, History and Religion, is investigating the search for meaning which she believes should inform the teaching of history.

Type of research project developed by students: Students are required to investigate the effectiveness of special education services at their host school and to compare their findings to best practice. The MAT program, however, is not essentially a research oriented program. All students complete portfolios which are both formative, showing growth over time, and summative, demonstrating their best teaching practices. The portfolio must also demonstrate how students transformed knowledge through their graduate level disciplinary courses for high school students.

Teachers of the concentration area methods courses: Adjunct faculty from: the Duke mathematics department; Durham public schools; and the North Carolina School of Science and Mathematics

Duration of methods course: The course is a three-unit summer school course taken prior to the internship. After students begin their full-year internship, they meet with their subject-area methods instructors several additional times during both first and second semester.

Required field work prior to student teaching: None.

Student teacher supervisors: The director, methods instructors, and a cohort of mentor teachers hired and trained by the program.

Frequency of student teacher observations: Varied, but all student teachers are observed at least weekly.

Others involved in supervision: Arts and sciences faculty who are appointed by the dean of the graduate school to serve on the MAT advisory committee provide some supervision for students.

Duration of student teaching: Twenty-eight.

University teaching roles, titles, or compensation provided to secondary classroom teachers who serve as mentors to student teachers: Mentors in the MAT program are designated instructors by the dean of the graduate school. They are paid $2,500 per year, and they are offered opportunities for continued professional development through the university. For example, MAT offers workshops on technology and its uses in the secondary classroom, effective discipline strategies, conducting Paideia seminars, cooperative learning, mentor training, and so on. Some mentor teachers are invited by arts and sciences faculty to develop curriculum that bridges secondary and post-secondary teaching. On occasion MAT mentors are invited to team teach a course at the university (for which they receive additional compensation). MAT mentors are also invited to participate in research and research grants with Duke faculty.

Decision-making roles of secondary teachers: Mentor teachers sat on the original committee which designed this version of the MAT program, and continue to sit on the MAT faculty advisory committee. Teachers selected to be mentors at Duke are given enormous responsibility within the program. Mentors meet with the director as a group three times during the year, and individually on an ongoing basis. All decisions about the direction, curriculum, and changes within the program are either initiated by the mentor teachers or approved by them. For example, when the university dictated that all master students, including MAT students, must complete a master's project, the mentor teachers determined that the most appropriate project would be a portfolio. Mentor teachers demanded the program include more full-time teaching as opposed to the half-day only requirement originally in place. Mentors provide an advising role to students as well, in all areas from course selections at Duke through job search.

Assistance to students in gaining employment: During the initial years of MAT, which was established in 1989, our placement record was good, but out graduates' staying power was bad. We determined that helping students make appropriate choices for their initial teaching years was critically important to keeping them in the classroom. We have, therefore, taken a very active role in helping students find positions that will be a good fit. The university has a career development counselor designated to help teachers. Students in MAT typically see her during the first semester. During first semester the director meets with each mentor/intern team to discuss placement. The mentor and director provide advice to the intern on the kind of school and classroom in which the student will likely be most successful. If that advice does not meet the students' vision of where he or she would like to be teaching, the mentor and director discuss with the student the ways in which the internship can be structured to best prepare the student. For example, during first semester this year, an MAT student expressed his desire to teach in inner-city schools in Washington, D.C. to his mentor and the director. To make sure he was prepared for that kind of career, the mentor and director jointly decided to switch his internship from a suburban high school to an inner-city school. Immediately prior to winter break, students are given a twenty-page packet on job search, with assignments they must complete over break. During the first week after break, students complete two workshops: one on the job search and one on completing resumes. The director then meets with each student individually and determines which parts of the country, which school systems, and which specific schools the student will apply to. The director offers to make personal contacts with each principal or school system to which the student is applying. Over the years we have established good relationships with a number of school systems around the country, and they welcome our graduates upon our recommendation.

Percentages of students who enter teaching and who remain in the profession after five years: Since its inception in 1989, about 75 percent of MAT graduates have entered the classroom after graduation. About 55 percent of those who did enter the classroom remain there. Our statistics in recent years are much better.

Brown Universtiy

Representatives: Larry Wakeford, Eileen Landay

Program length: twelve Months—starts in June, ends the following May.

Financial assistance available: We offer tuition scholarships and proctorships. A proctorship involves work within the education department. The average award for students is a sum equivalent to approximately one-half of the total tuition of $22,000.

Number of students admitted per year and their demographic makeup: twenty-five to thirty are admitted each year in three disciplines—English, history, and biology. We average twice as many females as males. Minorities generally total 20 percent.

Disciplines included in the program: English, history/social studies, biology.

Number of education faculty members teaching in the program: Three full-time clinical faculty are the principal teachers. One other education faculty member teaches a required course. Other education faculty teach the foundations courses which the students elect.

Admissions criteria and procedures: There are no special selection criteria. We are trying to attract students interested in urban education and, therefore, give some preference to candidates who express an interest in urban schools.

Number of courses taken in the concentration area/academic discipline: Four.

Number of research courses and a brief description: Only the biology students are required to take a research course. This entails a semester course of independent study with a biology researcher.

Type of research project developed by students: As part of the student teaching experience, all students are required to design "A Personal Inquiry" which involves identifying a question about teaching and learning which they investigate throughout the semester and give a final presentation to university faculty, cooperating teachers, and peers.

Teachers of the concentration area methods courses: Each clinical professor teaches his or her respective course. Since this is taught during the summer, local teachers who are involved in our summer program also share in the teaching.

Duration of methods course: It takes place over the seven weeks of the summer session and amounts to fifty hours, plus the forty hours of teaching in Brown Summer High School and the debriefing after each session with mentors.

Required field work prior to student teaching: Most students admitted to the program have done some work with adolescents in a school setting. Brown summer High School provides forty hours of teaching.

Student teacher supervisors: The three clinical professors and the cooperating teachers.

Frequency of student teacher observations: Clinical faculty observe four to six times. Cooperating teachers are expected to do two formal observations per week.

Duration of student teaching: thirteen weeks.

University teaching roles, titles, or compensation provided to secondary classroom teachers who serve as mentors to student teachers: Presently, the only recognition or compensation is $150.

Decision-making roles of secondary teachers: At present, the secondary teachers do a final evaluation of our students. Their assessment is taken into account as to whether a student passes, but the final decision is the university supervisor.

Assistance to students in gaining employment: The university does have a Career Planning office to assist. We have developed a network with Coalition of Essential Schools which hire a number of our graduates each year.

Percentages of students who enter teaching and who remain in the profession after five years: Greater than 90 percent enter teaching. We do not have a good estimate of the retention rate after five years.

Agnes Scott College

Representative Dr. Ruth S. Bettandorff

Program length: fourteen months for students with bachelors, in English.

Financial assistance available: Graduate students are charged one-half of undergraduate tuition and then are eligible for federal loans if qualified.

Number of students admitted per year and their demographic makeup: We admit approximately twenty students. 90 percent are full-time; 10 percent are part-time. 90 percent are women; 80 percent are white; 15 percent are African American; 5 percent are other, 60 percent are ages twenty to thirty; 25 percent are ages thirty-one to fifty; and 15 percent are over fifty; 20 percent are Agnes Scott graduates; 100 percent are U.S. citizens.

Disciplines included in the program: English; biology is being planned.

Number of education faculty members teaching in the program: four to five.

Admissions criteria and procedures: Minimum of 2.75 undergraduate GPA, interview with faculty committee, review of portfolio of writing samples, three letters of reference

Number of courses taken in the concentration area/academic discipline: nine.

Number of research courses and a brief description: No specific courses designated as research, however research components are embedded throughout.

Type of research project developed by students: No set project done by all; a variety of research projects in literature and pedagogy are done in various classes.

Teachers of the concentration area methods courses: A part-time faculty member with a degree in English education.

Duration of methods course: This is a four-hour course taught in fall semester. It includes classroom observation.

Required field work prior to student teaching: Classroom observation is required in the methods course.

Student teacher supervisors: Supervisors are Ph.D. level part-time faculty with backgrounds in English education; faculty from the English department also do occasional observations of each student.

Frequency of student teacher observations: Students are observed a minimum of three times by a supervisor (and more often if warranted) plus one or two times by English department faculty.

Others involved in supervision: Faculty from the English department.

Duration of student teaching: ten weeks.

University teaching roles, titles, or compensation provided to secondary classroom teachers who serve as mentors to student teachers: The classroom teachers are called Master Teachers but are not given compensation or instructor rank.

Decision-making roles of secondary teachers: The secondary teacher is basically in charge of the classroom experience and schedule and provides an evaluation of that experience which is counted as part of the grade. The college supervisor works closely with the classroom teacher to identify strategies for helping individuals and in resolving any problems.

Assistance to students in gaining employment: Mostly through the Career Planning and Counseling Center, which meets with all students, does mock interviews and résumé writing. School systems conduct interviews on campus. Often the Office of Graduate Studies or the Education department will receive calls about open positions which are passed on to students. Many students are placed at the schools where they do student teaching.

Percentages of students who enter teaching and who remain in the profession after five years: Approximately 95 percent enter teaching; we do not have data on percent remaining after five years since this program started in 1992 and that follow-up has not been conducted yet.

Furman University

Representatives: Hazel Harris and Leslie Quast

Program length: four years, typically. Students are increasingly choosing to extend their programs into the fifth year.

Financial assistance available: South Carolina has a teacher loan program that many students apply for and receive. Three scholarships are available through the Education department.

Number of students admitted per year and their demographic makeup: approximately eighty-five, primarily undergraduate.

Disciplines included in the program: English, art, drama, music, mathematics, chemistry, biology, physics, Spanish French, German, Latin, political science, sociology, history, physical education, elementary, early childhood, special education.

Number of education faculty members teaching in the program: eight.

Admissions criteria and procedures: 2.5 GPA, references from faculty in major and introductory education courses, basic skills assessment, supervised writing sample.

Number of courses taken in the concentration area/academic discipline: eight to eleven.

Number of research courses and a brief description: None required yet—elective as a collaborative effort with Furman Advantage or Undergraduate Research program with faculty sponsor.

Teachers of the concentration area methods courses: some taught within the academic discipline (languages, physical education, music). Others taught by education faculty with teaming by master teachers in discipline.

Duration of methods course: four credit hours (eight for English and languages).

Required field work prior to student teaching: Incorporated into three courses (tutoring, observation, whole-class teaching).

Student teacher supervisors: Team supervised by education and discipline specific faculty.

Frequency of student teacher observations: weekly.

Others involved in supervision: other education or discipline specific faculty as needed.

Duration of student teaching: fifteen weeks (three at the beginning of school, twelve during the fall or spring).

University teaching roles, titles, or compensation provided to secondary classroom teachers who serve as mentors to student teachers: Voucher for three-hour graduate course.

Decision-making roles of secondary teachers: secondary teachers from our professional development school actively participate in planning and improvements.

Assistance to students in gaining employment: we host an Education Career Day with thirty to sixty districts represented, and we work closely with local district personnel and principals.

◆◆◆◆◆

Trinity University

Representative John H. Moore

Program length: Trinity University features a five-year teacher education program. Students receive the Bachelor of Arts or Bachelor of Science degree at the conclusion of their undergraduate course of study and the Master of Arts in Teaching at the successful conclusion of the fifth year.

Financial assistance available: Financial assistance is available to students during their undergraduate studies and Interns in Teaching during the graduate fifth year on both a need and merit basis. Financial packages on average range from $2,000 to $12,000 per year.

Number of students admitted per year and their demographic makeup: Students apply to the teacher education program during the sophomore or junior year, and each year the Department of Education admits forty to fifty students to matriculate in the fifth year. Trinity students are recruited from across the nation and abroad, and approximately 20 percent of the population is minority.

Disciplines included in the program: Students pursuing elementary education major in the humanities, and students in secondary education choose from approximately twenty disciplines taught in the public or private schools.

Number of education faculty members teaching in the program: Eight full-time faculty from Trinity University are engaged in the teacher education program. In addition, each year approximately fifty classroom teachers from the professional development schools are appointed to serve on the clinical faculty as mentors to fifth year Interns in Teaching.

Admissions criteria and procedures: Admission criteria for the fifth year includes the successful completion of three practicum experiences in the professional development schools. Classroom teachers in these schools are involved in the assessment and admission process.

Number of courses taken in the concentration area/academic discipline: Students in secondary education complete a major consisting of thirty to thirty-six semester hours in the discipline(s) they will teach. Students in elementary education complete a thirty-six-semester-hour major in the humanities.

Number of research courses and a brief description: A specific research class is not required, but the topic is discussed in several courses during the fifth year.

Type of research project developed by students: Fifth-year Interns in Teaching complete a research project during the fall semester and share findings with interns, mentors, and other interested persons from the schools and school districts.

Teachers of the concentration area methods courses: Mentor teachers from the professional development schools and clinical faculty from Trinity University teach methods as part of the eight-month internship during the fifth year.

Duration of methods course: Methods of teaching are included during the eight-month internship scheduled the fifth year. The courses and the internship provide the Interns in Teaching with a balance of theory and practice.

Required field work prior to student teaching: Three practicum courses are required prior to the fifth-year eight-month internship. Students are in the professional development schools for approximately forty-five clock hours a semester for each practicum course.

Student teacher supervisors: Interns in Teaching are supervised by mentor teachers and clinical faculty from Trinity University during the eight-month internship

Frequency of student teacher observations: mentor teachers are with interns daily, and clinical faculty from Trinity are on site at the professional development schools virtually every day.

Others involved in supervision: Interns in Teaching are supervised only by mentor teachers and university clinical faculty.

Duration of student teaching: Interns in Teaching complete an eight-month internship.

University teaching roles, titles, or compensation provided to secondary classroom teachers who serve as mentors to student teachers: Each year Trinity University officially appoints some fifty classroom teachers to the clinical faculty and they serve as mentors to the Interns in Teaching. Mentor teachers are not paid, but Trinity provides a variety of professional development opportunities to them.

Decision-making roles of secondary teachers: Mentor teachers in the professional development schools are partners in the teacher education program at Trinity University. The teachers play a significant role in planning, implementing, and assessing the program.

Assistance to students in gaining employment: Trinity has a 100 percent placement rate for graduates seeking positions in teaching. The Department of Education has a placement office, and the clinical faculty and the chair are actively involved in assisting students secure teaching positions.

Percentages of students who enter teaching and who remain in the profession after five years: Currently more than 90 percent of Trinity's graduates enter the teaching profession and a high percent are teaching or in related positions after five years.

◆◆◆◆◆

Rice University, Master of Arts in Teaching Program

Representative Lissa Heckelman

Program length: The program lasts one academic year for course work, one summer of student teaching in the Rice University Summer School for Middle and High School Students, and one semester of full time intern teaching in a local accredited school in which the student has been offered employment.

Financial assistance available: Two full tuition remissions are usually divided among four students.

Number of students admitted per year and their demographic makeup: We have no limit on the number of graduate students admitted; usually we have six to twelve MAT students. We normally have one or two under-represented minority students, and one or two males.

Disciplines included in the program: Art, biology, chemistry, computer science, earth science, economics, English, French, geology, German, health sciences, history, Latin, mathematics, mathematical science, physical education, physical science, physics, political science, psychology, Russian, science (composite), social studies (composite), and Spanish.

Number of education faculty members teaching in the program: All four tenured or tenure track professors serve as teachers. The summer school director also serves as lecturer in education.

Admissions criteria and procedures: Applicants submit a completed application, including one essay, a statement of intent, GRE scores, and four letters of reference. All applications are reviewed by at least three, but usually four, members of the department.

Number of courses taken in the concentration area/academic discipline: Graduate students must complete thirty-three semester hours of upper division credit to earn the MAT and a Texas state teaching certificate. Eighteen of those hours, twelve hours of academic courses and six hours of student teaching, are required for certification. The remainder of the hours are completed for advanced preparation in the academic discipline and/or to learn more about the students in the schools of the surrounding area, including research, underrepresented minority literature and culture, and language courses.

Number of research courses and a brief description: Students are required to take "Fundamentals of Secondary Education" which involves a substantial group research report based on extensive observations in a selected urban school. Another course, "Studies in Teaching and Learning," is an optional course dealing with ethnographic research methods.

Type of research project developed by students: The Master of Arts in Teaching degree is a non-thesis degree, so research is completed in class. In "Fundamentals of Secondary Education" the students work together to create a portrait of a given urban high school, using ethnographic research methods to gather their data.

Teachers of the concentration area methods courses: Professors in the education department teach the majority of the methods courses. One professor from the human performance department teaches a section of the physical education methods course, and occasionally master teachers who are experienced with our student teaching program have been hired to teach a section of a course when a professor is on leave.

Duration of methods course: By Texas state law, the course is three semester hours. Students, however, may spend much more time than is represented by the number of course hours. They are creating curriculum for teaching in the Rice Summer School for Middle and High School Students while mastering the fundamentals of teaching methods.

Required field work prior to student teaching: Pre-student teaching field work includes the research described above and a total of forty-five observation hours in local schools.

Student teacher supervisors: Primary responsibility for supervision, during the summer school and during the internship, lies with the director of summer school. Professors of the discipline-specific-methods sections and the principal of summer school supervise summer classes as time allows. We also hire master teachers to supervise student teachers during summer school.

Frequency of student teacher observations: Master teachers observe and provide written reflective feedback to student teachers daily during the six weeks of Summer School. Rice faculty and the Principal visit each student teacher at least once during Summer School and the Director observes at least twice. During the internship, the Director observes each student at least once every three weeks during the semester.

Others involved in supervision: Only faculty who have taught the discipline-specific methods during the spring semester formally supervise the student teachers.

Duration of student teaching: Six weeks of summer school and one semester of internship are required.

University teaching roles, titles, or compensation provided to secondary classroom teachers who serve as mentors to student teachers: Secondary classroom teachers who supervise student teachers are hired by the university as Master Teachers. They receive compensation based on teaching responsibilities and experience with the summer school. The average salary is approximately $3,800.

Decision-making roles of secondary teachers: the secondary teachers participate in deciding whether a student teacher will be allowed to pursue an internship. We require all students to produce a portfolio during the summer school and secondary teachers serve on the review committees that approve the portfolios, thus playing a role in whether or not each student passes the course. Though the secondary teachers provide much input, the final decision for each of these rests with the university faculty.

Assistance to students in gaining employment: Finding a job is the student's responsibility, but we help by alerting the schools to the fact that our students are interested in their positions, announcing job openings weekly, writing references, and advising students during their searches.

Percentages of students who enter teaching and who remain in the profession after five years: All of our MAT students enter teaching since they must do so to complete the internship. We are currently surveying to find out what percentage remain after five years. We estimate that the number will be close to 65 percent. Many have returned to graduate school to seek administrative credentials and others have temporarily left the job market for health reasons, to raise families, or to seek teaching positions in new areas.

◆◆◆◆◆

Stanford University
Stanford Teachers Education Program (STEP)

Representative: Beverly Carter and David Fetterman

Program length: The length of the STEP Program is one calendar year from mid-June to mid-June. During the year, students earn an A.M. degree in Education, a California Single Subject Clear Professional Teaching Credential, and a possible CLAD Emphasis.

Financial assistance available: We offer approximately fifteen fellowships of from $3,000 to $5,000 each. Some teaching internships may be available for qualified students. (Students are limited to not more than one internship period paired with a student teaching period.)

Number of students admitted per year and their demographic makeup: The number of students admitted ranges from a high of eighty-two admitted in 1994-95 to fifty-eight admitted in 1997-98. The demographics of the group for 1997-98 include: By gender: Female 46 Male 12. By ethnicity: African American, 5 percent; Asian American, 12 percent; Mexican American, 12 percent; Other Hispanic, 5 percent; Caucasian, 57 percent; Undetermined, 9 percent.

Disciplines included in the program: English, foreign language, math, science, social studies.

Number of education faculty members teaching in the program: thirteen tenure line professors, including ten full professors (of a total of thirty-eight in the School of Education). Ten lecturers, all of them experienced teachers. Seven of these are current teachers. Two advanced graduate students who are experienced teachers and are preparing to become teacher educators.

Admissions criteria and procedures: Academic preparation—rigor and quality of the candidates undergraduate and graduate study. Subject matter preparation--applicant's ability to understand the subject matter for teaching. GRE Scores—Stanford School of Education has no minimum score requirement. CBEST (California Test of Basic Educational Skills)—passing scores required of all California candidates before admission. Out of state candidates may defer until the June administration. SSAT & PRAXIS or California Subject Matter Waiver Program—candidate must have passed one or more of the exams in its entirety or must have completed 80 percent of a subject matter waiver program before he or she may be admitted to STEP. Commitment to teaching—clarity, cohesion, and linkage between past experience, proposed teaching area, and future career plans. Match between candidate's interests and STEP goals. Interpersonal skills—candidate's ability to work in groups, to show leadership potential, to interact successfully with diverse individuals. Experiences (professional and other)—volunteer and/or paid positions with adolescents and young people (especially those that involve working with groups). Contribution to diversity and cross-cultural awareness—the candidate's potential contribution through diversity to STEP's educational program as well as his or her commitment to working in a diverse environment.

Number of courses taken in the concentration area/academic discipline: The design of the STEP program assumes that students will have met at least 80 percent of the requirements for subject matter competence before entering the program. Although students may take any course for which they qualify within Stanford University, most do not elect to take subject matter courses.

Number of research courses and a brief description: All of STEP courses endeavor to blend research and practice. We do not make a distinction between research related courses and others.

Type of research project developed by students: During the STEP year, students complete several research projects, ranging from analyses of language patterns in classroom discourse to case studies of their own teaching to action research. Students also participate in on-going research of Stanford faculty members. Some examples of projects include Lee Shulman's "Fostering a Community of Learners" study, Elizabeth Cohen's studies of group work, and James Greeno's studies of alternative ways of teaching mathematics.

Teachers of the concentration area methods courses: The concentration area courses (methods courses) are taught by teams of one university regular faculty member paired with a classroom teacher.

Duration of methods course: Each students must take two methods courses in their content area. These are offered in the summer quarter (the first quarter of STEP) and in the winter. STEP students also take a required practicum, "Secondary Teaching Seminar" during the four quarters of the year.

Required field work prior to student teaching: STEP looks for a stream of teaching and teaching-like experiences among its applicants. In addition, all students begin the STEP year in the Stanford Summer Teaching School, a school-university partnership between a school district and Stanford University. During this experience, teams of four STEP students work with a master teacher to teach twenty-five middle school students during a two-hour block period. This year, the Summer Teaching School will be at Peterson Middle School in Santa Clara Unified School District. Approximately 500 students entering grades 6 through 8 will attend the school. These will include the full spectrum of students who attend summer school in Santa Clara District, including second language learners, gifted and talented, special education, remedial, and average and above. The school is ethnically and economically diverse.

Student teacher supervisors: University supervisors are all experienced teachers. This year, there are sixteen, each with a quarter-time load of approximately four student teachers. About half of the supervisors are recently retired teachers. Another four are advanced graduate students with at least three years of experience. The rest include part-time teachers, teachers on special assignment, and teachers on leave. STEP university supervisors usually do not have more than one quarter-time assignment. A lead university supervisor coordinates the work of the university supervisors.

Frequency of student teacher observations: University supervisors must observe student teachers a minimum of nine full observation cycles a year (about once a month) between September and May. Three observations (one per quarter) must be videotaped. Students also conduct reciprocal observations twice a year. University Supervisors conduct weekly group discussions among their student teachers as a part of the Secondary Teaching Seminar. They also communicate informally with their students as often as needed.

Duration of student teaching: STEP students engage in five weeks of student teaching during the summer quarter, followed by year-long teaching placements, for four hours each day from August through June.

University teaching roles, titles, or compensation provided to secondary classroom teachers who serve as mentors to student teachers: Stanford does not pay intern teachers. They receive "Visiting Scholar" cards that entitle them to almost all the same privileges as other visiting scholars from other universities. These include access to athletic facilities, full library privileges in the Stanford library system (including ability to check out books), parking privileges (not free, but access), discounts on certain computer equipment, and discounts on tickets for athletic and cultural events. During the annual portfolio conference in May, STEP students honor the teachers and administrators who have worked with them most closely. They present them with certificates, small gifts, poems, songs, and other tokens of thanks.

Decision-making roles of secondary teachers: Cooperating teachers and resident supervisors advise the director of which STEP students should earn their teaching credential in the same way that university supervisors do. The recommendations of all the people in these roles carry equal weight. Cooperating teachers and resident supervisors are represented on the STEP advisory board. The Internship Council, made up of administrators who represent cooperating schools and districts, works with the placement coordinator to refine the placement system.

Assistance to students in gaining employment: STEP students officially work with the Stanford Career Planning and Placement Center to obtain employment. Former STEP students and STEP staff network informally to provide information about job fairs and openings in districts in the Bay Area, California, and beyond. STEP students also find their final portfolio projects are of great help in their interviews. We are fortunate to be living in an area where there are very great needs for teachers. During the last four years, almost every STEP student who wanted a teaching job has been able to find one. Some STEP students arrive with job offers already in their pockets. Others, with skills in high demand, begin receiving offers as early as January.

Percentages of students who enter teaching and who remain in the profession after five years: We do not know exactly how many STEP alumni are still in teaching five years after graduation. In a study of students over a ten year period who had received Mellon Fellowships, we found a range of from 60 to 80 percent of students who had graduated five or more years before were still in teaching. Very few had left the education sector. Many of those not in teaching were in school administration, policy analysis, and university teaching. Although these data suggest a pattern, it is risky to generalize these experiences to those of STEP students.

References

Christopher Roellke:

Burgess, C. (1990). Abiding by the rule of birds: Teaching teachers in small liberal arts colleges. In Goodlad, J., Soder R. and Sirotnik, K. (Eds.) *Places where teachers are taught* (pp.87-135). San Francisco, CA: Jossey-Bass.

Carnegie Forum on Education and the Economy (1986). *A nation prepared: Teachers for the twenty-first century.* Hyattsville, MD: Author.

Darling-Hammond, L. & Cobb, Velma L. (1996). The changing context of teacher education. In Murray, F. B. (Ed.), *The teacher educator's handbook: Building a knowledge base for the preparation of teachers* (pp. 14-62). San Francisco, CA: Jossey-Bass Publishers.

Davis, B.M. and Buttafuso, D. (1994). A case for the small liberal arts college and the preparation of teachers. *Journal of Teacher Education 45* (3), 229-235.

Goodlad, J. (1990). Connecting the present to the past. In Goodlad, J., Soder, R. and Sirotnik, K. (Eds.), *Places where teachers are taught* (pp. 3-39). San Francisco, CA: Jossey-Bass.

Farris, P. (1996). *Teaching, bearing the torch.* Madison, WI: Brown and Benchmark Publishers.

Hawley, W.D. (1987). The high costs and doubtful efficacy of extended teacher preparation programs: An invitation to more basic reforms. *American Journal of Education 95* (2), 275-298.

Holmes Group (1986). *Tomorrow's teachers: A report on the Holmes Group.* East Lansing, MI: Author. Nelson, J. L., Carlson, K., and Palonsky, S. (1996). *Critical issues in education: A dialectic approach.* New York: McGraw-Hill.

Soder, R. & Sirotnik, K. (1990). Beyond reinventing the past: The politics of teacher education. In Goodlad, J., Soder, R. and Sirotnik, K. (Eds.), *Places where teachers are taught* (pp. 385-411). San Francisco, CA: Jossey-Bass.

Traynelis-Yurek, E., Roellke, C.F., & Stohr, P. (in press). Teacher education and the liberal arts: A case study of the Department of Education at the University of Richmond. Yearbook of the International Council of Education for Teaching. Arlington, VA: Author.

Travers, E.F. & Sacks, S.R. (1989). Joining teacher education and the liberal arts in the undergraduate curriculum. *Phi Delta Kappan 70* (6), 470-474.

University of Richmond (1997). Interdisciplinary and integrative studies and activities at the University of Richmond: A report of a subcommittee of the university's planning and priorities committee. Richmond, VA: Author

Weingartner, R.H. (1993). Undergraduate education: Goals and means. Phoenix, AZ: IPT Oryx Press.

Angela Breidenstein:

Corcoran, E., and Andrew, M. (1993). A full-year internship: An example of school-university collaboration. *Journal of Teacher Education 39* (3), 17-23.

Darling-Hammond, L. (1997). *The right to learn: A blueprint for creating schools that work.* San Francisco: Jossey-Bass.

Grossman, P. L. (1990). *The making of a teacher: Teacher knowledge and teacher education.* New York: Teachers College Press.

Holmes Group. (1986). *Tomorrow's teachers.* East Lansing, MI: Author.

Holmes Group. (1990). *Tomorrow's teachers.* East Lansing, MI: Author.

Holmes Group. (1995). *Tomorrow's schools of education.* East Lansing, MI: Author.

Ishler, R. E. (1992). Teacher education policy: The Texas experience. In H. D. Gideonse (Ed.), *Teacher Education Policy: Narratives, Stories, and Cases* (p. 1-26). Albany: State University of New York Press.

National Center for Restructuring Education, Schools, and Teaching. (in press). Study of exemplary teacher education programs.

National Commission on teaching and America's Future. (1996). *What matters most: Teaching for America's future.* New York: Author.

Tyack, D. and Cuban, L. (1995). *Tinker toward utopia.* Cambridge, MA: Harvard University Press.

Tyson, H. (1994). *Who will teach the children?: Progress and resistance in teacher education.* San Francisco: Jossey-Bass.

Van Zandt, L. M. (1996, April). *Assessing the effect of reform in teacher education: An Evaluation of the MAT program at Trinity.*

University. Paper presented at the annual meeting of the American Education Research Association, New York.

Richard Card:

Card, Richard H. Field Notes, February 1998.
Clark, Richard W. *"Professional Development Schools: Costs and Finances"* (1996, working paper). New York, NY. CREST, Teachers College, Columbia University.
—— (1997). *Professional Development Schools: Policy and Financing.* Washington, DC: American Association of Colleges for Teacher Education.
Goodlad, John I. (1994). *Educational Renewal: Better Teachers, Better Schools.* San Francisco: Jossey-Bass.
Learning Results Support Initiative. (February 1997). "Our *Children: Our Future—Your Future."* Augusta, ME: Maine Leadership Consortium.
Professional Development Schools Standards Project. (March 1997). "Draft Standards for Professional Development Schools." (Discussion Draft). Washington, DC: National Council for Accreditation of Teacher Education.

Eileen Landay:

Berthoff, A. E. (1982). *Forming, thinking, writing: The composing imagination.* Montclair, NJ : Boynton/Cook.
Bissex, G. (1980). *GNYS at wrk.* Cambridge, MA.: Harvard University Press.
——. (1987). *Seeing for ourselves: Case studies of research by teachers of writing.* Portsmouth, N. H.: Heinemann.
Boomer, G. (1982). *Negotiating the curriculum.* Sydney: Ashton Scholastic.
Branscombe, A., D. Goswami & J. Schwartz (eds). (1992). *Students teaching, teachers learning.* Portsmouth, N.H.: Boynton/Cook Heinemann.
Britton, J. (1983). A quiet form of research. *English Journal.* April, 1983.
Bruner, Jerome S.(1962). *The process of education.* Cambridge, MA.: Harvard University Press.

Carini, P. (1975). *Observation and description: An alternative Methodology for the investigation of human phenomena.* Grand Forks: University of North Dakota.

Clay, M. (1982). Looking and seeing in the classroom. *English Journal 71* (February 1982). 90-92.

Dewey, J. (1933). *How we think, a restatement of the relation of reflective thinking to the educative process.* Boston: D.C. Heath and company.

Duckworth, E. (1987). *The having of wonderful ideas & other essays on teaching & learning.* New York: Teachers College Press.

Freire, Paulo. (1985). *The politics of education: Culture, power, and liberation.* Hadley, MA.: Bergin & Garvey.

Gardner, Howard. (1985). *The mind's new science: A history of the cognitive revolution.* New York : Basic Books.

Goswami, D. and P. Stillman. (eds.) 1987. *Reclaiming the classroom: Teacher research as an agency for change.* Portsmouth, N.H.: Boynton Cook.

Kutz and Roskelly. (1991). *An unquiet pedagogy: Transforming Practice in the English classroom.* Portsmouth, N.H.: Heinemann.

Myers, M. (1985). *The teacher researcher: How to study writing in the classroom.* Urbana, Ill.: ERIC Clearinghouse on Reading and Communications Skills.

Perrone, Vito. (1991). *A letter to teachers :Reflections on schooling and the art of teaching.* San Francisco : Jossey-Bass.

Schon, D. (1983). *The reflective practitioner: How professionals think in action.* New York: Basic Books.

____. (1987). *Educating the reflective practitioner.* San Francisco: Jossey-Bass.

Senge, P. (1990). *The fifth discipline: The art and practice of the learning organization.* New York: Doubleday.

Spindler, G. and L. Spindler, (1987). *Interpretive ethnography of education : at home and abroad.* Hillsdale, N.J. : L. Erlbaum Associates.

Leah McCoy and Robert Evans:

Interstate New Teacher Assessment and Support Consortium: http://www.ccsso.org/intasc.html

McCoy, L.P. (1995). *Studies in Teaching: 1995 Research Digest.* Winston-Salem, NC: Wake Forest University. (ERIC Document Reproduction Service No. ED 401 261).

National Board for Professional Teaching Standards:
http://www.nbpts.org/

Joseph McCaleb and Jeremy Price:

Berliner, D. (1987). Knowledge is power. In D. Berliner & B. Rosenshine (Eds.), *Talks to teachers* (pp. 3-33). Toronto: Random House.

Dewey, J. (1904/1965). The relation of theory to practice in education. In M. Borrowman (Ed.), *Teacher education in America: A documentary history*. NY: Teacher's College Press.

Dewey, J. (1933). *How we think*. Chicago: Henry Regnery.

Eisner, E. (1979). *The educational imagination*. NY: Macmillan.

Fenstermacher, G. (1986). Philosophy of research on teaching: Three aspects. In M. Wittrock (Ed.), *Handbook of research on teaching* (3rd ed.) (pp. 37-49). NY: Macmillan.

Fullan, M. (1991). *The meaning of educational change* (2nd Ed.). NY: Teachers College Press.

Hopkins, D. (1982). Doing research in classrooms. *Phi Delta Kappan 64*, 274-275.

Hopkins, D. (1985). *A teacher's guide to classroom research*. Milton Keynes, England: Open University Press.

McCaleb, J., Borko, H., Arends, R., Garner, R., & Mauro, L. (1987). Innovation in teacher education: The evolution of a program. *Journal of Teacher Education, 37* (4), 57-64.

McCaleb, J., Borko, H., & Arends, R. (1992). Reflection, research, and repertoire in the Master's Certification Program at the University of Maryland. In L. Valli (Ed.), *Reflective teacher education: Cases and critiques* (pp. 40-64). Albany, NY: State University of New York Press.

Zeichner, K. & Liston, D. (1996). *Reflective teaching: An introduction*. Mahwan, NJ: Lawrence Erlbaum Associates.

Charles Myers:

Eraut, M. (1994). *Developing professional knowledge and competence*. London: Falmer.

Lortie, D. (1995). *School teacher: A sociological study*. Chicago: University of Chicago Press.

John Mascazine

Brock, B. L., Grady, M. L. (1996). "Beginning Teachers Induction Programs." Paper presented at the Annual Meeting of the National Council of Professors in Educational Administration, Corpus Christi, TX, August, 6—10, 1996.

Darling—Hammond, L. (Ed.), (1994). *Professional Development Schools: Schools for Developing a Profession.* New York: Teachers College Press.

Haselkorn, D., Fideler, E. F. (1999). *Learning the Ropes: Urban Teacher Induction Programs and Practices in the United States.* New York: Recruiting New Teachers, Inc.

Holmes Group (1995). *Tomorrow's Schools of Education: A Report of the Holmes Group.* East Lansing, MI.

Johnston, M. (Ed.), (2000). *Collaborative Reform and Other Improbable Dreams: The Challenges of Professional Development Schools.* In Press, New York: State University of New York (SUNY).

Levine, M., Trachtman, R. (Eds.) (1997). *Making Professional Development Schools Work: Politics, Practice, and Policy.* New York: Teachers College Press.

Lux, D. G. (Ed.), (1990). "Reforming Education: The Holmes Agenda." Theory into Practice, 29(1).

Professional Development Schools at a Glance. Clinical Schools Clearinghouse (AACTE). August 1998. <http://aacte.org/glance.html>

Zimpher, N. L. (1990). "Creating Professional Development School Sites." Theory into Practice, 29(1).

Alan Reiman:

Book, C (1996). Professional development schools. In J. Sikula (Ed.), *Second handbook of research on teacher education.* (pp. 194-212). New York. NY. Macmillan.

Goodlad, J. (1993). School-university partnerships and partner schools. In P. Altback, H. Petrie, M. Shuhaa, & L. Weis (Eds.), *Educational policy: Volume 7, Number 1. Professional development schools* (pp. 24-39). Newbury Park, CA. Corwin Press.

Goodlad, J. (1990). *Teachers for our nation's schools.* San Francisco, CA. Jossey-Bass.

Guyton, E., Paille, E., & Rainer, J. (1993). Collaborative field-based urban teacher education program. *Action in Teacher Education. 15*(3), 7-11.

Guyton, E., & McIntrye, J. (1990). Student teaching and school experiences. In R. Houston (Ed.), *The handbook of research on teacher education.* New York, NY. Macmillan.

Howey, K. (1996). Designing coherent and effective teacher education programs. In J. Sikula (Ed.), *Second handbook of research on teacher education.* (pp. 143-170). New York, NY. Macmillan.

Joyce, B., & Showers, B. (1995). *Student achievement through staff development.* New York, NY. Longman.

McIntrye, J., Byrd, D., & Foxx, S. (1996). Field and laboratory experiences. In J. Sikula (Ed.), *Second handbook of research on teacher education.* (pp. 1710193). New York, NY. Macmillan.

Pogrow, S. (1996). Reforming the wannabe reformers. *Phi Delta Kappan. 77*(10), 656-663.

Reiman, A., & Parramore, B. (1993). Promoting preservice teacher development through extended field experience. In M. O'Hair and S. Odell (Eds.), *Diversity and teaching: Association of Teacher Educators Yearbook.* (pp. 111-121). Ft. Worth, TX. Harcourt Brace Javanovich.

Sarason, S. (1990). *The predictable failure of educational reform.* San Francisco, CA. Jossey-Bass.

Sprinthall, N.A., Reiman, A.J., & Thies-Sprinthall, L. (1996). Teacher professional development. In J. Sikula (Ed.), *Second handbook of research on teacher education.* New York, NY. Macmillan.

Index

Agnes Scott College, 25, 33, 45, 47, 139, 264
Arends, R., 178, 180, 183
Barnard College, 76
Berliner, D., 179
Berthoff, A.E., 163
Bissex, G., 163
Book, C., 154
Boomer, G., 161, 163
Borko, H., 178, 180, 183
Boyer, 116
Branscombe, A.D., 163
Britton, J., 161
Brown University, 87, 104, 107, 139, 145, 147, 159, 161, 193, 199, 221, 262
Bruner, Jerome S., 161
Burgess, C., 70
Buttafuso, D., 72
Byrd, D., 153
Carini, P., 161
Carlson, 73
Carnegie Forum, 79
Center for Educational Leadership, 117
Clark, Richard W., 126
Clay, M., 161
Cobb, Velma L., 80
Cornell University, 193, 256
Cuban, L., 123
Darling-Hammond, L., 80, 115
Davis, B.M., 72
Dartmouth University, 71
Dewey, John, 161, 178, 191
Duckworth, E., 163
Duke University, 18, 53, 87, 206, 215, 225, 258
Eisner, E., 189
Eraut, Michael, 200
Farris, P., 76
Foxx, S., 153
Freire, P., 161

Furman University, 193, 266
Gardner, Howard, 161
Garner, R., 180
Georgia Professional Standards Commission, 34, 46
Goodlad, John, 70, 126, 127, 155
Goswami, A.D., 163
Grossman, P.L., 115
Guyton, E., 154
Hargreave, A., 142
Harvard University, 14, 75, 87, 93, 139, 193, 251
Hirsch, E.D., 83
Holmes group, 79, 115, 116, 207
Interstate New Teacher Assessment and Support Consortium, 89, 101, 176
Ishler, R.E., 115
Kelman, Peter, 72
Kutz, 163
Lanier, 116
Lewis and Clark College, 87, 193, 221, 248
Liston, D., 178, 184, 187, 191
Lortie, Dan, 200
Mauro, L., 180
McIntyre, J., 153, 154
Myers, M., 161
National Board for Professional Teaching Standards, 7, 8, 10, 11, 85, 88, 174
National Center for Restructuring Education, Schools, and Teaching, 117
National Council for the Accreditation of Teacher Education, 89, 101, 117, 126
National Council for the Social Studies, 89
Nelson, 73
North Carolina State University, 56, 87
Ohio State University, 206, 207, 225
Paille, E., 154
Palonsky, 73
Parramore, B., 153
Perrone, Vito, 14, 163
Pogrow, S., 156
Rainer, J., 154
Rice University, 60, 61, 87, 91, 100, 269

Roskelly, 163
Sacks, Susan, 76
Sarason, S., 151
Schon, D., 161, 187
Senge, Peter, 167
Sirotnik, K., 77
Sizer, 116
Soder, R., 77
Spindler, G. and L., 161
Sprinthall, N.A., 156
Stanford University, 49, 87, 272
Stillman, P., 163
Stohr-Hunt, P., 80
Swarthmore College, 76
Thies-Sprinthall, L., 156
Travers, Eva, 76
Traynelis-Yurek, Elaine, 76, 80
Trinity University, 115, 135, 139, 147, 221, 267
Tyack, D., 123
Tyson, 115, 117
University of Maine at Orono, 4
University of Maryland, 159, 177, 202, 244
University of New Hampshire, 24, 39, 45, 48, 104, 134, 139, 240
University of North Carolina at Chapel Hill, 24, 27, 45, 49, 87, 193, 238
University of Richmond, 60, 69, 87, 96, 100, 139, 237
University of Southern Maine, 9, 87, 97, 104, 125, 135, 139, 147, 193, 221, 234
University of Virginia, 5, 87, 139, 193, 233
Valli, Linda, 184
Vanderbilt University, 25, 50, 57, 87, 139, 231
Van Zandt, L.M., 117
Wake Forest University, 17, 19, 20, 25, 53, 60, 81, 87, 88, 100, 104, 135, 139, 159, 171, 193, 201, 221, 229
Weingartner, Rudolph, 73
Wesleyan University, 71
Wise, 116
World Assembly of the International Council on Education for Teaching, 77
Zeichner, K., 178, 184, 187, 191